HAUNTED IMAGES

HAUNTED IMAGES

FILM, ETHICS, TESTIMONY AND THE HOLOCAUST

LIBBY SAXTON

WALLFLOWER PRESS
LONDON & NEW YORK

First published in Great Britain in 2008 by
Wallflower Press
6 Market Place, London W1W 8AF
www.wallflowerpress.co.uk

A catalogue record for this book is available from the British Library.

ISBN 978-1-905674-35-0 (pbk)
ISBN 978-1-905674-36-7 (hbk)

Book design by Elsa Mathern.

Printed in India.

Contents

Acknowledgements

My first debt is to Jean Khalfa, for his insight and guidance as supervisor of the doctoral research which led to this book. Emma Wilson, Colin Davis, Barry Langford and Sarah Cooper have responded astutely to drafts at various stages and offered advice, encouragement and inspiration; my second debt is to them. My third is to Claude Lanzmann, for his interest in the project, generosity with time and material, hospitality and patience with my questions. I am grateful to Yoram Allon, Editorial Director of Wallflower Press, who has been an energetic and discerning editor; to Editorial Manager Jacqueline Downs and all the staff at the press. Thanks are due also to the staff at the Cinémathèque in Jerusalem, in particular Shmulik Barkai, for their help and kindness. I would like to record my thanks to the Arts and Humanities Research Council for funding both the doctoral research during which this book was conceived and the sabbatical leave during which it was completed, and to the School of Languages, Linguistics and Film at Queen Mary, University of London for granting me this period of leave. Parts of chapter two have appeared in earlier forms in *Trafic*, 47 (Autumn 2003) and Michael Temple, James S. Williams and Michael Witt (eds) *For Ever Godard: The Work of Jean-Luc Godard 1950–2000* (Black Dog, 2004), and I am grateful to the editors of these publications for their permission to draw on this material here. I would also like to thank the many others who have offered advice, assistance and sustenance of different kinds along the way, including Raymond Bellour, Claire Boyle, Andrew Brown, Chris Darke, Jean-Michel Frodon, Louis Jackson, Sorley MacDonald, Alice Mann, Ruth Saxton, Nitza Spiro and James Williams.

This book is dedicated to C.J.D.

To argue for silence, prayer, the banishment equally of poetry and knowledge, in short, the witness of 'ineffability', that is, non-representability, is to *mystify something we dare not understand,* because we fear that it may be all too understandable, all too continuous with what we are – human, all too human.

Gillian Rose (1996: 43)

Introduction

Elida Schogt's award-winning experimental short film *Zyklon Portrait* (1999) explores the enduring impact of Nazi atrocities on three generations of women in her family. Two divergent narratives are interwoven in the film: an impersonal, detailed analysis of the scientific developments that facilitated the implementation of the so-called 'Final Solution' is juxtaposed with an intimate personal history revealing the human consequences of this policy. As these parallel narratives unfold, dazzling sequences of underwater photography become progressively associated, via their myriad blue hues, with a more dangerous hydrogen compound named after the intense pigment from which it is obtained: hydrogen cyanide, also known by the brand name Zyklon B.[1] Favoured by the Nazis because of its efficiency in mass killing, Zyklon B was used in the gas chambers at Auschwitz and Majdanek. In the build-up to the culminating sequence of the film, the cold monotone of the male narrator explains what happens when the chemical enters a living human body. As he describes the ease with which it penetrates mucus membranes and the physical symptoms it causes, the X-ray images of lungs that illustrate his account begin to disintegrate into abstract visual patterns, evocative of expiring organs, as if Schogt has inserted her camera inside a body succumbing to the poison. The image-track simultaneously starts to fragment; shapes flash up on the screen between black leaders, as if the celluloid is breaking up or the projection apparatus is breaking down. Suddenly, just as darkness threatens to engulf the screen permanently, the contours of a face become faintly visible and the filmmaker's mother speaks: 'Those last moments you do not want to visualise.'

This disturbingly beautiful and disarmingly moving sequence eloquently attests to persistent anxieties about the possibility of adequately representing the unprecedented violence that has been called the Holocaust, or Shoah.[2] *Zyklon Portrait* resolutely refuses to visualise this event directly. The film contains neither archive footage from the camps nor reconstructions of the atrocities. Moreover, as it approaches what has been variously described as the 'primal scene', 'nerve centre' or 'constitutive crime' of the genocide (Köppen 1997: 162; Didi-Huberman 2001: 237; Wajcman 2001: 47),[3] the collapse of representation seems imminent: the voices fall silent, the flow of images is interrupted and the light projected onto the screen quite literally flickers and dies. And yet the film does not end here; representation falters but ultimately persists. Schogt's disorientating, eviscerating visuals at once disturb and enable our vision, suggesting competing desires to respect the visual limit evoked by her mother and to invent an image of the epicentre of the event – to take us right inside the gas chamber.

Schogt's self-conscious investigation of film's capacity to bear witness to atrocity echoes and anticipates some of the questions about ethics and epistemology posed in recent debates about Holocaust representation. Over the past couple of decades, witnesses, artists and thinkers have become increasingly sceptical of the legitimacy of traditional religious and socially-constructed moral prohibitions on representation of the genocide. The idea that the Holocaust is beyond representation and the concomitant notions that it remains 'unspeakable', 'incommunicable' or 'incomprehensible' are being treated with growing suspicion. In the wake of interventions by Jorge Semprun, Gillian Rose, Giorgio Agamben, Jacques Rancière, Georges Didi-Huberman, Jean-Luc Nancy and others, rhetorics of 'ineffability' are rapidly losing critical currency.[4] Broadly speaking, then, the focus of critical discussion and artistic invention has shifted from the question of *whether* the event could or should be represented to the question of *how* it might adequately or responsibly be represented.

It is one of the underlying contentions of this book that the concern to articulate moral limits or interdictions on representation can become a strategy for evading a properly ethical confrontation with the event. *Haunted Images: Film, Ethics, Testimony and the Holocaust* rethinks the role of film as witness to history and as visible evidence in the light of this conceptual shift from prohibition and taboo to permission and responsibility. More specifically, I explore how filmmakers have negotiated the singular challenges posed by the near absence of photographs or film footage of the Nazi machine of mass murder in action. I suggest that Holocaust films may be haunted by these missing images in ways which are not fully articulated or directly represented. I show, moreover, how this haunting has served as a catalyst for aesthetic and ethical innovation, for an ongoing search for more responsible forms of witnessing. My readings approach these haunted images as sources of ethical as well as historical insight. While ethical issues have emerged as a pivotal concern in writings on Holocaust representation, they have only recently begun to receive explicit and sustained critical attention in film scholarship. This book argues that images of the Holocaust can bring film into focus as object and vehicle of ethical inquiry.

Questions about the ethics of representation are gaining urgency at a time when ever more diverse forms of Holocaust representation are emerging worldwide, and particularly in cinema. 'Over the past decade,' observes Terri Ginsberg, 'Holocaust films of nearly every generic and formal structure have been produced as well as distributed across an expanding global context, as Holocaust cinema has become an increasingly mainstream, international venture' (2004: 47). Films such as Steven Spielberg's *Schindler's List* (1993), Roberto Benigni's *La Vita è bella* (*Life is Beautiful*, 1997) and Roman Polanski's *The Pianist* (2002) have brought the events of the period to the attention of a wider international public. However, these incursions into the mainstream have regularly divided opinion and courted controversy, and thus prompted fresh stock-taking of the broader legacy of the camps in cinema.

Some of the most impassioned debates about film and the Holocaust in the last decade have taken place in France. A series of significant but often conflicting interventions by philosophers, historians, critics and filmmakers has confirmed that the place occupied by the genocide in French consciousness remains as contested today as it was in the late twentieth century. The roots of France's ongoing preoccupation with the events of World War Two have been extensively discussed. While the killing zones were located a long way from French soil and it lost a smaller proportion of its Jewish population (approximately one quarter) than the majority of other European nations (by way of comparison, Poland, Germany and Austria each lost ninety per cent of their Jews), France has struggled to come to terms with the extent of its institutional implication in the Holocaust through the Vichy regime's anti-Semitic legislation and deportation of Jews. Despite the publication of testimonies by survivors, both Jewish and non-Jewish, from the 1940s onwards, it was not until the early 1970s that France began to confront these facts in a concerted way and to question postwar mythologies of a nation united in resistance. It took events such as the Six Day War in 1967, the release of films debunking myths about the period from the 1970s onwards and high-profile war crimes trials in the 1980s and 1990s to bring the Holocaust and French complicity in it to the forefront of public consciousness and scholarly debate.[5]

In the last decade French critical discourse has opened up new perspectives on the representability of the Holocaust and the roles played by photography and film both during and after the event, without yet reaching any consensus on these issues. Nathalie Nezick has described the camps as 'the great blind spot in the history of cinema' (1998: 164). Jean-Luc Godard has suggested that cinema neglected its moral duty to testify to the camps and needs to redeem itself for this failure (see, for instance, Godard 1998a II: 336). Initially puzzling in the face of the ever-growing body of films which purport to deal with precisely this topic, such allegations reflect doubts about the films' historical fidelity and testimonial efficacy. Others offer a contrasting assessment of postwar cinematic history, arguing that the genocide has had a profound and constitutive impact on the development of the medium. Antoine de Baecque traces the original point of impact back to the first images of the camps to enter the public domain – the footage shot by Allied cameras just after the camps were liberated:

> Modern cinema was born out of those images, which have been cease-lessly at work in it, resurfacing in other forms, the to-camera look, the freeze-frame, documentary in fiction, the flashback, montage, contem-plation, malaise, those specifically cinematographic figures that testify to the obsessive presence of the concentrationary palimpsest. (2000: 66)

According to Gérard Wajcman, this residual holocaustal presence haunts not merely certain cinematographic figures but every contemporary image of the human form: 'Today it is impossible to eliminate from the image of a body the resonance of the attack on the human image perpetrated in the gas chambers ... Images are no longer as they were before' (1998: 25). Wajcman's contention is unverifiable yet in a sense irrefutable, since any image of the body could conceivably be read as bearing the imprint of historical violence. More illuminating in the current context is his insight that the Nazis' violation of the body has also led, in a sense to which I shall return, to a violation of the image. De Baecque's and Wajc-man's accounts intersect in the contentious and challenging idea that the violence of the Holocaust has radically transformed cinematic images and our relationship to them.

One of the broader contexts in which the particular interest in visual media shown by French critics might be viewed is the history of the deni-gration of vision in twentieth-century French thought, as charted by Martin Jay (1993). Jay demonstrates how many French thinkers of this period share a suspicion of the privilege traditionally accorded to vision and of the role it plays in different forms of political and social oppression, although he has little to say about the specific impact of the Holocaust on this history. One lengthy current in writing on the visual legacy of the genocide exhib-its a scepticism about images which intersects at crucial points with this tradition. Wajcman (2001), for example, contends that images of atrocities have a consolatory, placatory function which can act to shield us against the realities they portray. Critiques along such lines hint at the extent to which the history traced by Jay may be informed and underpinned by the legacy of the Holocaust. However, as we shall see, an increasingly powerful counter-current in recent debates argues for the rehabilitation of vision and defends the capacity of photography and film to grant us access to history without falsifying or betraying it. Didi-Huberman (2001 and 2003), for instance, suggests that close scrutiny of photographs taken in Auschwitz can challenge the discourses of invisibility and unrepresentability which have dominated much discussion of the genocide.

These issues lie at the heart of the recent dispute between Godard and Claude Lanzmann regarding the testimonial value and ethical import of archive images of the camps. Lanzmann's groundbreaking film *Shoah* (1985) and Godard's celebrated video-essay *Histoire(s) du cinéma* (1988–98) are informed by ostensibly opposing views of such images. While Lanzmann, who excludes them from his film, dismisses them as 'images without imagination' (1990a: 297), according to Godard they can have, on the contrary, a redemptive function, as his video-essay seeks to demonstrate. Over the past decade in particular, a series of competing interventions by the two directors have reinvigorated discussion of the ethical import of photographic and filmic images of the Holocaust. Furthermore, critical attention became refocused on these questions by the controversial photographic exhibition held at the Hôtel de Sully in Paris in March 2001, 'Mémoire des camps: photographies des camps de concentration et d'extermination nazis (1933–1999)' ('Memory of the Camps: Photographs of the Nazi Concentration and Extermination Camps (1933–1999)'). The photographs displayed in the exhibition have provoked heated discussions in French scholarship about the virtual absence of images of the extermination and its implications for historians and filmmakers. These discussions have thrown fresh light on the distinctive testimonial strategies adopted by Lanzmann and Godard, the status of the image as document and trace and the ethics of vision and blindness.

Given these illuminating recent developments, which have been largely overlooked by Anglo-American scholars to date, the time seems ripe to re-open the broader debate about the role of film as witness to the Holocaust. This book does not aim to offer a nationally or internationally comprehensive survey of films on the topic. A number of valuable studies of this kind already exist, and my readings are indebted to some of their insights. Works by Annette Insdorf, Judith Doneson, Ilan Avisar and André Pierre Colombat, amongst others, offer detailed, incisive and inclusive analyses of the eclectic strategies adopted by filmmakers in France, the United States and internationally to bear witness to the Holocaust.[6] My own concerns are more specific. *Haunted Images* focuses on a spectrum of films which contend explicitly or implicitly with the dearth of images of the murderous core of the genocide. I place these films in dialogue with critical conversations about the ethics of the image as witness. My particular focus on French films reflects the fact that some of the most productive of these debates are currently being conducted within the French intellectual context outlined above. This is not simply a question of Filmmaker A versus Filmmaker B; interlocutors include some of the most important figures in postwar cinema, including Godard and Lanzmann. The films and writings discussed here offer new perspectives on the film image as document, as evidence, as proof and as weapon, screen and shield, but, above all, as witness to the other's suffering, as testimony to injustice. In so doing, moreover, I suggest, they shed light on some of the under-explored ethical dynamics of cinema and spectatorship.

This book is aimed primarily at a readership with an interest in philosophical and film critical debates about Holocaust representation. Some may be offended by its engagement with such debates and ask what they have to do with the historical facts, with terror, hunger, filth, blood and murder. This is a book about images and mediation, about the betrayals that take place and the possibilities that open up when an event is captured by or recreated for a camera. In a society increasingly saturated with images of atrocities, I see an understanding of these transformations as crucial if we are to respond to such images in an informed and responsible way. Rather than abstracting suffering and death into philosophical lenses, critical discussions about ethics and representation can equip us with the tools to view these images differently, and bring us closer to the traumatic realities that lie behind them.

Beyond the 'unrepresentable'

To what extent does the singular barbarity of the Holocaust cast doubt upon the possibility of adequate representation? This question has remained a recurrent preoccupation of testimony and philosophy in the wake of the event. Such doubts have been fuelled by persistent claims that neither the experience nor the appearance of the event can be encapsulated in words or images, or that they should not be represented for moral or religious reasons. 'Auschwitz cannot be explained nor can it be visualised', insists Elie Wiesel, one of the best-known proponents of such a view (1978: 29). As Gillian Rose explains, certain currents in philosophy and theology have promoted the idea of 'ineffability' to articulate the ways in which the genocide calls language and other systems of representation into question:

'The ineffable' is invoked by a now widespread tradition of reflection on the Holocaust: by Adorno, by Holocaust theology, Christian and Jewish, more recently by Lyotard, and now by Habermas. According to this view, 'Auschwitz' or 'the Holocaust' are emblems for the breakdown in divine and/or human history. The uniqueness of this break delegitimises names and narratives as such, and hence all aesthetic or apprehensive representation. (1996: 43)

While the arguments advanced by these philosophers and theologians are sophisticated, nuanced and distinctive, they have regularly been bowdlerised and subsumed within more generalising discourses of 'unrepresentability' which have not always been attentive to their specificity. Broadly speaking, discourses of this kind emphasise the event's uniqueness, insist that it cannot be known or conceptualised in conventional ways and define it negatively in terms of its radical non-relation to representation and thought ('Auschwitz' is revered as 'unnameable', 'unsayable', 'unimaginable', 'unthinkable', 'unfathomable', and so on). In this view, any attempt to represent the Holocaust will involve some degree of *mis*representation. The obligatory reference in this context is Theodor Adorno's remark about poetry after Auschwitz, originally made in the late 1940s but later revisited and qualified (Adorno 1973: 355; 1974: 422; 1977: 30), which has become a convenient shorthand for the positions described above. However, some of Adorno's more careful readers have warned that this remark is frequently misread or misunderstood.[7] Dominick LaCapra argues that it 'is itself best seen not as a *Verbot* (prohibition) but as a statement concerning the difficulty of legitimate creation and renewal in a posttraumatic condition' (1998: 181). In line with this reading, he suggests that it is more helpful to discuss Holocaust representation in terms of obstacles and challenges rather than prohibitions and taboos. LaCapra's comments reflect a more general trend in debates about the legacy of the camps. With increasing frequency over the past two decades, survivors and scholars have expressed misgivings about prohibitions on representation and rhetorics of ineffability which have been variously criticised as imprecise, obscurantist, viciously circular or simply unfounded.

In *If This is a Man* Primo Levi remembers the first time he became aware that 'our language lacks words to express this offence, the demolition of a man' (1966: 21). However, in a later essay in *The Drowned and the Saved*, he appears to question the view that language is entirely inadequate to his experiences. While the essay focuses on linguistic barriers and their consequences in Auschwitz, it is prefaced by an affirmation of our ability to communicate in whatever situation we find ourselves. Taking issue with theories of 'incommunicability' advanced during the 1970s, which he charges with perpetuating 'mental laziness', Levi retorts: 'To say that it is impossible to communicate is false; one always can. To refuse to communicate is a failing; we are biologically and socially predisposed to communication, and in particular to its highly evolved and noble form, which is language' (1988: 68–9). For Levi, then, communication with others is at once a perpetual possibility and a moral obligation, though in this passage he does not comment explicitly on the particular difficulties of communicating the realities of life in the camp, either in speech or writing. In *L'Écriture ou la vie* Jorge Semprun challenges proponents of the ineffability topos more directly. Asserting that there is 'nothing exceptional' about the task of testifying to the Holocaust, he argues further that language is perfectly adequate to this task: 'In short, you can always say everything. The ineffable you hear so much about is only an alibi. Or a sign of laziness. You can always say everything, language contains everything ... You can tell all about this experience' (1997: 13). Semprun reiterates this position in an interview with *Le Monde des débats* where he also refuses *a priori* the concept of a prohibition on representation: 'No-one, no court, can pronounce in advance on whether this or that can or cannot be written or filmed. There can be no prohibition on this ... For me, no aspect of the camps is unsayable. Language permits everything' (in Delorme & Herzlich 2000: 11–12). Semprun does not suggest that it is easy or straightforward to speak about the camps; on the contrary, he emphasises that it requires immense courage and effort and perhaps infinite time – 'a boundless and probably never-ending account, illuminated – as well as enclosed, naturally – by that possibility of going on forever' (1997: 14). But crucially he insists that it remains possible nevertheless. For Semprun, the Holocaust is speakable, writable and legible in ways that do not diminish its horror.

The demystifying claims of these witnesses have been echoed, tested and developed in recent scholarship. Gillian Rose, Giorgio Agamben and Berel Lang have pursued intersecting lines of inquiry in the attempt to 'defigure' the figure of 'unspeakability'. In *Holocaust Representation: Art Within the Limits of History and Ethics* Lang points out an apparent inconsistency in recurrent discursive allusions to 'incomprehensibility' and 'ineffability': 'in these very discourses the "incomprehensible" is explained (at least the effort is made), the "unspeakable" and the "ineffable" are pretty clearly spoken (or spoken about), and the "unwritable" is written' (2000: 17). Lang suggests that at such junctures these discourses verge on the rhetorical figure of *praeteritio*, 'in which a speaker announces that he will not speak about something, when what becomes immediately evident is that the purpose of this denial is to do just that, in effect to say precisely what he has declared he will not be saying' (2000: 18). Rejecting this rhetorical strategy, he insists that the Holocaust 'has been, will be ... and, most of all, ought to be spoken' (ibid.). Rose, too, advocates 'the persistence of always fallible and contestable representation', and is suspicious of what references to the 'ineffable' may work to distract or shield us from, or disavow (1996: 41, 43). The epigraph to this book is taken from an influential passage in *Mourning Becomes the Law: Philosophy and Representation* where Rose attacks the 'Holocaust piety' she discerns in invocations of 'ineffability'. She suggests that this 'piety' protects us from recognising uncomfortable continuities between the Holocaust and other realms of human experience (1996: 43). Furthermore, in *Remnants of Auschwitz: The Witness and the Archive* Agamben draws attention to another danger inherent in insisting upon the 'unsayable' essence of the event. He argues that such rhetorics are redolent of 'euphemism', in the original sense of observing a religious silence: 'To say that Auschwitz is "unsayable" or "incomprehensible" is equivalent to *euphemein*, to adoring in silence, as one does with a god. Regardless of one's intentions, this contributes to its glory' (1999: 32–3). Later in his book, Agamben nuances this critique, urging those who promote this view to proceed with caution:

> If they mean to say that Auschwitz was a unique event in the face of which the witness must in some way submit his every word to the test of an impossibility of speaking, they are right. But if, joining uniqueness to unsayability, they transform Auschwitz into a reality absolutely separated from language, if they break the tie between an impossibility and a possibility of speaking that, in the *Muselmann*, constitutes testimony, then they unconsciously repeat the Nazis' gesture. (1999: 157)

To clarify this point, Agamben goes on to cite a passage from the preface to *The Drowned and the Saved* in which Levi transcribes what he was told by an SS guard in Auschwitz: 'None of you will be left to bear witness, but even if someone were to survive, the world would not believe him' (1988: 1). To revere the Holocaust as 'unspeakable' may be to concede a terrible victory to the perpetrators of a crime designed to foreclose the possibility of testimony, a crime designed to annihilate its witnesses, leave them speechless or strip them of credibility.

In two more recent essays entitled, respectively, 'S'il y a de l'irreprés-entable' and 'La Représentation interdite' Jacques Rancière and Jean-Luc Nancy turn their attention to the related issue of interdictions on representation. Like Semprun, they are sceptical of the validity of prohibitions and taboos, and subject the assumptions underlying them to critical scrutiny. Rancière is troubled by what he perceives as the 'inflationary' use of the concept of the 'unrepresentable' in a wide range of contexts.[8] With particular reference to Robert Antelme's literary testimony, *L'Espèce humaine* (*The Human Race*,

1947) and Lanzmann's *Shoah*, Rancière attempts to demonstrate not only that the realities of life and death in the camps can be described in language and syntax which pre-existed them but also, and crucially, that prohibitions on representation lack any philosophical foundation: 'There is no property of the event which prohibits representation, which prohibits art, even in the sense of artifice. Unrepresentability does not exist as a property of the event. There are only choices' (2001: 96). Nancy, too, warns that interdictions on representation tend to be marred by conceptual confusion. He identifies in particular a propensity to conflate two related but distinct propositions: that representation of the Holocaust is *impossible* (that it *cannot* be represented) and that such representation is *illegitimate* (that the event *should not* be represented). Nancy cites paintings and literary works which appear to discredit the former claim, and argues that the latter is grounded in a religious prohibition which it tends to take out of context and misapply. Denouncing what he calls the 'idolatrous mysticism of the "ineffable"', he concludes that '"representation of the Shoah" is not only possible and licit, but in fact also necessary and imperative' (2003: 61, 98).[9]

Along with the others outlined above, Nancy's and Rancière's interventions are cumulatively redefining the questions asked of Holocaust representations. Although some of these contributions have been faulted for a lack of attention to the complexities of the positions with which they take issue (see, for example, Crowley 2005: 17), they nevertheless represent important advances in thinking about the legacy of the camps. By alerting us to the risks and blind spots of discourses of 'unrepresentability' and to the realities they work to disavow, they facilitate more critical and inclusive approaches to the representations that exist and more sophisticated engagements with the politics and ethics of these representations. They therefore provide an important conceptual context for my reassessment of a range of competing representational modes and testimonial strategies in this book. The rehabilitation of representation of – and after – the Holocaust as possible, legitimate and necessary does not imply that anything goes, that all representations are as valid and effective as each other. Rather, it means we need to adjust the criteria by which we judge their validity and efficacy. Moreover, if we accept that no event is 'unrepresentable' *per se*, we need to consider why particular aspects of the Holocaust nevertheless pose persistent challenges to representation. Related to this is the much-debated question of whether such representations should respect certain limits or operate within certain constraints, whether epistemological or ethical.[10] For Lang, the limits of representation are 'at most conventional and thus open to continuing, even limitless variation', but the fact that they are 'often vague or unarticulated [is] less to the point than that they are appealed to and applied' (1992: 302; 2000: 6).

This book suggests that the appeal to such limits perpetuates a reductive moral framework which promotes the application of interdictions and taboos, while shielding us from more difficult questions about complicity and responsibility. The reduction of moral debate around Holocaust representation to the binary 'to show or not to show' can become an alibi for neglecting its complex ethical implications for artists, readers and viewers. Discussions of the limits of representation have frequently turned to the moving image and the special role it has played in the construction of personal and collective memories of the Nazi atrocities. There is a widespread consensus that more stringent limits apply in cinema than in other forms of cultural production, or, at least, that its images bring perceived limits into sharper focus. The readings in this book consider why this might be. They explore how Holocaust films posit, test and contest representational limits, revealing them to be shifting and unstable. Furthermore, they show how the observance of such limits and the invocation of prohibitions can lead to a disavowal of the ethical relations between filmmaker, viewer and imaged subject and a denial of their responsibilities. I turn now to the particular challenges facing filmmakers and viewers as they confront the Holocaust and its legacy in order to identify some of the specific ethical questions raised by filmic representations.

'An event without a witness'?

In their influential though controversial study, *Testimony: Crises of Witnessing in Literature, Psychoanalysis, and History*, Shoshana Felman and Dori Laub contend that the Holocaust precipitated a 'radical historical *crisis of witnessing*' (1992: xvii; emphasis in original); more precisely, that it must be understood as 'the unprecedented, inconceivable, historical occurrence of "an event without a witness" – an event eliminating its own witness' (ibid.). What do they mean by this? In her review of the book, Sara R. Horowitz urges caution and precision in making such claims: 'Given the presence of survivors, perpetrators, bystanders, rescuers, liberators, and others who saw the genocide close up, and given also the availability of photographs, films, and other records of the Nazi era, one should mean something particular and specific when one refers to the Holocaust as "an event without a witness"' (1992: 51). Felman and Laub refer variously in this context to the fact that the Nazis murdered the majority of their victims, their attempts to conceal the evidence of their crimes, the inadequacy of language to which survivors attest, the difficulty of recuperating the atrocity within a coherent testimonial narrative and obstacles to the meaningful reception of testimony. While the limitations of their arguments have been highlighted by subsequent commentators, whose concerns inform my own reflections here, Felman and Laub's remarks about vision and perception merit consideration in the context of my discussion of film.[11] In their account, one of the unique and most devastating aspects of the Nazi enterprise was its endeavour to destroy every trace and every body, alive or dead, that might later bear witness to it – in short, to build a retroactive invisibility and amnesia into the crime itself. Felman elaborates:

> The essence of the Nazi scheme is to make itself – and to make the Jews – essentially invisible. To make the Jews invisible not merely by killing them, not merely by confining them to 'camouflaged', invisible death camps, but by reducing even the materiality of the dead bodies to smoke and ashes [...] The Nazi plan is in effect to *leave no trace* not only of the crime itself of the historical mass murder, but of all those who materially witnessed that crime, to eliminate without trace any possible eyewitness. (1992c: 209–10, 226; emphasis in original)

Laub suggests that the resulting 'crisis of testimony' was exacerbated by the dehumanising structure of the event, which made it difficult for potential witnesses to grasp the significance of what they were seeing:

> Not only, in effect, did the Nazis try to exterminate the physical witnesses of their crime; but the inherently incomprehensible *and* deceptive psychological structure of the event precluded its own witnessing, even by its very victims ... [It was] the very circumstance of *being inside the event* that made unthinkable the very notion that a witness could exist, that is, someone who could step outside of the coercively totalitarian and dehumanising frame of reference in which the event was taking place, and provide an independent frame of reference through which the event could be observed. (1992: 80–1; emphasis in original)

Felman and Laub's analyses intersect in ways that they do not always fully acknowledge with ongoing debates about the Holocaust and its legacy. Many accounts of the Nazi project see an inbuilt capacity for self-erasure as one of the event's defining characteristics. Didi-Huberman describes the camps as 'the laboratories, the experimental machines of a *generalised disappearance*' (2001: 228–9; emphasis in original), which aimed to destroy not only the minds, the language and the bodies of their victims, but also the traces of these bodies and even the instruments of destruction.[12] Discussing the impact of the 'Nazi policy of concealment' on memory and its transmission, Wajcman suggests that a 'radical forgetting' 'enveloped the victims even before they were pushed into the "showers"' (2001: 54,

1998: 234). He argues further that in this respect the Nazis accomplished something unprecedented: they integrated into their act, as a 'parameter of its calculation', 'the very dimension of the aftermath, of the memory of the act, that of History' (1998: 235). Wajcman's suspicions are corroborated by the SS guard cited by Levi: 'We will be the ones to dictate the history of the Lagers' (1988: 1). Rancière, too, identifies the 'rigorous planning of the extermination and of its invisibility' as specific to this event, and, like Didi-Huberman and Wajcman, is concerned by its implications for representation; in terms which implicitly take issue with Adorno, Rancière concludes that 'after Auschwitz, to show Auschwitz, only art is possible, because ... it is art's job to make manifest the invisible' (1997: 64–5, 66).

According to Felman, Wajcman and Rancière, one of the cultural artefacts which has most effectively borne witness to this policy of self-concealment and self-negation is a film: Lanzmann's *Shoah*. In her reading of *Shoah* Felman argues that Lanzmann

> makes us *see* concretely – makes us *witness* – how the Holocaust occurs as the unprecedented, inconceivable historical advent of *an event without a witness*, an event which historically consists in the scheme of the literal *erasure of its witnesses* but which, moreover, philosophically consists in an accidenting of perception, in a *splitting of eyewitnessing* as such; an event, thus, not empirically, but cognitively and perceptually without a witness both because it precludes seeing and because it precludes the possibility of a *community of seeing*. (1992c: 211; emphasis in original)

For Felman, then, the 'crises of witnessing' precipitated by the Holocaust took place on a philosophical level as well as on a historical one. Not only did the event annihilate the majority of its witnesses, it also 'precluded' their seeing or disrupted their perception in ways she deems to be evident from the testimonies of those who survived. Felman draws attention at this juncture to the distinctive viewing positions of the victims, bystanders and perpetrators interviewed by Lanzmann, who nevertheless 'have in common, paradoxically, the incommensurability of their different and particular positions of not seeing', and are thus construed as 'witnesses *who do not witness*, who let the Holocaust occur as an event essentially unwitnessed' (1992c: 210–11; emphasis in original). Moreover, and crucially for my discussion here, these failures of vision or perception have particular implications for cinema, as the 'art *par excellence* which ... calls upon a *witnessing by seeing*' (1992c: 207; emphasis in original).

This book argues that the attempt by the Nazis to eradicate the visible evidence of their crimes, and the obstacles these posed to seeing and witnessing, define the singularity of the challenge the Holocaust presents to filmmakers. In the wake of this attempt, filmmakers are faced with the task of making the invisible visible and absence present. I suggest that one of their crucial responsibilities may be to reveal what lies beyond the visible: hidden traces, missing bodies, mechanisms of concealment and erasure and the skewing of perception they entail. The difficulty of this endeavour is compounded by the scarcity of photographs or footage depicting the 'Final Solution' in action. Symptomatic of the Nazis' concern for secrecy were SS and Gestapo chief Heinrich Himmler's ban on the filming of activities relating to the killing of the Jews and the ban on amateur photography in the camps (see About 2001: 29; Hirsch 2004: 2; Struk 2004: 104). Although photographs were taken at some of the camps for a variety of administrative, scientific, political and (in contravention of the ban) unofficial purposes, and some had on-site photographic studios and laboratories, almost none of the photographs that exist show the machinery of extermination.[13] Almost no images survive from the extermination camps at Chelmno, Belzec, Treblinka and Sobibor, where no official photographs were taken. The overwhelming majority of the images that have come to symbolise the genocide in collective memory were recorded by the Nazis in the ghettos for propaganda purposes or by the Allies as the camps were liberated. Images of emaciated survivors, gaping mass graves and bulldozers clearing away piles of entangled corpses, such as those shot by members of the British Army's Film and Photographic Unit at the concentration camp at Bergen-Belsen in April 1945 and recycled widely in films and on television, have come to occupy a key position in the iconography of the Holocaust. Yet, as Toby Haggith points out, 'the scenes at Belsen, however appalling, do not represent the Holocaust. The corpses and spectrally-thin people that were filmed at Belsen were a consequence of the neglect and cruelty of the concentration camp system, not the policy of "the Final Solution"' (2005: 33–4). However horrifying the realities they depict, such images remain metonymic traces of the Holocaust itself – they show only the preparations (in the case of the ghettos) and the aftermath (in the case of the recently liberated camps).[14]

The near absence of images of the extermination process prompts Wajcman to propose that the genocide should be understood not merely as 'an event without a witness' but also as an event 'without an image' (1998: 239). Taken literally, of course, both designations are inaccurate. Just as the atrocities took place before the eyes of numerous witnesses, some of whom survived to testify to what they had seen, so a search of the archives reveals that a handful of images of the extermination do in fact exist. (The few known exceptions to the rule, which include a single brief fragment of moving footage and a few photographs, are discussed in chapters one and two.) Interpreted more loosely as an allusion to a dearth of images, however, Wajcman's observation brings into focus one of the most immediate difficulties faced by filmmakers tackling the subject of the Holocaust. In the chapters which follow I examine the ethical implications of the different strategies they have developed in response to this paucity of visual documents. While many filmmakers, especially those making documentaries, simply re-deploy metonymic images of the kind described above, others create new images which work at times to shield us from and at others to attest to this lack of visible evidence. Moreover, while some regard the restoration of visual access to the past as cinema's primary responsibility as witness, others intimate that the most appropriate and veracious forms of witnessing may take place instead through gaps, ellipses, silences and lacunae, without thereby reiterating prohibitions and taboos. My readings suggest that the ethical vision of the filmmaker is articulated as much through what she or he leaves unseen as through what she or he shows directly.

Ethical visions, or 'le travelling de *Kapo*'

Two central and related contentions have inflected my discussion so far: that the camps not only remain susceptible to artistic representation but also charge it with ethical significance and responsibility. While variations on the latter contention underpin much writing on Holocaust representation, whether they are explicitly articulated or implicitly assumed, its particular implications for cinema merit further consideration. In what respects are filmmakers and viewers ethically implicated by the event? To put the question differently: if its unprecedented brutality has prompted filmmakers to experiment and innovate in search of more adequate and responsible forms of representation, what ethical priorities inform their aesthetic choices, and what can we learn from these choices about the ethical dimensions of cinematic form, content and spectatorship? More fundamentally, do ethical concerns always remain irreducible to aesthetic ones, or is it impossible to separate them from each other? Furthermore, where precisely, within the experience, apparatus and institution that is cinema, is ethical meaning to be located? Does it reside purely in the flow of images or emerge more urgently in the course of the circulation and reception of these images – in the multifarious encounters between audiences and films? This in turn raises questions about the ethics of the act of viewing: what would it mean for a film to solicit an ethical response and what kinds of responsibilities are incumbent on viewers?

While such questions have remained implicit perennial preoccupations of film criticism and theory, explicit analysis of the ethical dimensions of cinema has remained limited. Whereas ethical issues have been influential in Literary and Cultural Studies for over two decades now, since poststruc-turalism took what has been described as its 'ethical turn', Film Studies, in the Anglo-American tradition at least, has only recently started to bring ethical thought to bear on cinema. Film scholars have often privileged questions of ontology and epistemology over ethical concerns.[15] That said, a handful of important interventions have bucked this trend and subjected cinema to ethical scrutiny. It is worth examining some of the key claims made in this context with which I engage in my analyses of Holocaust films in subsequent chapters.

Serge Daney, an articulate and penetrating chronicler of the postwar history of the moving image as witness, has addressed some of the ques-tions formulated above from perspectives particularly pertinent to the is-sues at stake in this book. For Daney, any attempt to conceptualise cinema in ethical terms must be predicated on a dual recognition: that film has been a privileged witness to certain traumatic historical events, and that this privilege entails an ethical responsibility. In an account indebted to André Bazin's reflections on the moral dimensions of cinema's capacity to reveal reality, Daney argues that cinema is defined by its testimonial voca-tion, and suggests that there are certain historical phenomena, such as the death camps, which *only* cinema has witnessed clear-sightedly. Not only did the Nuremberg trials confirm the power of film as evidence; according to Daney, it is cinema alone, rather than literary testimonies, photographs or television, for example, which is 'capable of camping at the limits of a denatured humanity' (1992: 7).

Daney explains the responsibility this implies by means of a negative foil. What he describes as 'the indisputable axiom, the limit of all debate' (1992: 6), or what might be understood as the *a priori* of his ethics, is en-capsulated in a single filmic sequence to which he refers as 'le travelling de *Kapo*' ('the tracking shot of *Kapo*'). Ironically, while he repeatedly returns to this sequence in his writings, Daney admits he has never actually seen it or the rest of Gillo Pontecorvo's *Kapo* (1960) and while he makes it clear that this was a conscious moral choice, it nevertheless lays him open to the charge of critical irresponsibility. He bases his argument instead on a seminal critique of Kapo and Holocaust films in general, namely an es-say by Jacques Rivette entitled 'De l'abjection' which originally appeared in *Cahiers du cinéma* in 1961. Rivette's essay attacks a scene in *Kapo* where a suicidal Emmanuelle Riva throws herself against the electrified barbed wire surrounding the camp at Auschwitz. What troubles Rivette about this scene is the way the camera travels forward to reframe Riva's suspended, lifeless body from a slightly different angle and, in his account, positions her outstretched hand neatly in the corner of the shot, apparently in pur-suit of a more balanced, settled, pleasing composition. As will be clear from

the image here, Rivette slightly misre-
members the framing in question, and it
is on his misrepresentation that Daney
founds his own argument; yet this does
not in fact invalidate the broader critical insights the pair derive from it. For
Rivette, the reframing is abject because
it prioritises the aesthetic over the ethical or the true. Daney adds that it is 'immoral' and deceptive in the further sense

Kapo: the aestheticisation of death

that it places both filmmaker and spectator somewhere they never were in
reality (1992: 18–19). In these respects it is also symptomatic of what Rivette perceives as a more general problem with Pontecorvo's approach. *Kapo*
betrays history by transforming the camps into a 'spectacle' which renders
their reality 'physically bearable' for the spectator (1961: 54). Rivette argues
further that when it comes to representing the camps on screen, 'every effort [at realism] is necessarily *incomplete* ("thus immoral"), every attempt
at reconstruction or make-up derisory and grotesque, every traditional approach to the "spectacle" is a matter of voyeurism and pornography' (ibid.;
emphasis in original).

It is revealing that the terms of Rivette's critique are recapitulated almost
word for word over thirty years later by critics of *Schindler's List* (see, for
example, Godmilow 1997: 93). Meanwhile, in French cinephilic circles at
least, 'le travelling de *Kapo*' has become a critical topos and shorthand for
the ethical risks at stake in reconstructing the Nazis' crimes or other historical atrocities.[16] Rivette's and Daney's interventions thus intersect on at
least two levels with my own concerns here. On one level, Rivette's analysis
of Pontecorvo's tracking shot reformulates the often-quoted cinephilic dictum 'les travellings sont affaire de morale' ('tracking shots are a question of
morality').[17] This provocative, elliptical claim articulates the idea that it is in
film form, as much as in diegetic content (insofar as the two can be conceptualised separately), that ethical perspectives are embodied. Tracking shots
are of course only one of an infinite number of means by which a director's
ethical vision can be inscribed in a film. However, the reference to this particular shot reminds us that the mobile relations between camera, imaged
subject and viewer are charged with ethical meaning. My readings look
closely at these relations and attempt to unpack the broader implications
of Rivette's insight. On another level, by taking Pontecorvo's reconstruction
of the Holocaust as their zero-degree of reference, Daney's writings suggest
that representations of this event might constitute an important point of
orientation for ethical criticism of film. Like Rivette, Daney contrasts Pontecorvo's 'consensual aestheticisation' of the camps with the approach ad-

opted in *Nuit et brouillard* (*Night and Fog*, 1955) by Alain Resnais, another filmmaker whose tracking shots have long been the focus of ethical debate (see Rivette 1961: 54; Daney 1992: 11). While neither Rivette nor Daney attempts to elaborate a systematic ethics of cinematic representation, their texts provide, at the very least, suggestive points of departure for ethically-orientated reflection on film of, and after, the Holocaust.

Vivian Sobchack offers a more extended and methodical exploration of the 'ethical spaces' of cinema in an important essay on documentary, originally published in 1984. In her phenomenological account, it is first and foremost the unsimulated event of death, rather than a specific historical trauma such as the Holocaust, which brings the ethical dimensions of film and spectatorship into focus. Sobchack describes death as 'an event that charges the act of looking at it with ethical significance' (2004a: 254), in the face of which the gazes of both filmmaker and spectator become legitimate objects of ethical judgement. On the one hand, she analyses the ways in which documentary filmmakers inscribe their ethical stances towards the deaths they witness in their films, for instance through the movement or stasis of their cameras and the framing and duration of their shots. To facilitate evaluation of these stances, she proposes that documentary representations of death fall into a series of distinct categories, reflecting, respectively, an 'accidental', 'helpless', 'endangered', 'interventional', 'humane' or 'professional' gaze (2004a: 244). On the other hand, she examines the means by which spectators judge and respond to these gazes. 'Responsibility for the representation of death', Sobchack surmises, 'lies with both filmmaker and spectator – and in the ethical relationship constituted between the vision of each' (ibid.).

Bill Nichols tests and develops a number of Sobchack's propositions in his study of what he calls 'axiographics' in documentary, where he tracks the transformation of 'historical space' into 'ethical space' (see 1991: 76–106). His claim that style is 'intimately attached to the idea of a moral point of view' (1991: 80) echoes the observations of Moullet, Godard, Rivette and Daney; however, Nichols is interested in the distinctive ethical qualities of documentary discourse and grounds this claim in a systematic analysis of documentary form. A neologism derived from 'axiology', the study of values, 'axiographics' is defined by Nichols as 'the attempt to explore the implantation of values in the configuration of space, in the constitution of a gaze, and in the relation of observer to observed' (1991: 78). More precisely, axiographic inquiry, as he models it, considers the ethical, political and ideological implications of the filmmaker's perspective as revealed in his or her presence in or absence from the image, the camera's proximity to or distance from its subject, diegetic and extra-diegetic sound and other aspects of spatial organisation.

More recently, a number of critics have sought to enhance understanding of the relationship between film and ethics by rethinking film in the light of ethical discourses in psychoanalysis and philosophy. One of the recurrent points of reference in this emerging and fertile field of inquiry is the thought of the French philosopher Emmanuel Levinas. Despite Levinas's suspicion of art and visuality, his discussions of the relationship between self and other are currently proving enabling in a variety of film-related critical contexts. In *The Tarantinian Ethics* (2001), for example, Fred Botting and Scott Wilson draw in parallel on the insights of Levinasian philosophy and Lacanian psychoanalysis to examine the unpredictable, accidental encounters with the other staged in Quentin Tarantino's films. In the final chapter of her study of Patrice Leconte, 'The Ethics of the Couple', Lisa Downing reconsiders the director's representations of responsibility, sacrifice and love in the context of Levinas's conception of ethical relations (2004: 106–30). Levinas's work has also received attention in studies of documentary, notably in two chapters of Michael Renov's *The Subject of Documentary*, which argue that a Levinasian reading of the genre would privilege ethical issues over the epistemological ones around which much documentary theory revolves (2004: 148–67). The most fully-developed case to date for the capacity of Levinas's work to enrich analysis of cinema is made by Sarah Cooper in *Selfless Cinema?: Ethics and French Documentary* (2006). Cooper demonstrates how Levinasian thought, and in particular his concept of the 'visage', can offer compelling ethical perspectives on the images of Jean Rouch, Chris Marker, Raymond Depardon and Agnès Varda.[18]

This book, and especially its third and fourth chapters, draws in a variety of ways on the strands of ethical inquiry mapped out above, while pursuing them into new cinematic contexts. In chapter three I explore how Sobchack's and Nichols' writings on ethics and documentary can inform readings of Holocaust films, arguing that these films undermine some of the distinctions they draw between documentary and narrative fiction, while in chapter four I read images of trauma and alterity through a Levinasian lens. The first two chapters revisit two seminal filmic approaches to the Holocaust and contrasting responses to the challenge posed by Rivette in the light of the ongoing discussions about representability outlined above. Chapter one opens the debate with a reading of *Shoah*, a film which has been described as a 'monolith and touchstone of ethical representation' (Wilson 1999: 85). While Lanzmann's painstaking investigation of the extermination of European Jewry has acquired an exemplary status through public and scholarly reception, this chapter reconsiders the film as a particular, rather than definitive, attempt to bear ethical witness to historical trauma. In his writings on the Nazi project and its legacy in thought and art, Lanzmann remains one of the most forceful proponents of the view that the genocide cannot be recuperated into representation, and has suggested, moreover, that there is a prohibition on representation of the event. In line with this position, *Shoah*, along with Lanzmann's more recent films *Un vivant qui passe* (*A Visitor from the Living*, 1997) and *Sobibor, 14 octobre 1943, 16 heures* (*Sobibor, October 14, 1943, 4pm*, 2001), have most frequently been interpreted as legislating an unconditional refusal of representation. Lanzmann's decision to exclude images of the past, both reconstructed and documentary, from all three films lends weight to this reading. The chapter begins by evaluating the rationale for this decision in relation to the filmmaker's deep-seated suspicion of representation. It proceeds to argue, however, that *Shoah*'s retreat from representation may be less straightforward or consistent than is habitually intimated by its director or its commentators. Lanzmann makes processes of concealment and erasure visible and tangible and explores forms of re-enactment and mimesis in ways that call into question the film's association with taboos on representation and its alleged promotion of the *Bilderverbot* (or religious interdiction on creating certain kinds of image). Chapter one thus identifies a nexus of ethical perspectives with which the films and filmmakers discussed in the following chapters take issue.

Shoah's privileged status and uncompromising exclusions, as well as Lanzmann's provocative interventions in recent debates about the value of archive images and historical explanations, have angered a number of historians, philosophers and filmmakers. Chapter two stages an encounter between Lanzmann and Godard, one of Lanzmann's most vigorous critics. Godard has expressed concerns about what he sees as cinema's failure to bear effective witness to the camps, and he singles out Lanzmann's film and remarks he has made in other contexts for particular censure (1998a II: 146; in Bonnaud & Viviant 1998: 28). This chapter places *Histoire(s) du cinéma* and *Shoah* in dialogue with each other in order to investigate the broader implications of the directors' apparently opposing ethical agendas. Godard's reappropriation of images of the camps in *Histoire(s) du cinéma* attests to a faith in the redemptive, even resurrectory power of direct images and montage which appears to be directly at odds with Lanzmann's refutation of representation. In search of explanations for these differences, my reading turns to the missing images which seem to lie at the heart of the directors' dispute: a piece of footage shot by the Nazis depicting a gas chamber in action. Godard's and Lanzmann's contradictory claims about the significance of these hypothetical images raise questions about the evidentiary and testimonial status of film and photographs. It is no coincidence that these are precisely the questions which turn out to be at stake in critical debate about the 'Mémoire des camps' photographic exhibition.

Didi-Huberman's (2001) attempt to rehabilitate photographs as 'instants' or 'vestiges' of truth which undermine conceptions of the Holocaust as 'invisible' or 'unimaginable' works to validate Godard's project. Conversely, Wajcman's (2001) consideration of the veil-like properties of images of horror is informed by a viewing of Lanzmann's film. However, revisiting *Histoire(s) du cinéma* and *Shoah* in the context of these wider debates ultimately reveals common ground between them in the form of a shared refusal of the 'obscenity' of dominant forms of representation in the tradition of Rivette's critique of 'le travelling de *Kapo*'.

Implicit in the disagreement between Godard and Lanzmann over the missing reel of film are conflicting ideas about cinema spectatorship. Chapter three engages explicitly with this issue, approaching questions of ethics and responsibility from a different angle. The position of the spectator face to face with another's pain or suffering has remained a central preoccupation of ethical thought over the centuries. For Jean-Jacques Rousseau, it is the unbearable nature of such a position that constitutes the foundation of ethics, which derive, in his account, from an intuitive and spontaneous 'pitié' or compassion that makes us reluctant to cause or witness distress (1985: 84–7). This chapter explores how cinematic images of the other's suffering might help to reconceptualise encounters between viewers and films along ethical lines. The sociologist Luc Boltanski suggests that the mediated spectacle of suffering contemplated from afar by a 'distant and sheltered spectator' may be 'the only spectacle capable of posing a specifically *moral* dilemma to someone exposed to it' (1993: 38, 42; emphasis in original). The images which concern me here have little in common with the media pictures of poverty and war which are Boltanski's primary point of reference, but the ethical questions they pose to viewers suggest that his insight is also applicable to cinematic representations of suffering. My focus is on representations of the gas chamber in a range of fiction and documentary films. Disturbingly, this trauma scene has haunted Holocaust films more persistently than any other, attesting, I suggest, to an ongoing search for what Clément Chéroux has called an elusive '"integral" image' of the genocide (2001: 213). A recurrent and harrowing motif in Holocaust films is the spyhole or small window that was set in the chamber doors for observation purposes (a frame most famously exploited by Spielberg in *Schindler's List*). My readings examine how this motif calls the viewer's look into question, foregrounding the non-reciprocal structure of the confrontation between the inviolable body of the viewer and the vulnerable bodies viewed. While in certain films the view through the spyhole aligns our look with the sadistic, voyeuristic gaze of observing SS guards, in others we are positioned instead in the grey zone with members of the *Sonderkommandos*. But these positions do not define our emotional and ethical responses. I am interested here in particular in the strategies developed by filmmakers to destabilise the frequently posited correlation between film spectatorship and voyeurism and encourage more responsible and self-conscious ways of looking. My argument draws in this context on recent accounts of film spectatorship which emphasise the fluid and fragile nature of identifications and the responsibilities of viewers in relation to the spectacle on the screen. I suggest that the preoccupation with moral limits and interdictions exhibited by many Holocaust films, particularly as they approach the gas chambers, can distract us from the ethical import of the responses they solicit from the viewer.

The final chapter aims to draw the strands of my argument together by exploring in both theory and practice how film can bear witness to another's trauma without fully staging or appropriating it. Lanzmann's apparently paradoxical suggestion that a 'vigilant blindness' may be the prerequisite of facing and witnessing the Holocaust (1990a: 279) serves here as a point of departure for a discussion of the blind spots and hidden dimensions of filmic testimony. I draw in parallel on Jacques Derrida's (1990) writings on the affinities between blindness and witnessing, Agamben's (1999) discussion of the Muselmann as a lacuna in testimony and Levinas's (1961) account of the 'visage', or face, which offer a series of insights into the ethics of vision and blindness. While film is incapable of replicating the immediacy of the ethical encounter described by Levinas, the *face-à-face*, and while his term 'visage' does not primarily refer to an object of vision, I suggest that his thought can nevertheless illuminate some of the ways in which cinema contends with alterity. Looking both at and beyond the Holocaust with Levinas, this chapter analyses images of trauma and otherness in films by Marker and Resnais, arguing that Marker's investigation of the 'regard caméra' ('to-camera look') and Resnais' 'effacement' of the face can bear witness to an alterity that lies beyond the visible.

Each of these chapters offers a distinctive take on the neglected question of how ethical perspectives are articulated in moving images and the ways we view and theorise them. My concluding remarks take stock of cinema's past and present role as witness to the Holocaust and other atrocities and consider its future prospects. Concerns about the role of the visual media in general and cinema in particular in ongoing processes of commemoration and mourning are acquiring fresh urgency as our society is increasingly bombarded with images. Insofar as new technologies of visual representation threaten to drain the image of its testimonial power and loosen its bond with history, they further compel inquiry into cinema as the site of a persistent haunting as well as a potentially responsible witnessing.

1

(In)visible Evidence: *Shoah*

Since its release in 1985, *Shoah*, Lanzmann's nine-and-a-half-hour filmic meditation on memory, testimony, annihilation and oblivion, has become a prominent point of reference in debates about the ethics of representation of, and after, the Holocaust. The film focuses exclusively on the policy of extermination conceived and put into practice by the Nazi regime. Shot with a minimal crew and a single 16mm camera, it consists principally of a series of interviews with survivors, perpetrators and bystanders intercut with present-day images of the killing sites. But critical debate has also dwelt upon the implications of what Lanzmann decides not to show. Not only does he refuse to reconstruct the past, he also eschews archive footage. *Shoah* pointedly avoids direct images of the catastrophic event named in its title. Thus, while Lanzmann describes it as a film about 'death itself, the radicality of death' (in Blouin, Nouchi & Tesson 2001: 48), it does not present us with a single image of a dead or dying body. The same is true of Lanzmann's two most recent films, *Un vivant qui passe* and *Sobibor, 14 octobre 1943, 16 heures*, both of which are assembled from outtakes from *Shoah*. In all three films these missing bodies appear emblematic of a concerted retreat from representation, which Lanzmann views as potentially – if not *a priori* – hazardous in the context of historical trauma. In the case of the Holocaust, he states categorically that 'there is a prohibition on representation' (Lanzmann 1994: vii).

In the light of the mounting scepticism about the legitimacy of interdictions on representation discussed in the introduction to this volume, it seems time to reopen the debate about *Shoah* and the broader implications of its investigation of representability. Lanzmann's uncompromising directorial choices have acquired something of a monumental, even monolithic status through public and scholarly reception of the film. If screenings of *Shoah* frequently take on a ceremonial or ritual quality,[1] the ever-growing interdisciplinary body of texts devoted to the film attests to what Jean-Michel Frodon has dubbed the 'Shoah effect' (1997a: 27). For many of its commentators, the film's form and, above all, its traumatic content render the traditional tools of critical analysis inadequate or simply inappropriate. Moreover, while *Shoah* has rightly been accorded a privileged place amongst films about the genocide and heralded as redefining the parameters of Holocaust representation, it has also, and in my view less justifiably, been credited by some with setting a series of definitive, non-negotiable standards against which all other films on the subject should be judged. Wajcman, for example, asserts that 'in a certain respect [*Shoah*] *regards* … and sheds light on all art before it' (1998: 224; emphasis in original), while for Pierre Sorlin, who has certain reservations about the film, this 'unique oeuvre [has nevertheless] discredited all previous enterprises' (2001: 183). Such verdicts echo Lanzmann's own conviction, which itself seems to echo and reformulate Adorno's famous dictum, that 'there was a "before" and an "after" *Shoah* [and] after *Shoah* there were a certain number of things that couldn't be done' (a conviction that was shaken, he acknowledges, by the release of *Schindler's List*) (1994: vii).

Nevertheless, a number of dissenting voices have challenged the validity of these hyperbolic claims and questioned the prevailing tendency to accord an exemplary status to the film. In an important essay on *Shoah* LaCapra attributes the widespread reluctance to subject it to critical analysis to a readiness to grant priority to the ideas articulated in Lanzmann's many essays and interviews as the primary framework through which his film should be interpreted (1998: 95–138). LaCapra is suspicious of the 'prevalent critical practice of using [Lanzmann's views] to initiate, substantiate, or illustrate the critic's own conception of the film without subjecting them to critical scrutiny' (1998: 97). It is on these grounds that LaCapra takes issue with the 'authorised' reading of the film offered in Felman's influential essay from 1992, which approaches the film in what he finds to be a spirit of 'celebratory participation' that remains 'undisturbed by critical judgement' (1998: 111–12). In *Images malgré tout* Didi-Huberman lays a similar charge against Wajcman and Elisabeth Pagnoux, two of the film's most committed proponents, arguing that their texts merely recapitulate rather than evaluate Lanzmann's own pronouncements (Didi-Huberman 2003: 118; Wajcman 2001; Pagnoux 2001). As a corrective to such approaches, both LaCapra and Didi-Huberman seek to disentangle *Shoah* from Lanzmann's own interpretations of it in order to open a space for critical debate and intervention.

While I have reservations about some of the criticisms levelled against *Shoah* and Lanzmann by LaCapra and Didi-Huberman, and would query whether LaCapra is entirely successful in disengaging it from the filmmaker's extrafilmic discourse, my own analysis is informed by their appeal for the development of interpretative frameworks independent from Lanzmann's own. In beginning this study with a reading of *Shoah*, it is my intention to interrogate, rather than simply reaffirm, its status as a 'touchstone of ethical representation' (Wilson 1999: 85). LaCapra's essay is in fact predated by several incisive analyses of the film's perceived shortcomings. Marianne Hirsch and Leo Spitzer (1993), for example, draw attention to the near absence of women among the Jewish survivors interviewed and suggest that in certain respects the film recapitulates the attempted erasure of gender differences that was one of the instruments of dehumanisation and oppression employed by the Nazis.[2] Tzvetan Todorov (1991: 250–2), meanwhile, is critical of the way in which Lanzmann's overly schematic treatment of Poles and Germans 'revives Manichean values', promoting a 'thesis of collective guilt' (1991: 253–4).

Above all, however, it is Lanzmann's rejection of direct images of the past and hostility towards representational practices that have riled the film's critics. The filmmaker has been accused, variously, of 'sacralising' the Holocaust, perpetuating Adornoesque proscriptions and pernicious rhetorics of ineffability, advocating the destruction of historical archives and even 'book-burning'.[3] Warning against the temptation to 'make the Holocaust into a taboo', Semprun argues that 'an extreme, fundamentalist formulation of this attitude is to be found in the work of Claude Lanzmann' (in Delorme & Herzlich 2000: 11). LaCapra reiterates this charge whilst acknowledging that the filmmaker has attempted to distance himself from such a practice: 'Lanzmann returns to what he explicitly denies, represses or suppresses: a tendency to sacralise the Holocaust and to surround it with taboos' (1998: 100; see, for example, Herzlich 2000: 14). Discerning manifestations of a 'displaced secular religiosity' in the film, LaCapra asserts further that Lanzmann 'especially affirms a *Bilderverbot*, or prohibition on images, with respect to representation' (1998: 100). LaCapra is one of a series of commentators, including Miriam Bratu Hansen, Michael Rothberg and Joshua Hirsch, who postulate a connection between the doubts about representability that inflect *Shoah* and the Second Commandment (Hansen 1996: 301; Hirsch 2004: 72). In Rothberg's view, 'Lanzmann's argument derives explicitly from a certain understanding of the ban on graven images', and his observance of the *Bilderverbot* leads him to impose 'representational limits' which are 'contradictory, imprecise, authoritarian and ill-suited to describing the heterogeneity of modes of Holocaust representation' (2000: 232–3).[4]

In this chapter I would like to suggest that some of these critical misgivings are more pertinent to Lanzmann's off-screen reflections than to what we hear and see on the screen during *Shoah*. Sporadic failures to preserve a clear distinction between these two discursive spaces may have contributed not only to the aversion to critical analysis identified by LaCapra, but also to a propensity to overlook the presence of slippages and discrepancies between film and extrafilmic commentary, or at least the possibility of viewing the film differently. The provocative positions that Lanzmann has defended in essays and interviews and, in particular, his often polemical interventions in ongoing debates about the limits of representation deserve consideration on their own merits, but do not fully account for the singular form and content of the film. This chapter begins by addressing Lanzmann's discussions of the pitfalls of fiction and the use and abuse of archive images before analysing the alternative strategies he develops in *Shoah*. While my analysis draws in places on his commentary, I argue that the refusal of representation which is often understood as the film's foundational ethical principle may be more ambivalent, conditional and conflicted than either Lanzmann's own pronouncements or some of his critics' interpretations allow.

'False archives' and 'images without imagination'

The persistent allegation that *Shoah* propounds a *Bilderverbot* rests primarily on Lanzmann's decision to exclude direct images of the past. *Shoah* breaks with the conventions established by previous films about the genocide by evoking history without recourse to reconstructions or atrocity footage. Lanzmann's reservations about reconstructing the past are perhaps most succinctly expressed in his critique of *Schindler's List*. He writes:

> The Holocaust is unique firstly in that it erects around itself, in a circle of flames, a limit which cannot be crossed because a certain absolute of horror is intransmissible: to claim to do so is to become guilty of the most serious transgression. Fiction is a transgression; I profoundly think that there is a prohibition on representation. (Lanzmann 1994: vii)

For Lanzmann, the unprecedented if not unique horror of the Holocaust defies adequate representation and therefore renders every attempt at representation 'transgressive' or unethical. Since its reality is 'intransmissible', representation will always involve a degree of fictionalisation and, worse, assume a domesticating function. What bothers Lanzmann about historical fictions such as Spielberg's is that they purport to offer us unmediated access to a reality which they in fact reconstruct, narrativise, sanitise and trivialise. He accuses Spielberg not merely of constructing fictions but also of fabricating 'false archives' (in Herzlich 2000: 15; see also Lanzmann 1994: vii); in Lanzmann's view, the more realistic the reconstruction, the more treacherous it becomes – the greater the risk that it will usurp the position of history. Much of the passage cited above recapitulates verbatim Lanzmann's attack on the American television series *Holocaust* (1978), where he argues that the historical reality of the camps 'defies every fiction to give an account of itself' (1990b: 309). In the face of this reality, fiction amounts to 'a fundamental lie', 'a moral crime', 'an assassination of memory' (ibid.). If Lanzmann's insistence on the inseparability of epistemological and ethical questions is compelling, both his conflation of representation with fiction and his claim that all fiction is morally suspect in such a context remain contentious. Other filmmakers have exploited the potential of narrative, fiction and fantasy to reveal hidden truths about the experience of the genocide. For Lanzmann, however, the interdiction (on representation) precedes the transgression (of fiction) and defines it as such; it assumes the status in his commentaries of an *a priori* ethical principle.

As Lanzmann's condemnation of Spielberg's 'false archives' intimates, concerns about the liability of representations to misrepresent and falsify also inform his attitude towards the visual archive. With the exceptions of a photograph of SS officer Christian Wirth, which Lanzmann uses to goad his former assistant Joseph Oberhauser, and a brief series of photographs of Dachau and of the deceased relatives of some of the survivors from Corfu, *Shoah* does not recycle pre-existing images. Lanzmann has regularly attempted to explain and defend the motives behind this exclusion (see, for example, in Chevrie & Le Roux 1990: 296–97; in Guerrin 2001b). To begin with, he points out that, to all intents and purposes, there were simply no relevant images to include. *Shoah* focuses predominantly on phenomena that, due to rigid Nazi restrictions on photographic activities in such contexts, were rarely captured on film: the 'Final Solution' and the barbarous machinery devised to implement it, rather than the processes of persecution and concentration that accompanied and facilitated it. Alongside Auschwitz-Birkenau, Lanzmann concentrates on camps where no official photographs were taken to document the activities: Chelmno, the Nazis' first extermination camp and the first where gas was used, and the Operation Reinhard extermination camps at Belzec, Sobibor and Treblinka. However, contrary to Lanzmann's claim that 'there were no archives' (in Chevrie & Le Roux 1990: 297), a few images of the extermination have survived. These include four photographs displayed in the 'Mémoire des camps' exhibition, whose status as direct witnesses to the killing has provoked renewed debate about Lanzmann's decision to turn his back on the archive, as we shall see in chapter two. The only known moving images of the mass murder, which last approximately two minutes, were shot by Reinhard Wiener, a German naval sergeant, and depict an execution of Jews by firing squad in Liepaja, Latvia in 1941.[5] The fact that Lanzmann viewed this footage during the preparation of *Shoah* and chose to discard it suggests that something more than a straightforward lack of availability is at stake in his avoidance of archive images. Indeed, Lanzmann acknowledges that even if he had found what he considered to be 'relevant' material in the archives, he would not have used it in his film (in Chevrie & Le Roux 1990: 297).

On what grounds, then, does Lanzmann object to the reappropriation of such images? It is useful at this point briefly to consider his position in the context of film theoretical accounts of the epistemological status of found footage and the ethical questions raised by its redeployment. Writing on collage techniques in cinema, Paul Arthur contrasts persistent views of appropriated images as objective, transparent, essentially value-free bearers of meaning (he alludes here to comments about newsreels by Siegfried Kracauer, Parker Tyler, Béla Balázs, Thomas Waugh and Nichols) with calls for analysis of the way in which they are shaped by context and ideology. In this latter view, the critical problem facing filmmakers using such images is 'the interrogation of ideologically-motivated signifiers embedded in and disseminated through the original material' (1998: n. p.). Yet many film and television documentaries about the Holocaust neglect, or even wilfully impede, such interrogation. In recycling footage shot by Nazi cameras without reference to the original source, for example, they make it more difficult for viewers to identify and take account of the ideological biases inscribed in these images. One of the most renowned culprits is Hugh Burnett's television documentary *The Warsaw Ghetto* (1968), which used to be screened in classrooms across the UK. Burnett borrows images from Fritz Hippler's *Der ewige Jude* (*The Eternal Jew*, 1940), a notoriously virulent anti-Semitic propaganda 'document' made at the request of Nazi Propaganda Minister Joseph Goebbels, which exploits footage depicting the abjection of ghetto life in order to confirm stereotypes of Jewish degeneracy (see Dawidowicz 1978). But the film fails to inform its viewers of the origins of this footage and to warn them against misreading the images as merely generic and illustrative. Other critics are concerned by the way that Nazi film records replicate the perspective of the original camera-operator whether or not their source is identified to the viewer. According to Joshua Hirsch, for example, such footage 'positions the spectator as a victimiser, potentially eliciting a voyeuristic or sadistic response' (2004: 72).

Doubts about the legitimacy of such viewing positions and viewers' capacity to read this kind of image against the ideological grain constitute one possible motivation for Lanzmann's decision not to include the Wiener film in *Shoah*. These issues are also implicitly at stake in the following widely-cited remarks:

> I used to say that if there had been – by sheer obscenity or miracle – a film actually shot in the past of three thousand people dying together in a gas chamber, first of all, I think that no one human being would have been able to look at this. Anyhow, I would never have included this in the film. I would have preferred to destroy it. It is not visible. You cannot look at this. (Lanzmann 1991: 99)[6]

While these comments remain at the level of speculation and hypothesis, they have proved singularly inflammatory. In particular, Lanzmann's suggestion that he would destroy such a film has alarmed a number of his interlocutors. Semprun dismisses his statement as 'absurd', pointing out that Holocaust revisionists have exploited the absence of such documentation and of witnesses. He also suggests that this absence accounts for the perceived taboo on representation: 'It's the only massacre in history which left no survivors or witnesses in the strict sense. This explains the prohibition which hangs over it, partly of a religious nature, close to the interdiction of representation in the Jewish religion' (in Delorme & Herzlich 2000: 11). Noting that Lanzmann repeats these observations in his attack on *Schindler's List*, shortly after a reference to the 'circle of flames' surrounding the event, Rothberg argues that Lanzmann's 'rhetoric of destruction by fire cannot but create an uneasy echo of Nazi book burnings and crematoria and of the Nazis' own injunction against filming the genocide' (2000: 233). This interpretation serves to bolster Rothberg's broader critique of Lanzmann's 'activation' of the *Bilderverbot* and, as we shall see, proves difficult to reconcile with *Shoah*'s probing investigation of the legacy of the Nazis' destruction of visible evidence. Nevertheless, Rothberg's remarks draw attention to the implicit links between Lanzmann's exclusion of archive images and his deep-seated mistrust of representation.[7]

Lanzmann's remarks about the limitations of existing archive material offer further insights into these links. He dismisses the Wiener footage in disparaging, but revealing, terms: 'I call these images without imagination. They are just images, they have no force' (in Chevrie & Le Roux 1990: 297). Elsewhere, he elaborates upon this notion: 'I have always said that archive images are images without imagination. They petrify thought and stifle all evocative power' (2001a: 274). For Lanzmann, as indexical traces of profilmic realities, images of this kind may transmit knowledge, but they fail to stimulate the imagination and thus remain of limited mnemonic and testimonial value. Like the hypothetical footage of the gas chamber, which would constitute 'a piece of information, and nothing else' (2001a: 275), they seem to show at once too much and not enough; in rendering the past representable they diminish its real horror. Lanzmann's dismissal of archive images and the larger questions it raises about visible evidence and referentiality have aroused suspicion on the part of a number of his critics, prompting a series of attempts to rethink such images from perspectives more attentive to their role as testimony. Questions about their ethical status lie at the heart of the dispute between Lanzmann and Godard, and I examine Godard's and others' objections to Lanzmann's position as well as the alternative accounts they offer in chapter two. The rest of this chapter turns to *Shoah* itself to evaluate the relationship between Lanzmann's critiques of fiction, representation and the archive and the form and content of his film.

The *mise-en-scène* of erasure

'The film is not at all representational', insists Lanzmann of *Shoah* (1991: 97), a declaration which has often been accepted at face value but which merits further attention in the current context. *Shoah* may avoid atrocity footage and reconstructions, it may not image the past directly, yet this refusal in itself does not disqualify it as representational art, any more than it imposes a general prohibition on representation of the genocide. From this perspective, the salient questions, I would suggest, are not *whether* but *what* the film does (and does not) represent and *how* it does so. Querying the legitimacy of the 'discourse of unrepresentability' so often invoked in the context of *Shoah*, Rancière answers these questions as follows:

> In what sense does this film bear witness to the 'unrepresentable'? What it affirms is not that the fact of the extermination is concealed from artistic presentation, from the production of an artistic equivalent ... What is to be represented ... is the process of a double deletion [*suppression*]: the deletion of the Jews and the deletion of the traces of their deletion. Now that is perfectly representable [...] So the reality of the genocide that is filmed is the reality of its disappearance. (2001: 94–5)

According to Rancière, *Shoah* neither confirms the impossibility of representing the genocide nor places any interdiction on the attempt to do so. The film represents not the past but its enduring legacy in the present, a legacy shaped by the perpetrators' attempts to cover up or 'delete' the traces of their crimes, and shows this process of erasure to be fully representable. 'The point of departure for the film', Lanzmann explains, 'was ... the disappearance of traces: nothing remains but a void, and it was necessary to make a film out of this void' (in Chevrie & Le Roux 1990: 295). Many of the different methods used by the Nazis to hide or eradicate the traces of their activities are mentioned in the film by the witnesses. The former SS *Unterscharführer* Franz Suchomel recalls the deployment of inmates in so-called 'Camouflage Squads' at Treblinka to conceal the murder sites from future victims and other potential witnesses:

> Woven into the barbed wire [surrounding the *Schlauch*, or 'tube', leading from the reception section to the extermination area] were branches of pine trees ... It was known as 'camouflage'. There was a Camouflage Squad of twenty Jews. They brought in new branches every day from the woods. So everything was screened. People couldn't see anything to the left or right. Nothing. You couldn't see through it. Impossible.

A few minutes later, Suchomel's account is corroborated by Abraham Bomba, a survivor of Treblinka, who remembers that the route was 'all covered with gates, barbed wire and trees covering the gates so that nobody should see there is a gate, or a place going into the gas chamber'. Earlier in the film, Bomba relates how on arrival at the camp he was ordered to clear up the piles of clothes and shoes left by other new arrivals: 'and in no time this was as clean as though people had never been on that place. There was no trace, none at all, like a magic thing, everything disappeared.' Other witnesses give accounts of the techniques used to dispose of the victims' bodies. Richard Glazar, another Treblinka survivor, recalls the moment when he realised that the dead would no longer be buried, as he watched blazing pyres at the camp in November 1942. Echoing the words of the SS guard quoted by Levi in *The Drowned and the Saved*, Glazar informs us that 'no one was supposed to be left to bear witness'. Motke Zaïdl and Itzhak Dugin, survivors of Vilna, remember opening up the mass graves at Ponari in January 1944 in order to disinter and burn the bodies, citing the order of the head of the Vilna Gestapo that 'absolutely no trace must be left of them'. Simon Srebnik, a survivor of Chelmno, describes how the bones that were too large to burn were crushed into powder and dumped into the River Narew. Jan Piwonski, a Pole who worked at the station at Sobibor, tells us that in the winter of 1943, after the camp was liquidated, the Nazis planted young pine trees to camouflage its traces.

But it is the disjunctive, fluctuating relationships between the witnesses' words and the images that accompany them that make the 'void' alluded to by Lanzmann tangible – if never fully graspable – to the viewer. The film is punctuated by prolonged, leisurely tracking and panning shots of the murder sites in the present, which invite us to search for evidence of the violence that took place there. Sometimes we discover material remains: railway lines and sidings, fences, barracks and watchtowers, cemeteries and gravestones. But we see how these remnants are being eroded over time by the elements; the buildings are derelict and decaying, the gravestones crumbling and the ground rubble-strewn, overgrown and nibbled by rabbits. Sometimes there is almost nothing left to see. In the grassy clearing in the Chelmno forest which Srebnik recognises as the place where the bodies of the asphyxiated were incinerated, all that remains of the furnaces are nondescript, harmless-looking foundations. As we listen to Srebnik remember in voice-over the moment when he first understood the purpose of the buildings that once stood there, we watch him silently roaming around the clearing and sifting clods of earth through his fingers. Like him, we scan the ground for physical traces, tangible remnants of its barbarous history, but, aside from the foundations, the visible evidence that might link this scene to his simultaneous narrative eludes us. Lingering shots of such abandoned sites recur throughout the film, unsettling us by arousing a desire for visual presence that they leave frustrated. It is the non-coincidence between word and image, between the atrocities recounted by the witnesses and the deceptive serenity, sometimes banality, sometimes beauty of the sites at which they occurred

Shoah: Simon Srebnik searching for traces at Chelmno

that makes manifest the progressive dematerialisation of the traces of the extermination. 'By its persistence in the present', observes David N. Rodowick, 'the landscape gives visible testimony to what cannot be represented in the voice. In turn, the voice excavates a past entombed in the landscape and hidden from sight' (1997: 148). What can neither be recounted by the voice nor shown by the images is figured instead in their non-relation. Yet as we realise that the earth in the Chelmno clearing is in part composed of the bodies that were burnt there, image and word, present and past collide, traumatically, in the physical evidence in Srebnik's hands.

Felman maintains that 'to understand *Shoah* is not to *know* the Holocaust, but to gain new insights into what *not knowing* means, to grasp the ways in which *erasure* is itself part of the functioning of our *history*' (1992c: 253; emphasis in original). While Felman accepts Lanzmann's assertion that the film is 'not at all representational', I would argue that in the ways outlined above *Shoah* continuously *represents* the process of erasure she describes, a process which defined the Holocaust. By juxtaposing oral accounts of the atrocities with the sight of traces under erasure and empty graves, *Shoah* makes disappearance and absence disarmingly present to our eyes and ears. Hirsch coins the term 'unerasure' to describe this mode of representation: the endeavour 'to reverse the effects of [the perpetrators'] attempted erasure by remembering it, by rewitnessing it, by recognising the site of the erasure now made almost unrecognisable by its own erasure' (2004: 77, 176). In certain sequences, moreover, the representation of erasure – which connects the past to the present – appears to coincide with a movement towards representation of the past, a movement which is addressed in the remaining sections of this chapter.

'Fictions of the real'

Another way to approach the vexed issue of representation in *Shoah* is through questions about cinematic genre and *mise-en-scène*. One of the difficulties facing the film's commentators is its apparent resistance to straightforward generic classification. The diverse representational strategies employed by Lanzmann challenge traditional understandings of the form and content of the documentary film. While the absence of reconstructions appears to mark the film as a work of non-fiction, many of the staple components of documentary, such as archive footage, a voice-over commentary, a chronological or linear narrative structure, are also missing. Moreover, Lanzmann's evident staging of some of the scenes involving witnesses reveals a readiness to resort to artifice and subterfuge that, for certain critics, belies the claims to objectivity conventionally associated with the documentary form. LaCapra describes *Shoah* as a 'disturbingly mixed generic performance' (1998: 96), arguing that Lanzmann is correct to reject the label 'documentary' in the limited sense that certain scenes are carefully constructed (see 1998: 98). But, as Janet Walker reasons, this does not in itself disqualify the film as a documentary; after all, virtually all documentary interviews are staged in the sense that they 'would not be occurring if not for the purpose of being filmed' (2005: 135–6). Indeed, in staging the events he films Lanzmann is employing a traditional documentary technique.

Lanzmann himself suggests alternative ways of conceptualising (if not categorising) his work and its propensity to undermine the stability of generic boundaries. Rather than as a 'historical film', he argues that *Shoah* should be understood as 'a kind of originary event' (in Chevrie & Le Roux 1990: 303), since it was filmed in the present, deals exclusively with the present and is constructed purely out of 'the traces of traces' (in Chevrie & Le Roux 1990: 304). Moreover, rather than asserting its non-fiction credentials, he posits his film provocatively as 'a fiction of the real' (see, for example, Chevrie & Le Roux 1990: 301).[8] How are we to interpret this seemingly paradoxical designation? Is Lanzmann simply refuting persistent claims that there is a meaningful distinction between 'non-fiction' and 'fiction' films? Or does his formula articulate a deeper insight into the role of artifice in the construction and transmission of truth? And if so, what is the difference between his 'fiction of the real' and the types of fictionalisation involved, for example, in *Holocaust* or *Schindler's List*, which he attacks as forgetful and mendacious? In short, on what basis are certain forms of artifice more acceptable than others?

One of the ways in which we might understand Lanzmann's phrase 'fiction of the real' in the context of the evidence supplied in his film is as an attempt to distinguish on ethical grounds between two types of films about the genocide: on the one hand, those such as *Shoah* which 'fictionalise the reality' of the camps through staged testimonies and, on the other, those which endeavour to authenticate a (historical) fiction. Emblematic of this second type of approach are the many films which exploit documentary techniques and motifs in a bid to validate a fictional narrative. Margaret Olin observes that documentary interpolations in Holocaust narratives 'have the rhetorical function of a metonym or index, seeming to ground a narrative in reality by displaying some real object directly connected with that reality' (1997: 8). In Olin's view, this is the function of the leap to present-day Israel that typically concludes what she dubs 'Holocaust escape films'. Thus in Peter Lilienthal's *David* (1979), Andrzej Wajda's *Korczak* (1990) and Agnieszka Holland's *Europa, Europa* (1991) Israel becomes 'the place where the film asserts its claim to truth' (ibid.). A similar function is served by the closing scene of *Schindler's List*, which depicts the real survivors, accompanied by the actors who play them, placing memorial stones on Schindler's grave in Jerusalem. According to Rothberg, this ending 'offers both a surplus of reality meant to supplement and confirm the realism of the film's narrative and a syncretism of fiction and reality that destabilises both the real and the fictional' (2000: 239). Indeed, the distinctions between these two representational modes are progressively destabilised throughout the Spielberg film, which exhibits a preoccupation with documentary style and its validating potential. While its black-and-white images, often shot with a handheld camera, have prompted laudatory comparisons with the work of Sergei Eisenstein, Italian neorealism and even *cinéma vérité*, they have aroused critical misgivings in equal measure. Jill Godmilow sums up the concerns of many of the film's detractors when she accuses Spielberg of producing 'out of all that veracity ... only a pornography of the real' (1997: 93).[9] Revealingly, it is not only fiction films that resort to strategies of authentication. Christopher

Olgiati's documentary *Child of the Death Camps: Truth and Lies* (1999) examines the controversial case of Binjamin Wilkomirski, whose best-selling and singularly graphic testimony *Bruchstücke* (*Fragments: Memories of a Wartime Childhood*) has been exposed as a fraud. Olgiati offers two alternative narratives, the former recounting Wilkomirski's version of events and the latter uncovering and correcting the former's lies and self-deceptions. Yet the film imports harrowing archive footage from the camps, as if to authenticate a testimony that it has already revealed to be fraudulent; Wilkomirski was never inside a working death camp. Perversely, Olgiati's ambiguous deployment of visible evidence further obscures the distinctions between the truths and the falsehoods that his film purports to separate.

Shoah's 'fictions of the real' can be read as a response and corrective to this widespread and, in Lanzmann's view, pernicious compulsion to document fiction. Rather than strategically 'claiming the real' in order to verify a fiction, Lanzmann contends that it is more ethical to approach reality through fictional constructs. 'To make images starting from the real is to make holes in reality' (in Chevrie & Le Roux 1990: 298), he observes, acknowledging the unstable relationship between reality and its representation. He goes on to underline the subjective decisions that shape his film, and describes his work as a process of 'continuous creation', involving scenes that are 'practically always constructed … always staged' (in Blouin, Nouchi & Tesson 2001: 54–5).

In *Shoah mise-en-scène* plays a crucial role both in the puncturing of reality and the production and transmission of truth. As often as possible, Lanzmann returns his witnesses to the sites where the events they recount occurred, in the hope that memories will resurface as they contemplate and explore these places in the present. Sometimes he uses props or other people to facilitate the process of recollection. In one of the film's most famous sequences, Henrik Gawkowski, a Polish train-driver who drove death transports to the camps, retraces his journey to Treblinka in a hired locomotive with Lanzmann. As he catches sight of the station sign, Gawkowski silently draws his finger across his throat, involuntarily re-enacting the ambivalent gesture which some of the Polish villagers suggest was intended to warn those in the trains of their impending fate, but which, Lanzmann implies, is more likely to have been an expression of unmitigated sadism or at least *Schadenfreude*. Emphasising that Gawkowski's gesture was entirely spontaneous, Lanzmann refers to it as an 'image which has become truth', next to which archive footage becomes 'unbearable' (in Chevrie & Le Roux 1990: 300).

Amongst the most elaborately staged sequences of the film is a much-discussed excerpt from Lanzmann's interviews with Bomba. A barber by

Shoah: Abraham Bomba returning our look

training, Bomba was selected in Treblinka to cut the hair of those who were about to be gassed. Bomba is now retired, but Lanzmann rents a barber's shop in Tel Aviv and places a pair of scissors in his hands and a customer in front of him. As Bomba relates how he waited in the gas chamber while women and children came in from the undressing huts, Lanzmann interrupts with a question that marks a departure from his customary preoccupation with concrete, technical specifics: 'What did you feel the first time you saw all these naked women?' Seemingly unsatisfied with Bomba's response, Lanzmann urges him to imitate the actions he performed under duress in the camp and repeats his question almost verbatim several minutes later. This time it prompts Bomba to explain that all feelings were rapidly deadened by such work and then to recount an incident which appears to contradict this assertion. As he describes the arrival of a transport of women from Czestochowa, his home town, many of whom he was close to and who included the wife and sister of one of his friends and fellow barbers at Treblinka, his words become choked and his hitherto coherent testimony breaks down under the pressure of resurfacing trauma. He falls silent, wipes his face and turns away from the camera. But the camera zooms in closer until his face almost fills the screen, and Lanzmann, ignoring Bomba's request that they stop, repeatedly urges him to keep going: 'We have to do it. You know it … You have to do it. I know it's very hard. I know and I apologise … Please. We must go on.' It is nearly three-and-a-half minutes before Bomba is ready and able to pick up his story.

Arnaud Desplechin describes this sequence as 'a definitive cinematic scene … Perfect *mise-en-scène*' (cited in Herzlich 2000: 15). The ethical issues raised by Lanzmann's tendency to direct and manipulate his witnesses from a prominent on-screen position, to channel their testimonies through his own point of view and to continue filming even when they do not appear to consent and attempt to hide from the camera have been the subject of extensive debate. Many viewers are uncomfortable with the ruthlessness of these strategies. Todorov argues that Lanzmann's interview techniques verge on the coercive, betraying a disrespect for the wishes and dignity of the individual which perpetuates values belonging to the ideology the film condemns (1991: 252–4). For LaCapra, who is also disturbed by 'the intrusive, if not inquisitorial and violent, nature of Lanzmann's questioning' (1998: 123), the filmmaker's direction of Bomba is symptomatic of a questionable investment in the acting out of trauma which informs his approach throughout the film. In LaCapra's view, Lanzmann is more interested in inducing the survivors to become retraumatised and relive the past in the present than in helping them to work their traumas through. An alternative reading is offered by Hirsch, who contends that the film fulfils a key requirement of working through by according the witness a safe space in which to speak and a community of attentive, receptive, sympathetic listeners (2004: 84). Other critics argue that Lanzmann's ends justify his means. Noting that the morality of Lanzmann's decision to film Suchomel covertly and break his promise not to disclose the witness's name tends to divide student audiences, Walker maintains that Lanzmann's choice not to conceal his subterfuge from his viewers confirms his integrity as filmmaker and historian (2005: 135).

Rather than taking sides in this ongoing debate, however, I would like to draw attention here to another aspect of Lanzmann's 'fictionalisation of the real'. While, for Felman, the fact that Bomba is filmed cutting the hair of a male rather than female customer confirms that the staging of this scene is 'not representational' (in Lanzmann 1991: 97), I would offer an alternative reading. Lanzmann's insistent prompting of an increasingly distressed Bomba, his decision to keep the camera rolling when Bomba is no longer able to speak and to include the entirety of Bomba's silence unedited in *Shoah*, and the fact that he cuts to another scene almost immediately after Bomba has recovered his self-composure sufficiently to resume his account all arouse the suspicion that the director is interested not only in the facts and events recounted but also in what is communicated non-verbally. Commenting on this sequence, Renov writes: 'the kernel of trauma, buried and of the Real, erupts less as language, more as signs of bodily distress' (2004: 127). Lanzmann's own commentary on the scene lends further weight to this reading. He refers to Bomba's relatively coherent narrative and deadpan delivery in the earlier stages of the sequence as 'neutral and flat'; 'he transmits things, but he transmits them badly ... He transmits only knowledge' (in Chevrie & Le Roux 1990: 297). Lanzmann suggests, however, that something shifts as soon as he asks Bomba to imitate the physical action of hair-cutting: 'It is starting from this moment that the truth is incarnated and he relives the scene, that suddenly knowledge becomes incarnated' (in Chevrie & Le Roux 1990: 298). Elsewhere, the director appears to identify this process as the telos of the film: 'The purpose of *Shoah* is not to transmit knowledge, in spite of the fact that there is knowledge in the film ... I would say that the film is an *incarnation*, a *resurrection*' (cited in Felman 1992c: 213–14; emphasis in original). I would suggest that this process of 'incarnation' or 'resurrection' might be understood, precisely, in representational terms – more specifically, as an attempt to access past realities through a form of mimesis that avoids the pitfalls of and obviates the need for archive images or reconstruction. Lanzmann's identification of Bomba's and Gawkowski's physical gestures as privileged moments of revelation attests to an investment in mimesis as a vector of memory and vehicle of truth. Rather than his words, it is the witness's body, and in particular his hands, that become the locus of representation and testimony; the manual imitation or miming of past actions in the present precipitates the 'incarnation' of truth. Moreover, Bomba's act of representation is reflected in the mirror beside him, whose prominent presence in the frame implies, for Nico Israel, that Lanzmann may be 'attempting to get at the repression through a kind of mimesis or recollection' (in Lanzmann 1991: 97).

The theatrical terms in which Lanzmann describes the role of his witnesses seem to corroborate this reading, implicitly locating their 'incarnation' of truth within a representational regime. 'In a certain respect', he observes, 'it was necessary to transform these people into actors. It's their own story that they tell. But telling was not enough. They had to act it out, that is, that they had to de-realise [*irréalisent*]' (in Chevrie & Le Roux 1990: 301). Lanzmann's reconceptualisation of witnessing as a form of acting or 'de-realisation' invites us to reconsider the relationship between testimony and fiction and the moral values he ascribes to each in the critiques of reconstruction cited above. How can the witness speak truthfully if he or she is required to act out a part? And to what extent can his or her face and body represent anything but the appearance, rather than the reality, of a past experience? For Lanzmann, it is only by acting that the witness can effect the 'abolition of all distance between the past and the present' (ibid.) which is the primary goal of his film. In other words, when the witness begins to act, past and present are no longer distinct moments in a temporal continuum but become simultaneous, at which point the image becomes truthful. Involuntary, irresistible and devoid of conscious artfulness, the act thus undermines its own artifice; indeed, rather than *acting*, it is as if the witness *is acted* by the past in the present.

In *Shoah*, then, fiction becomes the condition of possibility for authentic testimony while a past that is never reconstructed is nonetheless represented through the bodies of the actor-witnesses as they relive, re-enact, are acted by or 'incarnate' their traumas. From this perspective, Lanzmann's 'fictions of the real' and Spielberg's historical fiction might be rethought as alternative representational strategies. The differences between Spielberg's actors and Lanzmann's actor-witnesses and between Spielberg's sets and reconstructions and Lanzmann's *mise-en-scène* bring into focus the directors' divergent conceptions of ethical representation and of the role that fiction can play in accessing truth.

The return of representation

At the centre of the 'circles of hell' mapped out by *Shoah* (Lanzmann 1991: 83), at the heart of the machinery of extermination described by Bomba and the other witnesses, and at the root of Lanzmann's doubts about the possibility and legitimacy of representation, lies the gas chamber. This is the site of the primal trauma scene which the film incessantly asks us to face but refuses to show us directly: 'you cannot look at this'. Lanzmann's verdict on the hypothetical film identifies the threshold of the gas chamber as the limit of the representable and the viewable. However, in spite of Lanzmann's assertion that the violence perpetrated there 'is not visible', and in spite of the multiple precautions taken by the SS, there were, of course, a handful of prisoners who witnessed the gas chambers or the gas vans from the inside and survived to tell the tale, several of whom testify in *Shoah*. Srebnik, Michaël Podchlebnik and Filip Müller are survivors of the Chelmno and Auschwitz *Sonderkommandos* (literally, and euphemistically, 'special units'), work details of exclusively male, mainly Jewish deportees who were forced to work in and around the gas vans (at Chelmno) or the gas chambers (at Auschwitz and other camps). The appalling daily tasks of the *Sonderkommandos* included preparing other deportees for gassing while concealing the fate that awaited them and removing and interring or, later, incinerating their corpses. Podchlebnik describes coming across the bodies of his wife and children while unloading the asphyxiated from gas vans into mass graves during the 'first period' at Chelmno. Srebnik recounts burning the bodies of the dead and not quite dead in open-air ovens during the 'second period' of killings at the camp. Life expectancy for the members of the *Sonderkommandos* was even shorter than for inmates assigned to other duties. Some committed suicide, unable to live with the collaborative role they were compelled to play in the annihilation of their own people. Others fell victim to the regular 'liquidations' carried out the by SS to ensure that none who had seen their killing machines first-hand would survive to bear witness.[10] In discussions of *Shoah* Bomba and Glazar are sometimes referred to alongside Müller as *Sonderkommando* survivors, a designation which is strictly incorrect. However, most of the slave workers in Treblinka and the other Reinhard camps were directly involved in one way or another in the extermination process, since this was the sole purpose of these camps, and in this respect their function bears comparison with that of the Auschwitz *Sonderkommandos*. Moreover, Bomba insists that he spent up to ten days working actually inside the gas chamber, before the barbers were relocated to the undressing huts.[11] It is Podchlebnik's, Srebnik's, Müller's and Bomba's privileged position as eyewitnesses to the production line of death that prompts Lanzmann to track them down and persuade them to speak about their experiences in *Shoah*. For Lanzmann, deportees employed in these ways were 'the only direct witnesses to the extermination of their people' (in Frodon 2007b: 115). There is also something miraculous about their testimony; 'promised to death', they bear witness now as 'revenants', or ghosts, who speak 'from beyond the threshold of the crematorium' (Lanzmann 1980: 9, 13; in Frodon 1997b). In a similar vein, Felman calls them 'spokesmen for the dead', witnesses who 'have seen their own death – and the death of their own people – face to face' and who thus 'address us in the film both from inside life and from beyond the grave' (1992c: 280).[12]

In a series of lengthy interview extracts interpolated at different points in *Shoah*, Müller, a Czech Jew who survived five 'liquidations' of the Auschwitz *Sonderkommando*, delivers an excruciatingly detailed account of the workings of the crematoria and gas chambers. Not only is he able and willing to describe scenes of almost inconceivable horror with the utmost precision, such as the sight which confronted his team when they reopened the doors to the chambers after the gassings, but he also reflects lucidly on the specificity of the predicament of the *Sonderkommandos* who daily witnessed the murder of thousands of innocent people, as well as on how this experience has informed his understanding of the value of human life and hope. One of the many things that is remarkable about Müller's performance as a witness is his apparent self-possession; his account is articulate, coherent and linear and his delivery calm, assured and measured, though never detached. Indeed, next to Bomba, who makes few concessions to rhetoric, Müller appears an eloquent storyteller. He spends time setting the scene, allows suspense to build (for example, by punctuating his narrative with the adverb 'plötzlich' ('suddenly')) and employs figures of speech such as similes even in the most unlikely contexts (likening, for instance, the compressed corpses of the asphyxiated to slabs of basalt). In these ways and in marked contrast to Bomba's, Müller's testimony prompts us to question the universal validity of the ineffability topos invoked by Lanzmann ('I started precisely with the impossibility of telling this story' (in Chevrie & Le Roux 1990: 295)) and explicitly affirmed at the beginning of the film by Srebnik: 'No one can describe it. No one can recreate what happened here.'

While Müller's evocative descriptions invite us to visualise in our imagination what Lanzmann tends to refuse to show us in images, there are a number of points in his testimony when word and image intersect in ways that I would argue call further into question Lanzmann's understanding of the film as non-representational. Unlike Bomba, Müller is not encouraged by Lanzmann physically to re-enact what he describes. Nor is he interviewed in a setting that bears any visible relationship to his past (he testifies from the comfort of a sofa at his home). At certain moments, nevertheless, Müller's voice is accompanied by images which stage the events he relates in respects that remain unacknowledged and unauthorised by Lanzmann's commentary. As Müller recounts his discovery of the crematorium in Camp 1 at Auschwitz, a handheld camera retraces his journey along the same street, through the gate, into the crematorium, down the dark corridor and into the incineration chamber. A new relationship is established between word and image and between past and present during this sequence. Not only are the shots of the camp carefully synchronised with Müller's account; the camera also simulates his point of view, aligning our viewing position with his by moving in precisely the way he describes doing himself and at precisely the moment we hear him do so. The images thereby assume an imitative or referential function which draws us in, builds suspense and heightens their affective impact. They invite us to share vicariously in the bewilderment and horror experienced by Müller as he entered the crematorium and witnessed it in action for the first time. Subjective shots of the camp also accompany other segments of Müller's testimony, including his description of the crematoria at Birkenau. Part of this account is narrated from the viewpoint of the arriving victims, during which a handheld camera leads us down some steps into what remains of Crematorium III and wanders haltingly through the overgrown, snow-covered ruins of the undressing room towards the gas chamber. Like Müller's words, in time with which it moves, the camera encourages us to contemplate the scene from the perspective of the condemned.

In a discussion of these sequences, Rothberg (2000: 234–7) draws parallels between the imitative function of Lanzmann's handheld camerawork and the realist strategies deployed by Spielberg. Finding in *Schindler's List* and *Shoah* 'related attempts to create a mimetic correspondence between text and event, albeit with very different effects', he contends that the sequences in question perform 'a reenactment of the type [Lanzmann] complains about in Spielberg' (2000: 224, 234). While he acknowledges that, unlike Spielberg, Lanzmann maintains 'an unbridgeable gap between testimony and "being-there"' thereby marking 'the desire for the real without arousing the suspicion that he might attempt to simulate it', Rothberg reads the handheld tracking shots as a 'mimetic gesture' which 'suggests a desire to touch the real in a more direct way' (2000: 237, 238). Although I would argue that this 'mimetic gesture' remains at odds with Spielberg's realist aesthetic, Rothberg's argument intersects with my own in the contention that representation returns to *Shoah* – or *Shoah* returns to representation – in ways and at moments that merit further attention.

As Rothberg concedes, the handheld shots during Müller's narrative remain anomalous, their unsteadiness and jerky twists and turns contrasting sharply with the smoothly panning impersonal landscape shots that dominate the image-track. Yet there are a number of other moments at which the camera reproduces the historical perspective of the victims and survivor-witnesses. The film is punctuated by sequences filmed from moving vehicles, including vans, trucks and even boats, as they retrace the itineraries of the deportees. There are several images of the entrance to the Auschwitz camp shot from a camera that approaches slowly and steadily along the tracks that lead up to and through the gate. In one particularly unsettling sequence, the station sign at Treblinka is filmed from inside the darkness of a freight truck. Like the images that accompany Müller's testimony, shots of this kind have a mimetic or representational function which implicates and repositions the audience in disturbing ways. By adopting the point of view of those arriving on the death transports, they seem to invite us to identify with the victims in their plight, staging that 'detour through the other that defines a self' which, for Diana Fuss, structures identification (1995: 2).

At the same time, however, the distancing strategies employed by Lanzmann foreclose this detour, exposing the cognitive and experiential gulf that separates survivor from viewer rather than pretending to bridge it. In an illuminating commentary on the first of the handheld sequences described above, Rodowick argues that the 'mimetic relation ... between camera and voice' constitutes

> neither an attempt to identify with Müller's former place nor to construct a subjective perspective for the spectator to occupy. The camera accompanies the voice in a free indirect relation ... The camera follows the visual traces in the present that coincide with the linguistic traces Müller follows in memory, while acknowledging that the two can never be fully present to one another. (1997: 147)

Rodowick concludes that the relation between image and sound in such sequences is 'incommensurate yet complementary' (ibid.). For while we see the settings and some of the props to which Müller alludes – the crematoria chimney and door, the pillars in the undressing room, the silhouettes of ovens – the crucial components of his testimony cannot be visualised. The images do not show us the noise, stench and smoke, the piles of suitcases and crystals of Zyklon B. Nor do they show us the protagonists of his narrative: the human bodies, Jewish and Nazi, alive and dead. Like the disjunctive cuts between the decaying landscapes and the witnesses' traumatised faces, the incommensurability of their words with the uneasy silence of the empty atrocity sites insists upon the limits of the images' referentiality. It reminds us that, as viewers of *Shoah*, we are merely vicarious or belated witnesses to events we hear described but can never fully come to grasp or know. As if to acknowledge this impossibility, the camera reverses away from the Auschwitz gate almost as often as it approaches it, distancing us physically from the place of death and metaphorically from the fate of the victims. What is more, as Barry Langford points out, the camera never crosses the threshold from the undressing rooms into the gas chambers themselves (1999: 31). In pulling up short at this threshold, in surveying the ruins only from the out-side, it appears to mark the physical and psychological limit at which identifica-tory bonds are definitively sundered.

Shoah: model of Crematoria II and III at Auschwitz-Birkenau

All the more unexpected and discon-certing, then, are two sequences which bring us face to face with the horror on the other side of this threshold. Müller's description of the Birkenau crematoria is introduced by a shot of the scale model of Crematoria II and III in the Auschwitz museum. Lanzmann delays the title identifying the model, and for the first few seconds of this shot it is not entirely clear what kind of representation we are being shown; due to its stasis and monochrome tones it may initially be mistaken for an old photograph. As Müller details the layout and capacity of the complex, the camera pans over the model in time with his narration, slowly, patiently but relentlessly following the passage of the condemned across the yard, down the steps, through the underground undressing rooms and into the gas chamber. For the first time in the film, we are confronted with a direct representation of violence being inflicted upon the human body. Unlike the deserted, aban-doned ruins that so often occupy the screen, the miniature buildings are in perfect working condition and replete with tiny, roughly-hewn plaster figures waiting, descending, undressing and dying. The camera comes mo-mentarily to rest in a close-up on a group of naked, contorted, entwined bodies inside the gas chamber, before zooming out to reveal the thousands suffocating there with them, as well as the ovens beyond. While these fig-ures do not actually move, they are disturbingly evocative of motion; the model captures in three dimensions the final instant of desperate turmoil and chaos before the bodies are stilled by death.

Reflecting on the incongruity of this sequence, Langford writes 'it seems paradoxical that, at the very moment when both representational conven-tions and Lanzmann's own ethos ought to require the eye to avert itself, representation should return to *Shoah*' (ibid.). It is indeed striking that visual access to the past – albeit via iconic, rather than indexical, signs – should be restored to us as we contemplate the gas chamber. Although this is a plaster model rather than a celluloid imprint, it nonetheless constitutes a mimetic or figurative representation of the scene which, according to Lanzmann, 'is not visible', at which we 'cannot look'. At precisely the instant when sight should elude us, we find ourselves able to see. Moreover, part of the shot of the model is recycled in a later sequence, directly after the habitually self-composed Müller evokes the final moments of the Czech Jews from the 'family camp' at Theresienstadt, the memory of which is so painful that, for the first and only time in the film, he finds himself at a loss for words, unable to go on. The cut from Müller's tear-stained face back to the plaster figures in the throes of death establishes a new degree of referentiality between sounds and visuals while reasserting the primacy of the image. In this sequence it is at the point where language fails and testimony breaks down that direct vision, representation and the missing body return.

In an essay on *Schindler's List* Hansen warns that Lanzmann's attack on Spielberg's film 'reduces the dialectics of the problem of representing the unrepresentable to a binary opposition of showing or not showing – rather than casting it, as one might, as an issue of competing representations and competing modes of representation' (1996: 302). My own reading of *Shoah* has attempted to complicate this binary opposition not by collapsing the distinctions between Lanzmann's approach and Spielberg's, for example, but by attending to signs of a recalcitrant representational impulse that is not only difficult to reconcile with aspects of Lanzmann's critique of representation but also begins to challenge the prevailing critical consensus about his film. *Shoah*'s *mise-en-scène* of erasure and exploration of processes of staging, re-enactment, incarnation and mimesis interrupt its retreat from representation in ways that undermine readings of the film as straightforwardly anti-representational. Analysis of these strategies can open up new perspectives from which we might also reconsider the extent to which the film affirms the *Bilderverbot* with which it is often associated. Lanzmann's careful avoidance of indexical images of the past amounts to neither a refusal of representation *per se* nor a prohibition of such images. Unlike Lanzmann's extrafilmic interventions, *Shoah* itself offers a series of challenging insights into the ethical dimensions of the image without laying down any proscriptive or prescriptive moral rules. As Didi-Huberman observes, Lanzmann's formal choices are 'specific, therefore relative … they do not decree any law' (2001: 231).

Shoah's singular contribution to ongoing conversations about the Holocaust and its legacy derives, I would suggest, not from any interdiction on representation but from the capacity of Lanzmann's ethical choices to stimulate engaged reflection and debate. The possibility that his role is Socratic – that, effectively, of an irritant provoking discussion and invention amongst other filmmakers – provides a point of orientation for the chapters which follow. As we shall see, *Shoah*'s structuring preoccupations and obsessions return insistently in other films, not least as sources of suspicion. Indeed, the next chapter suggests that the film's legacy may be at its most aesthetically and ethically fertile precisely when it provokes the most antagonistic responses. If *Shoah* can serve as a paradigm for exploration of the challenges the Holocaust poses to representation, this is not in the privileged capacity of an ethical monolith, but, rather, because it opens up a space for us to explore conflicting ideas about what it means to bear ethical witness. As its images unfold into the future, the film, and the shattering testimonies that it presents, become, in Lanzmann's words, 'a place of meeting' (1991: 84), of encounters which call us as reflective and reflecting ethical subjects, as spectator-witnesses, while constantly putting that place at risk.

2

The Missing Reel and the Unimaged Real: Godard/Lanzmann

'It showed nothing at all' (1998a II: 146): thus Godard, always the *provoca-teur*, dismisses Lanzmann's film *Shoah*. One of the most troubling – though under-explored – claims underpinning Godard's critical take on cinema's history is that the medium has failed to honour what he perceives as its ethical obligation to bear witness to the Nazi camps. While the first chap-ter of his celebrated eight-hour video-essay *Histoire(s) du cinéma* admits a brief citation from *Shoah*, Godard's reluctance to pay any more than cur-sory lip-service to a work that would widely be considered to undermine his argument raises some important questions. In the light of the evidence outlined in chapter one, the contention that *Shoah* 'shows nothing' surely attests to a radical misreading of the film which empties both its images and its lacunae of their resonant meanings and testimonial power. This misreading is particularly perplexing given certain striking affinities be-tween the work of the two filmmakers. Sharing a penchant for polemic and ellipsis, both Godard and Lanzmann have courted controversy by creating resistant, challenging, provocative films which reflect directly on the ethics of representation. Both have abandoned narrativity to explore cinema as a way of rethinking time, memory and history when fractured by atrocity. For both, moreover, the moving image remains a privileged witness to the alterity of historical trauma, capable of producing ethical moments where self-conscious fiction collides with the shock of the real.

However, the collaborative filmic project proposed in 1999 by Bernard-Henri Lévy for the 'Gauche/Droite' series on Franco-German television channel Arte ('Lanzmann–JLG chez BHL', 'Le fameux débat', or 'Pas un dîner de gala') was intended to give both directors an opportunity, in a film where directorial responsibility was equally shared, to explain and debate certain deep-rooted differences that have long been latent between them and have more recently begun to surface. Since Godard's attack on Lanzmann in an interview for *Les Inrockuptibles*, where he aligns the latter's misgivings about representation with Adorno's original comment about the barbarity of writing poetry after Auschwitz (see Bonnaud & Viviant 1998: 28), interaction between the two directors has been characterised by mutual mistrust, with periodical outbursts on Godard's part met by hostile silence on Lanzmann's. The collaborative film was eventually abandoned, ostensibly due to Lanzmann's eventual loss of patience with Godard's many alterations to the 'rules of the game', as well as to secondary questions such as the choice of editor.[1] Viewed from a broader perspective, however, the failure of this project would seem testimony not merely to the mutual suspicion which reduced all attempts at dialogue to a twisted rhetorical duel, but also to a shared conviction that there was simply no common ground between the two that might provide the basis for an encounter.

It is my aim in this chapter to test this conviction by staging just such an encounter. At stake in the directors' dispute, I suggest, is much more than a rhetorical game. For their distinctive conceptions of the ethical status of traumatic images offer fresh perspectives on the relationship between ethics and aesthetics that is a central concern of this study. As we shall see, their arguments also intersect with wider debates in recent scholarship on Holocaust representation and testimony in a number of illuminating ways. My concern at this juncture is not only to examine the merits and limitations of the position of each filmmaker (insofar as their positions can be fixed at all) but also to identify points of difference and coincidence that can help us to rethink the relations between history, images and spectators. By reading *Histoire(s) du cinéma* and *Shoah* against each other, I would like to query the extent to which Godard's histories of cinema challenge Lanzmann's rejection of images of the past. Conversely, to what extent might Godard's attack on cinema's amnesia with regard to the Holocaust be redefined by films such as Lanzmann's that privilege a temporal present to cultivate, precisely, the *an*amnesis that is a prerequisite of mourning? To rephrase the question using Godard's terms: if only belated testimony to the camps could afford the medium the 'redemption' it seeks, what, then, would such a 'redemptive' cinema be like, and how different would it be from *Shoah*?

Redemptive images

Godard's and Lanzmann's respective approaches to the Holocaust might be understood as divergent responses to the same two concrete and related problems. Firstly, both see conventional forms of representation as unable to bear witness to the horror of the camps and consequently embark on a search for new kinds of image and cinematic forms more adequate to this challenge. Secondly and in so doing, both confront a dearth of images: the scarcity of photographic and film records of the machinery of extermination that is the legacy of the Nazis' attempt to conceal their crimes. As discussed in chapter one, this lack of what he deems to be appropriate material is one of the motivations for Lanzmann's decision to exclude archive images from *Shoah*, although it does not fully account for his more general suspicion of such images. Godard, in direct contrast, affirms the testimonial and mnemonic power of the archive by collecting Holocaust-related footage and recycling it in films including *Une femme mariée* (*A Married Woman*, 1964), *Allemagne année 90 neuf zéro* (*Germany Year 90 Nine Zero*, 1991), *The Old Place* (with Anne-Marie Miéville, 1999), *Notre musique* (*Our Music*, 2004) and *Histoire(s) du cinéma*. Unlike *Shoah*, which remains resolutely in the present, *Histoire(s) du cinéma* is composed largely of images, words and sounds gleaned from pre-existing sources, which Godard re-edits and reassembles in a collage.

While the Holocaust is by no means Godard's *only* subject in *Histoire(s) du cinéma*, as it is Lanzmann's in *Shoah*, it remains one of the pivotal preoccupations of the video-essay. Godard's particular concern to prolong the afterlife of images of the camps and faith in their capacity to bear witness derive from one of his most challenging histories of cinema, a narrative of amnesia, sin, death and resurrection that is couched, intriguingly, in quasi-religious, as well as ethical, terms. In Godard's video-essay cinema is put on trial and found guilty, convicted of a failure to film Auschwitz (or other twentieth-century atrocities of war: as an intertitle puts it in chapter 4B, 'you saw nothing at Hiroshima, at Leningrad, at Madagascar, at Dresden, at Hanoi, at Sarajevo'). In an interview given in 1995, while he was working on *Histoire(s) du cinéma*, Godard comments:

> Naively, we believed that the New Wave would be a beginning, a revolution. Whereas in fact it was already too late. It was all over. The culmination was the moment when we didn't film the concentration camps. At that instant, cinema completely neglected its duty. Six million people, mainly Jews, were killed or gassed, and cinema was not there … In not filming the concentration camps, cinema completely gave up. (1998a II: 336)

For Godard, moreover, cinema is doubly culpable as it not only neglected to film the camps, but also failed to recognise that it had inadvertently announced their imminent violence. Specifically, he refers in this context to sequences, read by him as prophetic, such as the rabbit hunt and death dance in Jean Renoir's *La Règle du jeu* (*The Rules of the Game*, 1939) and the round-ups in Charlie Chaplin's *The Great Dictator* (1940). (At this juncture, Godard's history of cinema is at once at odds and in agreement with Daney's, discussed in the introduction, which identifies the Holocaust as one of those twentieth-century events that only cinema has seen.) Stressing the connections between escapist narrative and totalitarian horror, Hollywood and Hitler, Godard argues that cinema's documentary roots became fatally diseased by the spectacular dictates of Eros and Thanatos (as he puts it early on in *Histoire(s) du cinéma*, quoting D. W. Griffith, 'a film is a girl and a gun'). In 1939, however, according to his voice-over in chapter 1A of his video-essay, the real began to wreak revenge on the movies for sacrificing it: 'For almost fifty years ... the people of cinema's darkened rooms have been burning up the imaginary to reheat the real. Now this real is taking its revenge, and wants real tears and real blood.' Cinema thus found itself implicated in the bloodshed, but failed to make amends by relinquishing its pursuit of spectacle and attending to reality. In Godard's account, Hitler the movie-star can only be removed from under the sweeping beams of the Twentieth Century Fox klieg lights by a penitent cinema willing to retrace its steps and renew its documentary charge in a long-overdue communion with history.[2]

None of this is strikingly new. Godard's ever erudite *histoires* recall and reconfigure not only Adorno's concerns about poetry and Paul Virilio's (1984) analysis of links between the moving image and warfare, but also Gilles Deleuze's segmentation of cinematic history and insights into the pleasure in spectacular self-stagings binding cinema to fascism (see 1985: 214, 344–5). However, where Godard departs dramatically from this eclectic philosophical heritage is in his confidence in the possibility of cinema's self-'redemption' (see, for example, Godard 1998a II: 316). Amongst the series of claims about the properties and potentialities of the image which punctuate *Histoire(s) du cinéma*, often surfacing explicitly in the form of slowly evolving intertextual citations, one of the most insistent refrains is a prophecy attributed to St Paul: 'the image will come at the time of the resurrection'. The metaphor of 'resurrection' has recurred in various suggestive permutations in Godardian discourse, both on-screen and off-screen, for some two decades now. Reflecting on its significance, James S. Williams argues that Godard's primary aim in *Histoire(s) du cinéma* is 'to privilege and celebrate the resurrecting potential of film, the process whereby cinema ... sacrifices the real by putting it to death and then mourning it. Although "killed off" the real does not totally disappear, since the sacrifice returns the real to us and allows us to regain access to it. The projected image is effectively resurrected into light' (1999: 311). This restoration of past presence acquires an ethical dimension in the dual contexts of twentieth-century genocide and Godard's history of an art that has lost its way and must seek redemption.

Crucial to cinema's capacity to revive the past and raise the dead is montage: 'For me', asserts Godard, 'montage is the resurrection of life' (1998a II: 246). The opening chapter of *Histoire(s) du cinéma* confronts us with a collage of images of war and suffering, including footage of Hitler and Nazi rallies, details from Pablo Picasso's *Guernica* (1937) and Francisco Goya's *Disasters of War* series (c. 1810–14) and extracts from Andrzej Munk's film *Pasazerka* (*The Passenger*, 1962) and a West-German porn film showing a dog fighting with a deportee. Towards the climax of this section there is a sequence which appears to activate the redemptive powers that Godard attributes to montage in a particularly disconcerting way. Three different types of image and body are juxtaposed with each other here: two still, colour images showing a pile of corpses and an emaciated face contorted in death, victims of a convoy from Buchenwald to Dachau in April 1945, are linked, via a black-and-white stop-started film excerpt featuring a bathing-suit-clad Elizabeth Taylor, to a colour detail from a Giotto fresco depicting Mary Magdalene. The sequence is accompanied by a melodious viola playing a Paul Hindemith sonata. On a superficial level, at least, this montage has an internal narrative logic, which Godard spells out for us in voice-over: 'And if George Stevens hadn't used the first sixteen-millimetre colour film at Auschwitz and Ravensbrück, Elizabeth Taylor's happiness would probably never have found a place in the sun.' Prior to directing *A Place in the Sun* (1951), the Hollywood feature which Godard samples here, Stevens was one of the first cameramen to advance with the Allied forces and one of the few to film the camps with colour footage. If Godard's voice-over indicates one way in which we might read this sequence, by inviting us to consider how Stevens' experiences during the war informed his later work, to scan the scenes for signs of cause and effect, such a reading does not fully account for the suggestive meanings produced by the montage. Sundered from their original contexts and recontextualised within *Histoire(s) du cinéma*, the images establish disruptive new relationships which begin to produce a compelling logic of their own. As Taylor cradles Montgomery Clift's head tenderly in her lap, a series of dissolves and cuts creates the illusion that she is also caressing the corpses from the Dachau convoy. Moreover, the detail from Giotto's fresco is rotated by 90 degrees, so that the figure of Mary Magdalene is no longer reaching out towards a saviour who rebuffs her – *Noli me tangere* ('do not touch me') – but down to the earth with what now looks more like an angelic promise of new life. In a fascinating commentary on this sequence, Rancière describes how Giotto's original image of separation, absence and an empty tomb is transfigured through Godard's montage, becoming instead an image of resurrection: 'Elizabeth Taylor stepping out of the water is a figure for the cinema itself being reborn from among the dead. The angel of the Resurrection and of painting descends from the heaven of Images to restore to life both the cinema and its heroines' (2006: 184). In short, we might read this sequence as a rhetorical inversion of St Paul's doctrine, where the image produces the resurrection, rather than vice versa.

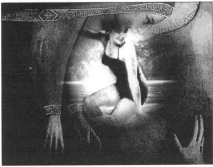

Histoire(s) du cinéma: montage as resurrection

For Rancière, this series of unexpected juxtapositions is emblematic of Godard's project in *Histoire(s) du cinéma*, which transgressively combines '"excessive" conceptual collage' with 'impossible visual collage' (1999: 58).[3] The foundations of this project are laid in Godard's earlier work: *Une femme mariée*, for instance, includes images from Resnais' *Nuit et brouillard* alongside advertisements for women's underwear. In *Histoire(s) du cinéma* too the sacred and the profane are recurrently juxtaposed. The Stevens/Giotto sequence is one of a number which explore the twentieth-century trajectories of the image in parallel with its religious significance and heritage, and which might be taken as evidence of what Agamben identifies as the 'messianic' perspective inflecting Godard's recent work (in Frodon *et al.* 1995: xi). Earlier in the same chapter, the videographic superimposition of two images transports nuns from Robert Bresson's *Les Anges du péché* (*Angels of the Streets*, 1943) to Auschwitz, where they appear to kiss the railway track that runs through the gate of the camp. Described by Williams as 'sublime crossings and transfigurations' (2000: 135), unauthorised encounters of this kind reconfigure filmic temporality, placing the plenitude of the present moment in tension with a 'messianism' that orients the images towards an end (a 'resurrection'). Fictions such as Taylor's visit to the camps, where the falsity of the *eidôlon* (Taylor the movie star) recruits to itself the veracity of the *eikôn* (Mary Magdalene the saint), testify to Godard's faith in the intrinsically multiple or composite 'Image' created in their collision as a vehicle of truth and revelation ('I believe in images', he proclaims, quite simply (cited in Carr 1985: 28)).[4]

Such a faith is unfamiliar in a visual era noteworthy, according to Régis Debray, for its propensity to 'desacralise the image while pretending to consecrate it' (1992: 61–2). Godard's eschatological reworking of cinematic history using current technology marks *Histoire(s) du cinéma* as a utopian project. Besides being ascribed the power to restore to life, the miracle-working Image is repeatedly linked in Godardian discourse via medical metaphors to notions of healing.[5] Raymond Bellour has described some of Godard's recent rhetoric as 'iconophiliac', a term which evokes a faith in the reality of the Incarnation (the acceptance of Christ as the visible image or face of an invisible God) and in the capacity of the image to restore presence.[6] Frodon argues that the term 'idolatry' more accurately characterises Godard's current relationship to images: 'The idolater is someone who believes that the image (the object which figures a non-object) is endowed with powers of its own' (2004: 22). Godard's insistence on the revelatory potential of montage does indeed seem to attest to his belief in such powers. In chapter 4B of *Histoire(s) du cinéma* the voice-over informs us that the plenitude of the Image is 'capable of denying the void', while at the culmination of the Stevens/Giotto sequence in chapter 1A, Godard proclaims: '39–44 – martyrdom and resurrection of the documentary. Oh what wonder to be able to contemplate what we cannot see! Oh sweet miracle of our blind eyes!' In their celebration of the Image as a vehicle of 'resurrection', Godard's histories seem to coincide (a coincidence reinforced through explicit reference) teleologically with a Proustian narrative of mnemonic recuperation, in which time is regained and redeemed in the present.[7] In this respect, the multiplicity of stories invoked by the bracketed plural in the title of the video-essay ('toutes les histoires', in the words of the title of chapter 1A) threatens to coalesce into a unified History ('une histoire seule', in the words of the title of chapter 1B). What is more, this history appears to echo a widespread impulse in post-Holocaust discourse to ascribe a redemptive function to art. From this perspective Godard's project raises broader questions about the role of cinema in the aftermath of the Holocaust. Is the redemptive impulse an appropriate or adequate response to the paucity of visual traces of mass death in the extermination camps? And in what sense are images capable of 'redeeming' an absence of images?

'La pellicule maudite'

In *Arrêt sur histoire* Jean-Louis Comolli identifies resurrection and disguise as the two defining motifs of cinema, and argues that each motif is merely a version of the other (see 1997: 35, 38). This binding of resurrection to false images, indeed, to *mis*representation, further compels the questions I am raising around the image-redemption equation, questions that have specific historical roots. Read through the lens of *Histoire(s) du cinéma*, Godard's dismissal of *Shoah* begins to make more sense. If cinema has a responsibility to atone for its past neglect by showing the suffering endured in the camps directly, then Lanzmann's avoidance of images of the past amounts to a dereliction of the filmmaker's duty to history. But when Godard identifies *Shoah* with cinema's failure to film the camps, he fails to acknowledge the disturbing possibility which underpins Lanzmann's formal choices: that the dearth of images of the extermination may cast doubt upon the redemptive capacity of those images we have of the camps. Godard's avowed faith in their ability to bear witness and resurrect is directly at odds with Lanzmann's suspicion of such images, which derives from his awareness of what they do not show.

Ironically from this perspective, as discussed in chapter one, it is Lanzmann rather than Godard who has come under fire for 'sacralising' the genocide through his images. Godard himself is the author of one of the most caustic critiques in this vein, which accuses Lanzmann not merely of 'pronouncing interdictions', but also of 'preventing people from filming' and 'burning books' (in Bonnaud & Viviant 1998: 28). Symptomatically, the conflict between the two directors has centred on a hypothetical fragment of film which Jean-Jacques Delfour has aptly named 'la pellicule maudite' ('the confounded reel') (2000a).[8] In dispute here is the existence and testimonial status of footage of a working gas chamber that may or may not have been shot by the Nazis. While, as we have seen, Lanzmann claims that were such images ever to be discovered, he would prefer to destroy them rather than include them in his work, Godard's remarks hint that he might do just the opposite. Alluding to the Nazis' bureaucratic obsession with recording and documenting every detail of their operations, he has repeatedly insisted that footage of actual gassings must be buried in an archive somewhere. In an interview coinciding with the release of *Histoire(s) du cinéma* in 1998, for example, he states: 'I have no proof of what I'm suggesting, but I think that if I set to work with a good investigative journalist, I would find images of the gas chambers after twenty years. You would see the deportees enter and you would see the state in which they emerge again' (in Bonnaud & Viviant 1998: 28).[9] Some critics have suggested that Godard's insistence on the existence of film of the gas chambers reflects an unease about historical events which are unwitnessed by the camera, conceivably fuelled by revisionists' exploitation of the absence of such footage, and a concomitant affirmation of the image as guarantor of truth, as mark of the real. Wajcman has suggested that Godard's claims about the missing reel of film are rooted in a 'logic of proof' (1999: 122) which, according to Jean-François Forges, amounts to the simple equation 'there is no existence without images' (2000: 31). Indeed, it is this logic which appears to inform Godard's reflections on digital technology when he contemplates the possibility of its abuse by Jean-Marie Le Pen to retouch images of the camps, in which event the image would 'no longer constitute evidence [*une preuve*]' (Godard, cited in Niney 2000: 303). As Frodon (1999) and Sylvie Lindeperg (2000: 268) have pointed out, however, such logic appears to contradict Godard's famous formula 'pas une image juste ... juste une image' ('not a just image ... just an image') (Godard 1998a I: 348).

Lanzmann's approach is grounded in a categorical refusal of the 'logic of proof' that, according to Wajcman and Forges, informs Godard's words and images. Indeed, as Godard's own remarks acknowledge, this logic seems increasingly dubious at a time when new technologies of representation are undermining the status of the image as visible evidence, as a reliable witness. What Felman describes as the paradox of the Holocaust as 'an *utterly proofless event*' (1992c: 211; emphasis in original) is revealed not only through *Shoah*'s missing bodies (the presence of a corpse is generally accepted as irrefutable proof that a crime has taken place), but also through its ambivalent attitude towards historical documentation (the word 'document' is etymologically related to notions of proof, evidence and epistemology). With rare exceptions such as the industrial memorandum and Nazi *Fahrplanordnung* from which Lanzmann and the historian Raul Hilberg read, *Shoah* excludes written documents. But it is the absence of photographic and filmic documents, specifically visual records that pre-exist the film, that is particularly striking (in *Shoah*, of course, Lanzmann has created a new filmic document). Lanzmann's critique of archive images, outlined in chapter one, questions both the testimonial value of such material and its traditional function in cinema as guarantee of a narrative's authenticity.

In the light of their contrasting views of the evidentiary and testimonial status of archive footage, it becomes clearer why the elusive 'pellicule maudite' constitutes more than a historical footnote for Lanzmann and Godard. At stake here are both epistemological and ethical questions. The missing reel becomes the locus of Godard's concerns about the potentialities of film as document and witness and Lanzmann's anxieties about the limits of the visible and the viewable. This footage would not only bring us face to face with the 'primal scene' of the genocide; it would also be shot from the perspective of an invulnerable observer who is complicit in its violence: the SS guard/camera-operator. In this respect at least, the 'pellicule maudite' has something in common with another hypothetical film discussed by Godard. In an essay written in the early 1960s, he asserts that the only veracious film on the genocide would adopt the perspective of the perpetrators:

The only true film about [the camps] – which has never been made and never will be because it would be intolerable – would show a camp from the point of view of the torturers, with their daily problems. How to fit a two-metre human corpse into a fifty-centimetre coffin? How to clear away ten tons of arms and legs in a three-ton truck? How to burn a hundred women with only enough petrol for ten? … What would be unendurable is not the horror that would emanate from such scenes, but their perfectly normal and human appearance. (1963: 2)

Godard elaborates on these remarks in a later text, where he suggests that such a film might narrate 'the story of the typist who, day in day out, would type "four gold teeth, five hundred grams of hair"' (1980: 321). The implied equation of 'normality' and 'humanity' in the earlier passage recalls the debates provoked by Hannah Arendt's study of the 'banality of evil' (1964) and would probably be refuted by Lanzmann (arguably, part of the fascination of *Shoah* lies in the way individuals such as Suchomel appear normal yet *in*human).[10] Nevertheless, Godard's conclusion that the filmic project he outlines remains unrealisable because it would be 'intolerable' anticipates Lanzmann's verdict on the 'pellicule maudite': 'you cannot look at this' (1991: 99). Albeit in different contexts, both directors posit limits to representation deriving from a shared intuition that witnessing the event through the eyes of the perpetrators would present insuperable cognitive challenges to viewers. However, whereas what would be unendurable about the missing Nazi reel for Lanzmann would be its horror, what would be intolerable about Godard's unrealisable film would be instead its very banality.

Yet Godard does not say the same of the hypothetical footage of the gas chamber. Despite their intersecting concerns with representational limits, the directors' respective attitudes towards the 'pellicule maudite' remain irreconcilably opposed. Both their comments on this film and the interpretations of their positions advanced by others (including myself) exemplify some of the difficulties inherent in the attempt to develop any kind of critical perspective on images that remain imaginary. The 'pellicule maudite' assumes the status in these discussions of a ghost-film, a 'fantasy' (Didi-Huberman 2003: 124) or a 'screen' (Chéroux 2001: 216) onto which each interlocutor can project their individual desires and fears. Nevertheless, I am arguing that these fantasy images, at once overdetermined and undecidable, serve to bring into focus the very real ethical differences between Godard and Lanzmann. As demonstrated in chapter three, they also persistently haunt the work of other directors, where they exert an uncanny influence on the images we see on the screen.

'Images in spite of everything'

An alternative barometer of the anxieties aroused by these missing or imaginary images is the ongoing debate in French scholarship about the real images displayed in the 'Mémoire des camps' exhibition. If it is no coincidence that this debate has become polarised around the positions defended by Lanzmann and Godard, interventions by scholars working in a variety of disciplines have also served to contextualise the directors' dispute within broader currents in contemporary thinking about the visual legacy of the Holocaust. One of the initial sources of controversy was that while nearly all the photographs in the exhibition showed the concentration camps, as opposed to the extermination camps, this imbalance was not pointed out to visitors nor acknowledged by the exhibition's subtitle: 'Photographies des camps de concentration et d'extermination nazis' ('Photographs of the Nazi Concentration and Extermination Camps'). Criticising this failure, Michel Guerrin regretted that the exhibition organisers neglected to leave a space for 'the "void of images" [of the extermination camps] in front of which we find ourselves' (2001a: 28).[11] Only four photographs dealt directly with the extermination, and it is their contents, status and value that have proved of particular interest and concern to commentators.

In an important essay in the exhibition catalogue, Didi-Huberman, one of the key participants in the ensuing debate, offers a detailed analysis of what he describes as 'four scraps of film snatched from the jaws of hell' (2001: 219). Two of the images in question show the incineration of bodies in an open-air ditch framed by a doorway; another depicts naked women being marched towards a gas chamber; and in the last, which is indistinct, it is just possible to make out the tops of birch trees. By scrutinising these photographs and drawing on other sources, Didi-Huberman reconstructs the history of their creation, preservation and afterlife. He describes how they were taken secretly in Auschwitz-Birkenau in August 1944 by a Greek Jew called Alex (whose surname remains unknown) assisted by other members of the *Sonderkommando*, who had decided to attempt to document the atrocities, despite the extreme personal risks involved; how the film was smuggled out of the camp in a toothpaste tube; and how the images have since been used, reframed and retouched.[12] What is particularly significant in the current context is that the angle from which the two photographs of burning corpses were taken shows the photographer must have been hiding inside the gas chamber in Crematorium V. 'From the darkness of the gas chamber', writes Didi-Huberman, 'Alex in fact brought to light the nerve centre of Auschwitz, that is the destruction of the Jewish populations of Europe, which was supposed to leave no remains' (2001: 237). In another essay in the catalogue, Chéroux, who curated the exhibition and edited the catalogue, goes as far as to claim that these four photographs are the missing images sought by Godard (2001: 217). Chéroux points out that while they were taken by deportees rather than Nazis and do not show the gassing process itself, they allow us to witness 'the deportees enter' and 'the state in which they emerge again' (Godard in Bonnaud & Viviant 1998: 28).[13]

However tenuous the link made by Chéroux between these real and hypothetical images, the 'pellicule maudite' makes its spectral presence felt at many points in Didi-Huberman's argument, which intervenes in the debate between Godard and Lanzmann in illuminating ways. His essay bears in epigraph a quotation from chapter 1A of *Histoire(s) du cinéma*: 'Even scratched beyond recognition, a simple rectangle of thirty-five millimetres saves the honour of all the real' (2001: 219). As this epigraph suggests, the broader aim of Didi-Huberman's essay intersects with Godard's in *Histoire(s) du cinéma*: to redress what he perceives as a persistent neglect of the documentary and testimonial value of photographic traces. While Didi-Huberman acknowledges that, like survivor testimonies, Alex's images 'have a fragmentary and lacunary relationship to the truth to which they bear witness' (2001: 234) – that they *do not tell* "the whole truth"' (2001: 236; emphasis in original) – he affirms their status as 'instants' or 'vestiges' of veracity and highlights the political and ethical dimension of the *Sonderkommando* members' actions:

It is in the fold of ... two impossibilities – imminent disappearance of the witness, certain unrepresentability of testimony – that the photographic image appears. [...] The four photographs snatched from Auschwitz by the members of the *Sonderkommando* were thus, also, four *refutations* snatched from a world that the Nazis wanted to offend: that is to say without words and without images. [...] What the SS wanted to destroy in Auschwitz was not only the life, but also ... the very form of the human being, and with it the human image. In such a context, the act of resistance became identified as a result with the act of *preserving this image in spite of everything* [*maintenir cette image malgré tout*]. (2001: 221, 228, 239; emphasis in original)

Didi-Huberman argues further that the *Sonderkommando* members' 'act of resistance' challenges discourses of 'invisibility' of the kind popularised by readings of *Shoah*, as well as the concomitant notions that the Holocaust remains 'unspeakable', 'unimaginable' and 'unrepresentable'. He asserts that Lanzmann's formal choices in *Shoah* 'do not allow us to make any peremptory judgement about the status of photographic archives in general' (2001: 230–1). In Didi-Huberman's view, the very existence of the four photographs refutes Wajcman's claims that 'the Shoah was and remains without an image ... an absolute disaster absolutely without a gaze' (1998: 239, 248). What is more, they also confirm the event's representability: 'Thanks to these images, we have a representation *in spite of everything* which, from now on, will be essential as the representation *par excellence*, the necessary representation of what August 1944 was at Crematorium V at Auschwitz' (Didi-Huberman 2001: 236; emphasis in original).

Given the boldness of contentions such as this, it was only to be expected that Lanzmann would take issue with Didi-Huberman's thesis. In an interview for *Le Monde* he questions the historical accuracy of some of Didi-Huberman's claims and accuses him of 'fetishising' the four photographs (in Guerrin 2001b: 29). Didi-Huberman responds to Lanzmann and others who contested his argument in a book published in 2003 under the same title as his catalogue essay, *Images malgré tout*. Here he clarifies that he did not intend to dismiss *Shoah*, a work he admires, in the earlier essay, but proceeds instead to attack Lanzmann's off-screen comments about the limited value of the archive (see 2003: 117–25, 141–3). Specifically, Didi-Huberman queries the rigour of an argument that, from a legitimate premise (the paucity of traces of the extermination) and legitimate concerns about specific cases (the Wiener film, the 'pellicule maudite'), derives general principles, or, in his terms, 'improper rules' (2003: 119), pertaining to *all* archive images. In particular, he questions the validity of Lanzmann's characterisation of photographic and filmic traces as 'images without imagination', pointing out that imagination belongs to spectators rather than images (2003: 141–2). 'An image without imagination', Didi-Huberman counters, 'is quite simply an image we have not taken the time to work on' (2003: 149). More fundamentally, he attempts to dismantle what he identifies as the primary opposition posited by Lanzmann: between archive and testimony, 'proof' and truth, visual traces of the past and the witness's words (2003: 130). Images, he contends, have just as important a role as words to play in bearing witness to the Holocaust.

Didi-Huberman's overarching argument that photographs such as those taken by the Auschwitz *Sonderkommando* deserve our close attention is indisputable and timely. His analyses of these images cumulatively mount a powerful defence of the photograph's capacity to grant us visual access to historical violence, which acquires particular significance in the context of the Nazis' attempt to conceal and destroy the traces of their crimes. Without condemning Lanzmann's choices in *Shoah*, he suggests that alternative choices, such as Godard's, can be just as valid in the endeavour to evoke the horror of the Holocaust. Yet Didi-Huberman's texts have provoked a series of polemical responses, and not only from Lanzmann. The next section considers alternative accounts of the relation between images and history which help to redefine the relationship between *Histoire(s) du cinéma* and *Shoah* by drawing attention to some of the potential dangers of direct images of violence.

Protective shields and veils

'Images in spite of everything'? Often italicised for emphasis, the 'malgré tout' that is Didi-Huberman's persistent refrain (the four photographs constitute 'a representation *in spite of everything*' (2001: 236; emphasis in original); the members of the *Sonderkommando* are '*alive in spite of everything*' and produce '*testimonies in spite of everything*' (2003: 135; emphasis in original)) calls attention to a potential crisis of figurability and testimony that it simultaneously aims to avert. If what he perceives as the Nazis' attempt to destroy the human image prompts Didi-Huberman to affirm the importance of creating, preserving and studying images such as Alex's, it leads others to posit different ethical imperatives. Wajcman and Pagnoux deliver emphatic ripostes to Didi-Huberman in two articles in *Les Temps modernes*, the journal founded by Jean-Paul Sartre and Simone de Beauvoir and currently edited by Lanzmann. Reiterating Lanzmann's doubts about the value of archive images, Wajcman and Pagnoux argue that his decision to exclude them from *Shoah* is the only proper response to the Nazis' violation of the image and endeavour to silence the witness. 'To make us witnesses to this scene', writes Pagnoux of death in the gas chamber, 'is to distort the reality of Auschwitz' (2001: 106), which she, following Felman and Laub, and notwithstanding Alex's images, understands as an 'event without a witness'; 'it is to fill the silence' (ibid.). Wajcman states categorically that 'there are no images of the Shoah' (2001: 47), by which he appears to mean there are no images of the destruction of the Jews in the gas chambers. Wajcman contests Didi-Huberman's characterisation of the images taken by the Auschwitz *Sonderkommando* as an 'essential … representation *par excellence*' and rejects the idea that they show the Holocaust to be representable or imaginable (2001: 67). He warns, further, that images of horror can paradoxically assume a 'consolatory' function, distracting us from the even more terrifying possibility that there may simply be nothing to see (ibid.). Elsewhere he reflects that images are liable to falsify the essence of the Nazi crimes, insofar as 'the image always brings with it a little of the presence that once was. Every image is a sort of denial [*dénégation*] of absence' (1998: 243). In the light of these contentions it is no surprise that Wajcman has also intervened in the debate between Lanzmann and Godard on the side of the former (see Wajcman 1999).[14]

While his claim that the Shoah remains an event 'without an image' is plainly contradicted by the four photographs analysed by Didi-Huberman, which do not show death in the gas chamber but depict the moments immediately before and afterwards with painful clarity, Wajcman's argument nevertheless raises a series of important questions about the potential risks of images of atrocity. To what extent does the filmic reappropriation of visual traces to 'illustrate' the Holocaust involve using the image itself merely to paper over the Nazi attack on the image – on our image – so vividly described by both Wajcman and Didi-Huberman? To what extent do direct images (both the familiar footage of ghettos and camps shot by the Nazis and the Allies and the rare, even exceptional 'images malgré tout' of the extermination itself taken by eyewitnesses like Alex) work to deflect attention from and thus allay the anxieties aroused by this attack? In short, is it possible that images of atrocity might effectively shield us from the event itself, replacing a traumatic absence with a redemptive presence?

Slavoj Žižek has formulated these risks in different terms in the course of a discussion of traumatic images, where he draws some unexpected parallels between Wilkomirski's fraudulent testimony and the experience of soldiers involved in today's 'aseptic' technological warfare (see 2000a: 30–1, 33–4). Both suffer from forms of False Memory Syndrome, and Žižek, reworking Freud, argues that in both cases the subject's habitual tendency to invent benign fantasies as shields from trauma is inverted. While what Žižek reads as the benevolent 'symbolic fiction' with which Guido protects his son in Benigni's *La Vita è bella* (that the camp is a game, with rules, winners and prizes) invites us to read the film as a fictional shield designed to protect its spectators (2000a: 29), the cases of Wilkomirski and the soldiers are altogether more disturbing. Here, rather than a de-traumatised fiction of the real, it is the ultimate traumatic experience (life as a child in the camps for Wilkomirski and face-to-face combat for the soldiers) that is itself fantasised as a shield. In other words, they protect themselves from real trauma with a fictive trauma that they have never experienced; Wilkomirski has never seen the inside of a working camp, and the soldiers have never encountered the enemy except as a dehumanised dot on a radar screen. Crucially, according to Žižek, this pathological inversion of the protective fiction which sees us taking 'refuge in catastrophic scenarios' (2000a: 34) offers insight into one of the fundamental lessons of psychoanalysis: that 'the images of utter catastrophe, far from giving access to the Real, can function as a protective shield AGAINST the Real' (ibid.).

Žižek's argument alerts us to the uncomfortable possibility that imaginary images of trauma can work to screen us from the Real rather than allowing us to approach it. Reflecting on the horrific images that surface in our memory and imagination as we view *Shoah*, Wilson, drawing on Žižek, observes that 'the image we recall or imagine may be a defence against the yet unimaginable image of the suffering and death of the Other on which Lanzmann fixes our minds' (2005: 91). In their evocation of 'utter catastrophe', such images can all too easily blind us to their protective, consolatory function. If Žižek's insights give us cause to be wary of the fantasy images of the 'pellicule maudite', to what extent do they also apply to the real images, the photographic and filmic documents from which our imaginary images tend to derive? This is one of the pivotal concerns of Wajcman's response to Didi-Huberman:

> Every image of the horror lays a veil over the horror; every image, because it is an image, protects us from the horror … at the same time … as it uncovers something, it covers it up again just as efficiently; the image diverts us from what it shows us … Horror and images repel each other – such is their nature. (2001: 68)

As the operative metaphor changes from a shield into a veil, what in Žižek's text was a possibility becomes in Wajcman's an ontological given. Wajcman's argument is arguably undermined at this juncture by the generalising nature of its claims, its insistence that every direct image functions in the same suspect way, in whichever context it is displayed.[15] However, his affirmation of the placatory power of images in the face of a reality that, despite images such as Alex's, remains resistant to visualisation goes some way to accounting for the public success of the 'Mémoire des camps' exhibition as an emotional release and salve. It is easier to begin to mourn an event whose violence has been captured and contained in images that, according to Didi-Huberman at least, 'refute the unimaginable' (2001: 227). Moreover, Wajcman's warning that horror and images 'repel' each other also suggests that every filmmaker approaching the genocide must embrace an aporia of representation: the possibility that certain images may in fact conceal as much as they reveal. This aporia leads Wajcman to query whether there are no more appropriate means of bearing witness to the event: 'Is there no other remedy to the absence of images than the image itself?' (2001: 55).

It is the guiding principle of Lanzmann's films and writings on the subject that art should seek not to 'remedy' but to diagnose and attest to this (near) absence. This he achieves in *Shoah* not only by excluding archive images but also by creating new images that constantly remind us of those – whether real or fantasised – that he withholds. Mindful of the risks alluded to by Wajcman, he seeks to offer us a more intimate encounter with the Real of trauma without affording us protection from its horror by visualising it directly. *Shoah* bears witness to missing images and missing bodies and can be read, from this perspective, as a categorical rejection of (rather than substitute for or supplement to) the 'pellicule maudite', those elusive 'images of utter catastrophe' which risk shielding us from the events they show. Yet the film at the same time revolves around the absence of these hypothetical images and the violence they depict, which haunts the survivor testimonies and is glimpsed in the shots of the plaster model of Crematoria II and III at Auschwitz.

Despite Lanzmann's well-known reservations about *Nuit et brouillard*, parallels might be drawn in this context with the cinema of Resnais, another filmmaker whose seminal work on historical trauma has consistently questioned the referential capacity of images.[16] In *Hiroshima mon amour* (1959) he chooses to suppress what had already become the iconic image of the bombing: the mushroom cloud (despite the fact that it opened Marguerite Duras's original screenplay (Duras 1960: 21)). *Muriel, ou le temps d'un retour* (*Muriel, or the Time of Return*, 1963) also centres on a trauma and a missing body that it leaves unimaged, which may or may not have been recorded on another missing reel of film. Even *Nuit et brouillard*, which makes ample use of archive images, remains dubious about their referentiality.[17] Like *Shoah*, then, these are films which either cannot or choose not to show their central subject directly and call into question the capacity of images – whether direct or reconstructed – to restore access to the past. In this respect *Shoah* and *Nuit et brouillard* not only reject the 'iconophiliac' or 'idolatrous' agenda endorsed by *Histoire(s) du cinéma* (in Bellour's and Frodon's readings) but also distance themselves from the kind of 'super-production à grand spectacle' ('big-budget spectacular') which Godard has provocatively claimed he has always wanted to make about the camps (1980: 321). (It is worth noting this claim predates *Schindler's List*, which Lanzmann describes as 'an illustrated *Shoah*' (Lanzmann 1994: vii).) For Lanzmann, the antidote to 'iconophilia' is not 'iconophobia', as Godard's remark that *Shoah* 'shows nothing' implies. It was argued in chapter one that representation returns to *Shoah* in ways that distance it from the religious prohibition of figuration (the *Bilderverbot*) with which it has often been associated. What *Shoah does* show – and Godard apparently chooses to miss the point here – is the progressive erasure of the traces that Godard amasses and redisplays. Lanzmann's shots of desolate places and traumatised faces and recordings of witnesses' memories confirm that cinema can bear witness to the Holocaust without recourse to the archive. *Shoah* redefines the task of the image differently from *Histoire(s) du cinéma*, divesting it of its shield-like properties, liberating it from the confines of representation and reminding us that it can also reveal what lies beyond the visible.

Lanzmann, like Godard, has employed the term 'resurrection' in commentary on his work ('I would say that the film is an *incarnation*, a *resurrection*' (cited in Felman 1992c: 213–14; emphasis in original). But the two directors use this noun to designate different processes. Lanzmann does not share Godard's faith in montage images as imprints of presence endowed with redemptive powers and is referring instead to the way in which *Shoah* resuscitates past realities in the present via the fictive detours of *mise-en-scène*. Lanzmann observes that at the moment when Müller, remembering the final song of the Czech Jews, falters and breaks down, 'the past was resuscitated with such violence that all distance collapsed, producing a pure present, the very opposite of recollection [*souvenir*]' (Lanzmann 1980: 10). Rather than accumulating *souvenirs*, which hold the past at a safe distance, Lanzmann's fictions are catalysts of an anamnesis quite distinct from the redemptive process of remembering enacted by *Histoire(s) du cinéma*. *Shoah* explores how the 'involuntary memory' which intrigued Proust is reconfigured by traumatic experience. As a boat and a song, a locomotive and a station sign, or a pair of scissors and a barber's shop transport the witnesses back into the past, Lanzmann's time-images begin to imitate the singular temporalities of traumatic memory. These temporalities are fluid, discontinuous and unpredictable; the distance between past and present is alternately collapsed – as the repetition of a gesture produces momentary paroxysms of pure anamnesis – and reaffirmed – as the camera roams around the abandoned killing sites that Lanzmann calls 'non-lieux de la mémoire' ('non-sites of memory') (in Gantheret 1990: 281). In *Shoah* the image reveals time and memory whilst keeping history from sight.

A missed encounter?

Godard's perfunctory dismissal of Lanzmann's approach, his defensiveness with regard to the 'pellicule maudite' and his belief in the redemptive power of images, prompt Wajcman to cast Godard as St Paul opposite Lanzmann's Moses. In Wajcman's account, Lanzmann becomes the 'pariah' banished from Godard's 'Church of the Holy Image'. Why? 'Because [Godard] believes in the image', whereas Lanzmann remains 'the Unbeliever, charged with iconoclasm' (1999: 125). While this religious analogy wields rhetorical power, it remains limiting, I would suggest, in that it risks reducing the debate, once again, to the binary opposition image/no image. Certainly, *Shoah*'s avoidance of images of the past pits itself against the proliferation of visual traces we encounter in *Histoire(s) du cinéma*, just as Lanzmann's refusals and exclusions appear directly at odds with Godard's ethic of heterogeneity and inclusion. Absence against excess: two figures of the ineffable which punctuate discussions about the representability of the Holocaust.

This opposition acknowledged, the directors' dispute and Wajcman's binary might be reframed in terms of competing modes of representation, conflicting conceptions of the nature and properties of an image and concrete questions about montage. If Godard's contention that *Shoah* 'shows nothing' and thus perpetuates interdictions proves ultimately indefensible, it underlines the contrast between the two directors' understandings of what a cinematic image is and can or should do – between *Shoah*'s inflammatory images of the present and the 'redemptive' Images of *Histoire(s) du cinéma*. As we have seen, Godard and Lanzmann fundamentally disagree about the ethical status of a direct image of real violence – about whether, for example, it allows its viewers space to judge and, if appropriate, to refuse. Godard's conviction that the image is not necessarily a mechanism of fascination and thus, in effect, a negation of its subject derives, I have argued, from his ongoing investigation of the multiple, unstable Images produced by montage. This Lanzmann rejects on the grounds that direct images are an ineffective and risky means of restoring access to a traumatic past and that cinema's primary task is to reveal the attempt at self-erasure which defined the Nazi project. These conflicting positions translate on the screen into two contrasting forms of montage, which pose distinctive challenges to the viewer. While Godard bombards us with a bewildering array of sounds and images, fragmenting, manipulating and recontextualising them to produce new relationships and meanings, Lanzmann, in contrast, presents us with extended sequence shots which build slowly and patiently up to instants of anamnesis when terror is not shown but relived and intensity of experience is privileged over sight. Didi-Huberman proposes the terms 'centripetal' and 'centrifugal' (2003: 157) to describe the montage of *Shoah* and *Histoire(s) du cinéma* respectively; while Godard's images and words seem to whirl frenetically outwards, Lanzmann's circle gradually inwards, converging on a centre they never quite reach.

Each position and approach can be criticised, but likewise defended on its own ground. If we begin to consider, however, how little resemblance either Godard's Images or Lanzmann's images bear to the visuals of mainstream cinema, indeed, how both constitute sites of resistance to mainstream aesthetics, it becomes possible to view them as complementary, rather than purely antagonistic. That Godard shares Lanzmann's misgivings about Hollywood reconstructions of the Holocaust in general and *Schindler's List* in particular is intimated by his expression of regret at having failed 'to prevent Mr Spielberg from reconstructing Auschwitz' (Godard, cited in MacCabe 2003: 327).[18] The story of the Resistance veterans considering whether to sell their story to a company called 'Spielberg Associates and Incorporated' in *Éloge de l'amour* (*In Praise of Love*, 2001) is further testimony to Godard's concerns about American cinema's tendency to appropriate others' memory, of which he sees Spielberg's film as symptomatic. In his biography of Godard, Colin MacCabe summarises the director's objections to Spielberg's approach in terms which hint at the proximity of his concerns to Lanzmann's: 'Spielberg's *Schindler's List* is, for Godard's aesthetic, a genuine obscenity. It is impossible to film the camps now, because it is impossible to starve actors to the point of death. It is impossible to film the camps because the narratives we impose on them, which "explain" them, are necessarily misleading and actually prevent understanding' (ibid.). Godard's hostile reaction to *Schindler's List* is grounded, like Lanzmann's, in a conviction that the reality of the camps can neither be reconstructed nor accommodated within conventional narrative frameworks.[19] What unites *Histoire(s) du cinéma* with *Shoah* is not only a critique of Spielberg's presumption to trademark the subject of Auschwitz, but also a wider call for a systematic questioning of the obscenity of dominant representational forms.

This appeal echoes Rivette's critique of Pontecorvo's *Kapo* (an essay that has had an important influence on Godard's work). Indeed, both *Shoah* and *Histoire(s) du cinéma* reanimate and update the debate instigated by Rivette about how the relationship between ethics and aesthetics is redefined by historical trauma, even if they propose contrasting correctives to what Daney calls Pontecorvo's 'consensual' aesthetic (1992: 11). Despite his rhetoric of redemption, Godard, just as much as Lanzmann, prevents us from seeking refuge, consolation or closure in images of catastrophe. *Histoire(s) du cinéma* figures lack and absence as excess and overload; here it is through multiple juxtapositions that closure is deferred, that the iconography of the Holocaust is defamiliarised, and that the image is stripped of its propensity to shield us from catastrophe. Godard's privileging of the visible does not, like Spielberg's, 'evacuate inwardness' (Hartman 1996: 85), or mask invisibility. Furthermore, just as the memory of *Shoah* influences our viewing of *Histoire(s) du cinéma*, so Godard's histories can also inform our viewing of *Shoah*. One of Lanzmann's most powerful images of spontaneous anamnesis, the shot of Gawkowski leaning out of his locomotive and drawing a finger across his throat in front of the sign announcing 'Treblinka', has been differently appropriated by Spielberg and Godard. Shortly before the controversial shower-room scene in *Schindler's List*, Gawkowski's gesture is repeated by a small child actor, an image which is replayed in a slow-motion flashback a few seconds later. Contemplating the relationship between these two sequences and the possible motivations behind Spielberg's quotation, Yosefa Loshitzky observes that in *Schindler's List* 'the disturbing ambivalence invoked by Gawkowski's facial expression was replaced by an explicitly sadistic expression' (1997: 104). I would add that in *Schindler's List* the manual gesture is divested of the ambiguity which surrounds it in *Shoah* and serves primarily to fuel our expectation that the Jewish women and children are about to be murdered, an expectation exploited by the shower room scene.[20] The first chapter of *Histoire(s) du cinéma*, on the other hand, includes a few seconds of Lanzmann's original shot of Gawkowski. But Godard recycles it in extreme slow motion and replaces the original soundtrack with music from another source, thereby drawing attention to its materiality and manipulability. In this way, Godard reminds us that the images of *Shoah* have an afterlife; that Gawkowski, too, has entered the archive; and that an image of the present will always become an image of the past in the archive of the future. At the same time, by tracing the complex ways in which images circulate on screens and in our memories, Godard's work also invites us to consider just how much of *Shoah*'s anamnesiac power comes – in spite of Lanzmann's claims – from the archive, from the images of atrocity we remember from elsewhere (including Godard's video-essay) which play in our minds but are refused to our eyes as we watch the film. As Wilson points out, 'Lanzmann may withhold such images from us on screen but he still goes some way to screening them in our imagination' (2005: 91).

From these perspectives, then, *Shoah* and *Histoire(s) du cinéma* might be understood (in spite of their directors' assertions to the contrary) as films in dialogue whose images are constantly interfering with and correcting each other. This is not to imply, as has been suggested, that the dispute between Godard and Lanzmann is ultimately a 'false debate' (see, for example, Mandelbaum 2001). On the contrary, I have endeavoured to show that their differences remain real and illuminating. While it seems unlikely that they will ever see eye to eye with regard to the 'pellicule maudite', their divergent attempts to rethink cinema's ethical responsibilities in the light of the missing Nazi reel leave a germane legacy to other filmmakers, certain aspects of which are addressed in the next chapter. Neither film pretends to have completed the process of ethical reflection it initiates. Despite its redemptive *telos*, *Histoire(s) du cinéma*, like *Shoah*, ultimately remains a work in progress; a work, as it were, of endless resurrection, which implicates us as 'spectateur[s] attentif et "en attente"' ('attentive spectator[s] "in waiting"') (Bergala 1999: 11).

All the more revealing, then, that Godard should show signs of revising his verdict on *Shoah* in interviews given after *Histoire(s) du cinéma* (see, for example, Gaillac, Morgue & Guerand 2001: 10). What is more, *Vrai faux passeport* (*True False Passport*, 2006), Godard's latest video-essay, includes a lengthy extract from Lanzmann's interview with Bomba in the rented barber's shop.[21] If this apparent homage to *Shoah* is difficult to reconcile with the quotation with which this chapter began, it seems that Godard's reservations about Lanzmann's approach do not prevent him from recognising the Bomba interview at least as an extraordinary piece of cinema. It remains to be seen whether this gesture on Godard's part will open a new dialogue, or whether 'le fameux débat' is doomed to remain a missed encounter.

3

Through the Spyhole:
Death, Ethics and Spectatorship

Leszek Wosiewicz's little-known feature film *Kornblumenblau* (1988) is based on the true story of a Polish musician's survival in Auschwitz. Amongst the many horrors he witnesses in the camp is a public hanging of prisoners. The execution is attended by SS officials accompanied by a group of tittering women who have dressed up for the occasion, but we watch it through the eyes of Tadeusz Wyczyński, the central protagonist, who is hiding in a storeroom nearby and observes the scene through a window. There are competing demands on Tadeusz's attention: his gaze, represented by the subjective camera, flits back and forth between the condemned men, the raw onion he is ravenously munching and the white petticoat intermittently visible beneath the skirt of one of the women. In this sequence an array of incompatible looks intersects with our own on the gallows, reflecting, respectively, the satisfaction of the officials, the voyeuristic curiosity of the women, Tadeusz's conflicting sensations of terror, hunger and desire and, finally, the agony of the dying. The culminating sequences of the film depict another mass execution, but this time it is staged as a private spectacle watched by a single on-screen spectator. In one of the few sustained direct representations of this scene in cinema, Wosiewicz affords us a view through a small window into a working gas chamber.[1] While this view is prefigured in an earlier sequence where a shutter slams closed over a spyhole, alerting the protagonist to the fact that somebody has been watching him, this time there is no shutter to block our line of vision. Colour drains from the images as we witness not only the slow asphyxiation of the victims but also the aftermath of their death struggle when the doors of the chamber are eventually reopened by a member of the *Sonderkommando*. Wosiewicz's camerawork heightens the scene's visceral and affective impact on the viewer. A series of shots and counter-shots places us alternately inside and outside the chamber, aligning us in turn with the perspective of the dying and with the smug, mildly intrigued gaze of a young SS officer who contemplates the scene through the window while chomping nonchalantly on an apple. In positioning us, by turns, as unseeing victim and as voyeuristic persecutor, this sequence implicates us in its violence, deprives us of any innocent perspective and foregrounds our complicity in the spectacle.

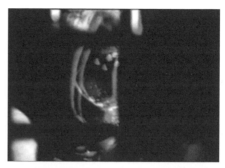

Kornblumenblau: the complicit viewer

In breaking the taboo on showing industrialised mass murder, Wosiewicz's harrowing reconstruction raises questions about the ethical position of the spectator face to face with suffering, violence and death. Furthermore, by casting its protagonists as observers and witnesses and by representing looking as a political and ethical act, *Kornblumenblau* invites us to consider the responsibilities conferred on viewers by the spectacle of violence, whether we are witnessing it first-hand, without mediation, or watching it on a screen.[2] The executions depicted by Wosiewicz might be contextualised within a long tradition in art of representing protagonists' anguish or death as subject to the look of more fortunate others. In her book *Regarding the Pain of Others* Susan Sontag notes that 'torment, a canonical subject in art, is often represented in painting as a spectacle, something being watched (or ignored) by other people. The implication is: no, it cannot be stopped – and the mingling of inattentive with attentive onlookers underscores this' (2003: 42). Sontag's remarks hint at the inherent ambiguity of the observer's relationship to the other's suffering. Simply to contemplate is morally suspect, or requires some form of moral justification, since the moral imperative is to attempt to intervene and alleviate the other person's distress. But to what extent does this ambiguity also pertain to the position of the viewer beholding mediated violence, real or reconstructed, in which he or she cannot intervene immediately if at all? Is such a position ever properly innocent or does it always imply a degree of complicity? To what extent does the fact of mediation absolve us from responsibility? Sontag warns against making premature generalisations about spectatorship of this kind, whether in the context of painting, photography, cinema or other visual media: 'No "we" should be taken for granted when the subject is looking at other people's pain' (2003: 7).

This 'we' and the various positions it might adopt in the face of imaged violence are implicitly at stake in the debates outlined in the previous chapter. The hypothetical filmic project described by Godard is grounded in his conviction that the only authentic film on the camps would consistently align its viewers with the perspective of the murderers, and yet that in reality this perspective would be unbearable. Moreover, Wosiewicz's reconstruction of the gas chamber is one of the closest things we have to a reconstruction of the 'pellicule maudite', the missing images at the centre of the dispute between Godard and Lanzmann. Reflecting on the significance these images have assumed in recent discussion, Chéroux writes:

> It seems that behind the multiplication of ... stereotypes there is the wish, on the part of photographers, to find a kind of 'integral' image (just as Primo Levi spoke of 'integral witnesses'), an image which would symbolise at once the insult of the deportation, the agony of the camps and the abomination of the gas chambers ... If the gas chamber is situated at the epicentre of the extermination, it seems logical that its image should also be the most appropriate representation of the genocidary enterprise. So this integral and radical image would probably be one which shows the deportees in the gas chamber in the throes of death. (2001: 213)

It is likely that both Lanzmann and Godard would be critical of the idea that there could be any 'integral image' of the genocide; both *Shoah* (by refusing images of the past) and *Histoire(s) du cinéma* (by multiplying them) arouse suspicion about formulations of this kind. Nevertheless, as we have seen, both directors remain preoccupied by the absent images of the gas chamber and their contrasting claims about the value of these images highlight deep-seated differences between their approaches. Moreover, as Chéroux's remarks imply and Wosiewicz's film confirms, Godard and Lanzmann are not the only filmmakers in whom these missing images have provoked anxiety. More than any other aspect of the genocide, it is what Manuel Köppen describes as 'the climax of the unimaginable ... the traumatic-perverse "primal scene" of the Holocaust' (1997: 160, 162) that has haunted cinema. As Gary Weissman observes, 'the gas chambers epitomize the Holocaust in the popular and scholarly imagination, and so the (re-created) gas chamber is imagined to be the quintessential site where the Holocaust could be witnessed' (2004: 176). Were a photographic or filmic record of this scene to be unearthed in an archive, which Godard and Chéroux insist remains a genuine possibility, it is conceivable that filmmakers would no longer feel compelled – or deem it possible – to reconstruct it. In the absence of such a record, however, they have repeatedly returned to this scene, presenting it either as a structuring absence, as something that cannot or should not be visualised but must be alluded to otherwise, or as the proper object of an 'integral image' that remains to be invented. Wosiewicz's gas chamber is merely one of the most unflinchingly literal instances of such invention. Whence an irony: what Felman and Laub describe as an 'event without a witness' and Wajcman as an event 'without an image' in fact produces an excess of filmic witness.

To avoid the gas chambers is arguably to avoid the Holocaust. Yet the vast majority of films dealing with the extermination assert in one way or another that it is neither appropriate nor legitimate to represent what happened inside the gas chambers directly. With the notable exception of *Kornblumenblau*, such films tend to respect and affirm the sentiments variously expressed by Wiesel: 'The last moments of the forgotten victims belong to themselves' (1978: 29); by Schogt's mother in *Zyklon Portrait*: 'Those last moments you do not want to visualise'; and by Lanzmann: 'You cannot look at this.' Furthermore, in certain films, direct or indirect images of this scene work to call the spectator's look and position into question. Wosiewicz's disruptive counter-shots in *Kornblumenblau* and Schogt's disintegrating images of the interior of the body in *Zyklon Portrait* are amongst the most unsettling examples of such interrogation.

Discussing vision and visibility in and of the gas chambers, Chéroux notes that a number of eyewitness testimonies refer to the guards' practice of switching off the lights just before the gas was turned on; the killing generally took place in darkness. Nevertheless, he informs us, numerous testimonies confirm the existence of glazed hermetic holes (variously described as 'eyepieces', 'judas holes', 'peep-holes', 'windows', 'fanlights', 'portholes', 'skylights' or 'panes' (2001: 214–15)) which allowed those outside to see what was happening inside the chamber. He quotes from the testimony of Josef Kramer, former commander of Struthof, who remembers switching the chamber lights on again in order to observe the effects of the gas (2001: 215). Chéroux likens the gas chambers to 'chambres noires', photographic darkrooms, a disturbing simile which links the death site to the possibility of vision and image-creation.

Critical debate around real and fantasy images of the gas chambers has dwelt on the implications of the fact that the only surviving first-hand witnesses to the executions were Nazis such as Kramer or members of the *Sonderkommandos*, and that the latter would not have been in a position to film them. In an essay defending Lanzmann's controversial remarks about the 'pellicule maudite', Delfour reinterprets them in the light of the dangers pertaining to witnessing the atrocities from the Nazi point of view:

> Lanzmann would destroy the film shot by the Nazis because it *contains and legitimises* the Nazi position; to watch it would necessarily mean inhabiting that spectatorial position, exterior to the victims, thus adhering *filmically, perceptually,* to the Nazi position itself, and then fixing its image in memory. Indeed, it would be like seeing the victims through the side of an aquarium, that is, at a distance which reduces the killing to a *piece of information* … [The porthole] is a technical tool producing information which, in this case, *neutralises* the factual and human import of what is happening on the other side and *banalises* the voyeuristic, irresponsible psychic position of the person observing through this scopic device. (2000a: 14–15; emphasis in original)

Delfour argues that the Nazi film would fix its viewers in a voyeuristic-sadistic relation to the violence it depicts: voyeuristic in the sense that it offers 'a pleasure of seeing without being seen and of being absolved from this on the grounds that what is to be seen is horrifying'; sadistic insofar as 'the other suffers before my eyes while I myself remain invulnerable' (2000a: 15). As a consequence, while the contents of the images would test the limits of spectatorial tolerance, the camera-operator's perspective would ultimately limit their traumatic force. Significantly, Delfour draws parallels on these grounds between the 'pellicule maudite' and Spielberg's reconstruction of a shower room in *Schindler's List*, which he describes as an '*iconic bandage* intended to neutralise the violence of the murders' (ibid.; emphasis in original). While Godard would probably be receptive to this critique of Spielberg's film, Delfour's argument is implicitly at odds with Godard's contention that the camps should properly be shown from the point of view of the perpetrators. Delfour's account intersects instead at this juncture with Wajcman's concerns about the propensity of images to screen or protect us from the horror of the very reality to which they pretend to give us access. Moreover, for Delfour, who, like Wajcman, mounts a powerful defence of Lanzmann's decision to privilege oral testimony over archive images, *Shoah* 'radically compensates for' the absence of the Nazi film, rendering it 'unnecessary and even pernicious' (2000a: 16).

It is my contention in this chapter that filmic representations of the gas chambers may solicit more complicated, challenging and dynamic responses than those outlined in Delfour's essay. Drawing on critical models of film spectatorship, I examine how a range of fiction and documentary films imagine, construct or revisit these sites of unconscionable atrocity. I am interested here, more specifically, in the means by which they disturb the voyeuristic-sadistic gaze described by Delfour and in the alternative viewing positions they make available. While conventional representations of this scene tend to keep the audience at a safe distance from the horror, insulating us in one way or another from complicity, others self-consciously collapse this distance and implicate us in the violence depicted. My primarily exploratory readings do not aim to outline an ethics of spectatorship but to offer some insights into spectatorial agency and responsibility by exploring how images of the gas chambers hold – or fail to hold – us to account.

Unwitnessed witnessing or responsible looking?

Windows in general and spyholes in particular are amongst the oldest motifs in film and film theory. At once aperture and frame, the window simultaneously facilitates and limits our vision; in this respect at least it might be understood as an allegory of cinema. What makes the spyhole a particularly rich and suggestive metaphor in a cinematic context is the secretive, furtive and potentially illicit mode of looking it sanctions. The architectural term for a peep-hole or secret opening for spying is a 'judas hole'. The reference to Judas Iscariot, the disciple who betrayed Christ with a kiss, links the spyhole to an act of violence disguised as an embrace, bringing notions of treachery and deception into play. Spyholes impede frank exchanges and face-to-face encounters, disrupting viewing relations between self and other in ways that arouse moral suspicion. In *L'Être et le néant: essai d'ontologie phénoménologique* Jean-Paul Sartre famously uses the scenario of the voyeur caught spying through a keyhole to explore the feeling of shame we experience in becoming the object of the other's look (1943: 317–19), a scenario which is subsequently revisited and reconfigured by Jacques Lacan in *Les Quatre Concepts fondamentaux de la psychanalyse* (1973: 79–80). To look through the spyhole is also to find one's look called into question as the object of another's ethical scrutiny.

In film theory the one-way, non-consensual looking licensed by the spyhole has proved conducive to reflection on the cinematic apparatus, for in cinema, too, the gaze is never mutual or reciprocated. Judith Mayne reminds us that those early films 'in which mostly men, but occasionally women, peek through keyholes [offer] bold demonstrations of the voyeuristic pleasure that has been central to virtually every theory of the cinema' (1990: 9). Insofar as it involves seeing without being seen, film spectatorship, like voyeurism, is, so to speak, unwitnessed witnessing. Christian Metz investigates these affinities in his canonical work *Le Signifiant imaginaire*, where he refers to cinema's inevitable 'effet de trou de serrure' ('keyhole effect'). Drawing on psychoanalytic accounts of subject-formation,

Metz argues that the spectator's 'solitude' in the cinema and the lack of communication between the spaces of the auditorium and the screen foster an '*unauthorised* scopophilia' (1982: 64, 63; emphasis in original). The absence of the object seen deprives us of 'rehabilitatory agreement, [a] real or supposed consensus with the other' (1982: 63). Metz draws parallels in this context between cinema and the primal scene described by Freud: 'For its spectator the film unfolds in that simultaneously very close and definitely inaccessible "elsewhere" in which the child *sees* the amorous play of the parental couple, who are similarly ignorant of it and leave it alone, a pure onlooker whose participation is inconceivable' (1982: 64; emphasis in original). According to Metz, the voyeuristic positioning of spectators is compounded by the combination of darkened auditorium and bright screen, which gives us the impression we are looking through a keyhole.

The parallels between film spectatorship and voyeurism also emerge as a preoccupation in feminist theory, notably Laura Mulvey's influential account, from 1975, of the relay of gazes structuring classical narrative cinema. Mulvey identifies voyeurism, along with fetishism, as strategies adopted by the male unconscious to contain the threat presented by the sexual difference of the woman on the screen. However, critics have subsequently challenged the comparatively fixed or one-dimensional models of viewing relations proposed by apparatus theorists such as Metz and Mulvey, pointing out that they cannot account for all our experiences of spectatorship. Summarising these developments, Linda Williams explains that 'whereas 1970s and 1980s film theory tended to posit … a *unitary* way of seeing, contemporary discussions of spectatorship emphasise the plurality and paradoxes of many different, historically distinct viewing positions' (1995: 3–4; emphasis in original). Such discussions have mobilised concepts of masochism, fantasy and negotiation in the attempt to develop alternative, less rigid accounts of spectatorial identification and pleasure more attentive to what Mayne considers as 'the competing claims of the homogeneous cinematic institution and heterogeneous responses to it' (1993: 79).[3] Reflecting on the broader implications of Judith Butler's critique of identity categories (1990), Caroline Evans and Lorraine Gamman argue that since identity is never fixed 'it is inappropriate to posit any single identification with images' (1995: 39); identifications must be rethought instead as 'multiple, contradictory, shifting, oscillating, inconsistent and fluid' (1995: 45).

While Metz's and Mulvey's arguments tempt us to posit a fixed correlation between the spectator and the Nazi voyeur he or she encounters in films such as *Kornblumenblau*, the recognition that identifications are multiple and mobile enables more circumspect readings of images of historical trauma which acknowledge the gap between the ways in which they address us and the more varied ways in which we actually respond to them.

In certain films, images of the gas chamber and the spyhole in particular destabilise rather than confirm our illusory position of mastery and transcendence over a vulnerable on-screen other who can neither return our gaze nor acquiesce in our looking. Notwithstanding the resonance of their insights here, however, recent discussions of spectatorship have remained surprisingly silent about the ethical dynamics of the fluid, shifting viewing relations they describe. Moreover, little has been said in this context about the specificity of viewers' encounters with traumatic images. One important exception on both counts is Michele Aaron, whose investigation of the pleasures and unpleasures of 'looking on' argues that film spectatorship is never neutral or innocent but 'intrinsically ethical', 'inherently … hooked on the "real" or imagined suffering of others' (2007: 112). In the introduction to this volume I mentioned two further seminal discussions of film and ethics by Sobchack and Nichols, which are of particular relevance to the issues at stake in this chapter. Nichols' analysis of 'axiographics' is framed as an attempt to revise Mulvey's account of classic narrative in terms more appropriate to documentary practice. In Nichols' text the emphasis is shifted from erotics to ethics and attention is paid to the moral implications of the diverse ways of looking inscribed in and solicited by non-fiction film. One of the questions Nichols raises in relation to observational documentaries and the strategies of textual organisation which shape our readings of them is whether it is possible for viewers 'to share the geographic perspective of a camera position but not necessarily to share the moral perspective of that position' (1991: 92). An affirmative answer would imply that Delfour's suspicions about the 'pellicule maudite' are unfounded, recognising that the moral alliance of viewers of this film need not be with the Nazi camera-operator.

Sobchack too is mindful of the potentially disjunctive relationship between filmmakers' and spectators' ethical positions. In her essay 'Inscribing Ethical Space: Ten Propositions on Death, Representation, and Documentary' she argues that in contemporary culture the event of death 'points to and interrogates the very limits of representation in all its forms' and 'poses an ethical question to vision' (2004a: 232, 255). More specifically, Sobchack proposes that documentary representations of death involve 'the visible constitution and inscription of an "ethical space" that subtends both filmmaker and spectator alike' (2004a: 255). She elaborates:

> Before the nonfictional screen event of an unsimulated death, the very act of looking at the film is ethically charged, and this act is itself an object of ethical judgement. That is, the viewer is – and is held – ethically responsible for his or her own visible visual response. The cinematic signs of the act of viewing death provide the visible grounds on which the spectator

judges not only the filmmaker's ethical behaviour in response to death but also his or her own ethical response to the visible visual activity represented on the screen – both its content and its form. (2004a: 244)

For Sobchack, then, both the filmmaker ('the immediate viewer') and the spectator ('the mediate viewer') find themselves ethically implicated by the event of death. Both the filmmaker's relation to this event, which is inscribed in his or her images through camerawork, montage and *mise-en-scène*, and the spectator's response to these images become subject to ethical scrutiny. Sobchack is interested here in the specificity of the ethical spaces constructed by documentary and argues that less stringent criteria for ethical judgement operate in fictional representations of death. In the face of death fiction film spectators are less 'ethically squeamish' than their documentary counterparts, she suggests, since fictional stagings of death do not demand the same kind of ethical justification as documentary representations and tend merely to play with the taboos surrounding the event (2004a: 242). But in a later essay, 'The Charge of the Real: Embodied Knowledge and Cinematic Consciousness', Sobchack acknowledges that these distinctions may not be quite so clear-cut. Here she investigates moments when fictional space becomes 'charged with the real' (2004b: 284) – an ethical charge which 'moves us from fictional into documentary consciousness [and] calls forth not only response but also responsibility – not only aesthetic valuation but also ethical judgement' (ibid.).

The insights of Sobchack's earlier essay are directly applicable to the hypothetical images of the 'pellicule maudite'. Further, we might examine the moral stance of the camera-operator as encoded in the images, although this complicit immediate gaze would be unlikely to fit into any of the categories of ethical behaviour she identifies (represented by the 'accidental', 'helpless', 'endangered', 'interventional', 'humane' and 'professional' gazes).[4] We might then consider whether any ethically acceptable position is available to the mediate viewer in the face of a film record and an atrocity of this kind. However, the readings of real images that follow suggest that it is not only the visible event of unsimulated death that charges filmmakers' and viewers' looks with ethical significance and responsibility. In certain films bodily violence, suffering and trauma too are liable to implicate us ethically, even when they are simulated by actors or not directly represented.

Reconstructing the gas chamber

Of the thousands of hours of film dedicated to the memory of the Holocaust, quite possibly the single scene that has generated the most commentary takes place in the shower room reconstructed by Spielberg for *Schindler's List*. On arrival at Auschwitz, the Jewish women and children whom Oskar Schindler is attempting to protect have their hair cut, are forced to undress and marched along a corridor into a large room marked 'Bad und Desinfektion' with showerheads attached to the ceiling. They are accompanied into the room by a handheld camera which adopts their point of view and conveys a sense of their disorientation. Spielberg then cuts to a shot of the doors being closed from the outside by female guards, and the camera reframes in close-up on a spyhole, through which we contemplate the terror of the women and children imprisoned inside for a full five seconds. In the next shot we are back inside the room amongst them. We watch them trembling with cold and fear and listen to them screaming in fright as they are plunged into darkness. Spielberg is playing games with spectatorial expectations here. The rumours of showers dispensing gas rather than water that circulate earlier in the film, the heavy metal doors with their spyhole, the abruptly extinguished lights and the ominous strains of an extradiegetic violin all conspire to mislead us, along with the women and children, into anticipating the worst. Finally, however, after the lights have been switched back on, water begins to flow from the showerheads and images of agony are replaced by a scene of euphoria. Ironically, Spielberg inverts the trick used by the SS to entice prisoners to their deaths without arousing their suspicions; instead of disguising a gas chamber as a shower room, he disguises a shower room as a gas chamber.

Critical commentary regarding this scene is punctuated by allusions to its 'voyeuristic', 'sadistic', 'indecent', 'pornographic' and 'obscene' tendencies.[5] For Rose, it is emblematic of the risks of a film which leaves its first-time viewers 'perpetually braced in fear of obscene excess of voyeuristic witness' (1996: 47). On more than one level, critics' responses to the shower room sequence recall the discussions prompted by 'le travelling de *Kapo*', not least because it is a movement forward by the camera to give us a better view of a spectacle of suffering (here, the shot which homes in upon the spyhole) that is once again the

Schindler's List: through the spyhole

central focus of debate. Delfour is troubled by the way in which the structure of this shot 'institutes filmically a position of sadistic voyeurism ... *protected and guaranteed*' rather than interrogated by the film (2000a: 15; emphasis in original). He goes on to identify this viewing position with what he hypothesises would be the voyeuristic-sadistic perspective adopted by the camera in the 'pellicule maudite'. While I share Delfour's qualms about the symbolic violence of Spielberg's shot, I would suggest that the sequence as a whole locates its viewers in more conflicted places than his reading admits. At least two contradictory identificatory positions are offered here: whilst the spyhole shot implicitly aligns us with the perspective of the guards on the outside, the handheld shots inside the chamber situate us in the midst of the terrified Jewish women, imitating their point of view as they glance fearfully up at the showerheads and around at each others' faces. Like Wosiewicz's shots and counter-shots of the gas chamber and the observing SS guard in *Kornblumenblau*, Spielberg's camerawork positions us alternately as powerless victim and omnipotent persecutor, yet the two sequences make different demands upon the viewer. Rothberg suggests that in *Schindler's List* 'the camera's movement inside/outside and above/within the scene of death indicates contrary desires to "testify" from within an impossible space and to distance the film from what has been judged socially unrepresentable' (2000: 238). While Wosiewicz transgresses this limit of representability by reconstructing a gas chamber, filling it with actors and inviting us to watch them simulate asphyxiation, his camerawork draws attention both to the indecency of a voyeuristic stance and the impossibility of any straightforward identification with the victims. In refusing us any innocent position from which to observe the scene of death, he compels us to confront the ethical implications of our looking. Here a *moral* line is overstepped in order to instigate an encounter which functions *ethically* to call our position into question. In contrast, Spielberg's scene finally respects the *moral* limit it repeatedly threatens to cross, but in so doing it evades *ethical* reflection. The alternately sadistic and masochistic viewing positions constructed by the camera work to downplay our agency and protect us from responsibility.

Schindler's List ultimately affirms the traditional moral prohibition on direct representation of the gas chamber. The subsequent scene reiterates this: as the women leave the shower room some of them notice another line of prisoners steadily descending the steps into the crematorium nearby. Following the gaze of one of the reprieved women, the camera lingers on the threshold where the less fortunate deportees pass out of sight, picking out the figure of a smiling child before she too is swallowed up by the building, and then panning upwards along the chimney to reveal the ash spewing from the top. Retrospectively, then, it becomes clear that the crisis of spectatorship precipitated by the shower room scene has as much to do with what we don't see as with what Spielberg actually shows; more precisely, it is a consequence of the relationship of substitution between the two: of water for gas, of Eros for Thanatos, of the sight of traumatised but disturbingly eroticised naked female bodies for the finally absent image of death in the gas chamber. Weissman suggests that the forbidden image of the eroticised Holocaust victim comes to stand in here for the even more forbidden image of the victims' death by gas (2004: 178–80).[6] Most problematic, in Rose's reading, is the substitution of water for gas, from which point onwards 'there is no decent position: … to show the death agonies would exceed the limit of permissible representation; but water not gas induces the regressive identification … with the few women who are saved' (1996: 47).[7] The film's duplicitous substitutions not only risk diminishing, even disavowing, the realities of the genocide; they also shore up the *moral* prohibition against its representation at the expense of an *ethical* confrontation with the event. Moral confusion is created as Spielberg deceives us into mistaking one trauma scene for another and exploits our fear that we are about to witness the prohibited image of asphyxiation. Yet the film ultimately guarantees the safety of our position as innocent onlookers, denying our investment in the violence and suffering shown. In *Schindler's List* the judas hole proves doubly treacherous; it offers false views both of the vulnerable other and of the irresponsible self, affording the semblance of moral clarity while exacerbating ethical disorientation.

Spielberg is not the first filmmaker to have moved perilously close to breaking while finally leaving intact the taboo on representation of mass murder by gas. In *Les Uns et les autres* (*Bolero*, 1981), a feature film which follows the lives of four families from different countries who become caught up in World War Two, Claude Lelouch affords us a momentary glimpse inside a gas chamber. In the scene in question, we see a group of naked boys and men, including one of the film's central protagonists, standing in a white-plastered room staring silently back at us, framed by an open window. But as the camera zooms out, we notice that there are showerheads attached to the ceiling, at which point an SS guard slides a metal shutter across the window, leaving us to imagine the scene of death it blocks from view. The film then cuts to a shot of other deportees clearing away clothes which have been left hanging next to a door marked 'Desinfektionsraum'. There is no diegetic sound; the scene is accompanied instead by melancholic violin music performed by the camp orchestra, which heightens our sense of unreality and disbelief. Robert Enrico leaves less to our imagination in his film *Au nom de tous les miens* (*For Those I Loved*, 1983), which reconstructs the true story of Martin Gray, a Polish Jew who escaped from Treblinka and survived the Holocaust. In one scene we watch a group of deportees, including Gray, being marched to a gas chamber and forced to wait outside until the killing is finished. Neither we nor Gray witness the victims' deaths, but we notice a yellow liquid draining out of the chamber and we share in the vision of horror which greets the surviving deportees when the doors are reopened. The extended scene which follows depicts Gray and his team removing the bodies one by one and depositing them in a purpose-dug ditch, and the camera dwells on the horrific details of their task. Unlike *Schindler's List*, *Les Uns et les autres* and *Au nom de tous les miens* avoid manipulating spectatorial expectations by arousing the suspicion that they are about to show the prohibited image of the death struggle itself. Lelouch's camera zooms out as the chamber window closes rather than homing in on a spyhole like Spielberg's, and Enrico's arrives on the scene at a point when the gassing is already almost over. Unlike Spielberg, neither Lelouch nor Enrico distract their viewers from the horror of the event itself by playing suspense games. Moreover, Lelouch and Enrico are also less duplicitous than Spielberg insofar as their gas chambers prove to be lethal; they offer neither an image of catharsis and redemption nor a substitute for the forbidden image they withhold. Nevertheless, in respecting the injunction against representing the atrocity itself, they too privilege a moral code over interrogation of the ethical implications of the position of the audience. In all three films depictions of the gas chamber avoid any reflection on the relation of viewers to the death depicted, on the complex dynamics of desire which keep them watching, or on the innocence or complicity of their looks.

Asserting provocatively that 'violence is a spectacle', the sociologist Yann Renaud argues that the logic of the violent relation implies the presence of a spectator or witness: 'Dual in its structure, the relation of violence nevertheless presupposes the presence of a third actor ... Violence generates a dramatic space and always possibly takes place under the gaze of this fascinated onlooking third party' (2001: 107). Renaud proceeds to analyse the ways in which spectators find themselves implicated in the violence they witness by the manner in which they look. While cinematically mediated violence is not Renaud's subject here, the triangulation of gazes he describes is repeatedly dramatised in filmic representations of the gas chamber. A recurrent motif or cliché in Holocaust films is the image of an on-screen spectator witnessing a gassing which goes unseen by the spectator in the cinema. Robert Young's feature film *Triumph of the Spirit* (1989) and the television series *Holocaust* offer ostensibly contrasting examples of scenes of this kind. Both works tend to be viewed, alongside films such as *Schindler's List*, as audience-friendly versions of history which do little to trouble the conventions of mainstream cinema and television despite the traumatic nature of their subject. *Triumph of the Spirit* tells the story of a Jewish Greek boxer, Salamo Arouch, who was imprisoned at Auschwitz and transferred to the *Sonderkommando* in preparation for an uprising. In one scene we see prisoners being prepared for gassing and SS guards donning gas masks and pouring crystals of Zyklon B into a gas chamber. But as the chemical begins to take effect, the film cuts to a close-up of Arouch's face on the outside as he witnesses the killing machinery in action for the first time. In *Holocaust* too the scene of death takes place off-screen and is reflected in the facial expressions of an on-screen eyewitness, but in this case his gaze is plainly complicit in the atrocity. In a sequence which both appeals to and refuses to satisfy the audience's voyeuristic impulses, Professor Pfannenstiel, a Nazi scientist visiting Auschwitz, observes a gassing through a spyhole and is irresistibly fascinated by what he sees. Rather than maintaining a horrified silence like Arouch, he attempts to put the experience into words, likening what he sees to Dante's *Inferno* and what he hears to wailing in a synagogue. Just as Müller's intricate description of the gassing process in *Shoah* supplies a corrective to Pfannenstiel's commentary here, so Arouch's expression of horror offers an antidote to Pfannenstiel's voyeurism. The contrasting viewing positions adopted by the *Sonderkommando* Jew and the Nazi scientist cast them respectively as resister and collaborator in the economy of violence. However, while the visual focus on the witness's face avoids a voyeuristic perspective on the unseen atrocity, these scenes and the films that contain them do little to deepen our understanding of the moral dilemmas faced by the *Sonderkommando* or the responsibilities of the Nazi collaborator. Once again, moreover, they evade self-conscious consideration of the ethical stance of the other onlooker, the film viewer, in relation to the violence hidden outside the frame.

A more challenging and nuanced representation of the spectator's role as potential actor in the intersubjective space configured by violence can be found in Constantin Costa-Gavras's *Amen* (2002), a thriller loosely based on Rolf Hochhuth's controversial play *Der Stellvertreter: ein christliches Trauerspiel* (*The Deputy: A Christian Tragedy*, 1963), which draws in turn upon real events. The film dramatises the story of chemist, SS lieutenant and protestant Kurt Gerstein, who supplies the Nazis with Zyklon B for what he assumes are solely disinfection procedures, until his discovery of the real purposes for which the chemical is being used leads to a crisis of conscience. *Amen* contains a representation of a gas chamber in the form of a diagram used in a meeting to discuss measures for improving the efficiency of gassing techniques. One of the SS officers present absent-mindedly sketches human figures inside the diagram, a detail that is twice picked out by the camera. Like the plaster model of Crematoria II and III in the Auschwitz museum that we encounter in *Shoah*, the pencil sketchings allude to the missing images of a scene which Costa-Gavras refuses to re-enact. But they also recall an earlier and pivotal sequence in which Gerstein and other Nazi officials visit a camp in Poland where gas is being tested on live victims, euphemistically referred to as 'units'. As the doors of the gas chamber start to rattle ominously, Gerstein and his companions take turns to look through the spyholes. A series of close-ups frame their faces in profile, inviting us to scrutinise their expressions. Most convey degrees of distaste (one remarks 'it's rather horrible'), but Gerstein, who has not been warned about the nature of the test, recoils in shock, before looking around in disbelief at his companions, who silently and steadily return his gaze. As in *Triumph of the Spirit* and *Holocaust*, the witnesses' faces come to stand in for the unimaged scene of death which viewers are invited to reconstruct instead in their imagination. But *Amen* offers more probing insights into the relations between seeing, witnessing and acting and the vital role of the eyewitness in the context of an event which consumed so many of its witnesses. As one of Gerstein's colleagues points out to him, 'there aren't ten people alive who have seen what you just saw.' Shortly afterwards, Gerstein tries to explain the significance and implications of his experience to his pastor: 'I saw it with my own eyes … I have seen what was not meant to be seen. There must be a witness. I shall be the eyes of God in that hell.' And, indeed, it is his single fleeting glance through the spyhole that prompts him to risk everything by attempting to alert the Vatican, the Allies and other Germans to the true nature of the 'Final Solution'. The film's commentary on the acts of witnessing and of bearing witness, which centres on the gas chamber scene, is self-conscious and knowing; it implicates its viewers too as witnesses even as it refuses to allow them direct visual access to its primal scene. The ethical question facing Gerstein and on which the narrative hinges concerns how the witness should act upon the traumatic knowledge of what he or she has seen, a question which Costa-Gavras also addresses to his audience, as spectator-witnesses, while the deepening ambiguity of his protagonist's chosen course of action saves the film from moral didacticism.

Amen: the witness as actor

The most detailed, sustained and unrelentingly brutal reconstruction of the activities of the *Sonderkommandos* and the operation of the gas chambers in any fiction film to date is provided by Tim Blake Nelson's *The Grey Zone* (2001). The film is adapted from a stage play, also written by Nelson, which was based in part on a memoir by Miklós Nyiszli, a Hungarian Jewish doctor and deportee who assisted Josef Mengele in his research on twins. Nyiszli's memories also inform the well-known essay by Levi from which the play and film borrow their titles (see 1988: 22–51). The film depicts the uprising of the twelfth *Sonderkommando* at Auschwitz in October 1944. A series of graphic scenes introduce us without warning or comment to the production line of death: a line of deportees descending into the crematorium to the strains of the camp orchestra; members of the *Sonderkomman-*

do reassuring the deportees that they are simply being taken for a shower; an SS officer emptying crystals into a gas chamber; the *Sonderkommando* removing the bodies, hosing down the chamber, extracting teeth, shaving hair, burning the bodies in the ovens and pits; ash spewing out of the chimney and coating the crematorium and the *Sonderkommando* in a layer of grey. Somewhat inevitably, despite the director's attention to historical detail, *The Grey Zone* has revived debates about the domesticating, trivialising function of the realist aesthetic; neither the star cast nor the extras are physically credible as deportees. If critics' misgivings echo aspects of Rivette's denunciation of *Kapo*, the film repeats 'le travelling de *Kapo*' in a more literal sense too. Just as in Pontecorvo's film, a deportee played by a beautiful actress (Natasha Lyonne) commits suicide by throwing herself against an electrified fence, and the camera reframes her in a more attractive composition, this time from a distance, but following the rule of thirds. The straightforward visual parallels between the two scenes suggest that this is unwitting recapitulation rather than a knowing intertextual reference. However, *The Grey Zone* includes quotations from other visual documents that indicate an engagement with the broader problems which concern Rivette. A brief establishing shot showing the *Sonderkommando* at work in front of a burning pit appears to be modelled directly on one of the photographs taken by the Auschwitz *Sonderkommando* in

August 1944 (images whose exceptional status as witnesses to the killing machine in action were discussed in chapter two), right down to the positioning of figures within the frame. This meticulous reconstruction unsettles the distinctions between documentary and fiction and tests, even if it ultimately validates, Rivette's claim that recreating the camps will always betray them. Despite its unflinch-

The Grey Zone: reframing death

ing and systematic depiction of the killing machine and its concerns with authenticity, *The Grey Zone* follows cinematic convention in respecting the prohibition against showing the death struggle in the gas chamber. There is one exception: an abrupt two-second flashback in the memory of a girl who miraculously survives the twenty minutes of gas, but returns mute, unable to bear witness to her experience, only to be executed in the final moments of the film. Unlike Spielberg, Nelson does not call attention to the images he withholds, never leading us to expect that we are about to witness the moment of death. Throughout the film we watch events from the perspective of the *Sonderkommando*, while camera angles and sounds are used to insinuate the murder that is taking place off-screen. By positioning us in the grey zone with the *Sonderkommando*, the film avoids the compensatory or redemptive trajectory traced by *Schindler's List*, disrupting Manichean oppositions between good and evil, innocence and guilt. The viewing positions we are offered solicit identifications with the *Sonderkommando* members while allowing us to establish a critical distance from which to evaluate their actions. Less explicitly than *Amen*, *The Grey Zone* contemplates the inextricability of onlooking and acting, refuting the myth of the neutral or guiltless bystander and implicating its viewers in this process.

Although all but two of the films discussed in this section respect the interdiction on representation of death in the gas chamber, in reconstructing the killing sites in a conventional realist narrative mode, the majority violate the ethical injunctions variously laid down by Rivette, Lanzmann and Godard. In so doing, they highlight and contend with the difficulties of recreating either the appearance or the experience of the death camps. But the ethical stances adopted by these films are not fully determined by the fidelity of their reconstructions. Ethical meaning resides just as much in the relationship between what they show – the preparations, the aftermath, the witness's face – and what they leave unimaged – the death scene itself – and in the positions they make available to the viewer. What makes these scenes instructive with regard to spectatorial ethics is that they dramatise the activity of looking on, its pleasures and unpleasures and, in certain cases, question the possibility of neutral bystanding. With the exception of Spielberg, each of these directors takes steps to avoid positioning us voyeuristically in relation to the other's suffering, most often by refusing to represent it directly. In some cases voyeurism is made untenable precisely by aligning us through the camerawork with the point of view of the Nazi perpetrator, which alerts us to the symbolic violence of such a perspective, apparently validating Godard's proposed filmic project while calling Delfour's argument into question. This said, the majority of these films avoid explicit commentary on the ethical implications of watching reconstructions of the genocide. While they arouse varying degrees of horror and pity in the audience, this in itself does not necessarily constitute an ethical response, and indeed can actively distract us from responding in such a way. As Aaron points out in a discussion of images of another kind of violence (the graphic Normandy D-Day landings sequence in Spielberg's *Saving Private Ryan* (1998)), 'being moved … marks the experience as moral but not ethical: involuntary emotion is the opposite of reflection and implication' (2007: 116). *Kornblumenblau*, *Amen* and *The Grey Zone* are noteworthy in this context for the ways in which they disturb viewing relations, and encourage us to think more (self-)critically about our responsibilities as mediate viewers, as vicarious witnesses to atrocity.

Documentary approaches

Documentary filmmakers are confronted with a distinct though not un-related set of ethical questions as they approach the threshold of the gas chamber. In the absence of historical footage showing a chamber in use – the contested images of the 'pellicule maudite' – they are obliged to seek alternative strategies to bear witness to the atrocities that took place there. As pointed out in chapter one, Lanzmann's solution is to interview survivors of the *Sonderkommandos* and others whose work in the crematoria positioned them as first-hand witnesses to the murder. Other directors have followed suit, inviting those rare survivors who, through a variety of circumstances, were unfortunate enough to see the gas chambers for themselves to speak about this experience on camera. In Thomas Mitscherlich's *Reisen ins Leben: Weiterleben nach einer Kindheit in Auschwitz* (*Journey into Life: Aftermath of a Childhood in Auschwitz*, 1995), for example, we meet Yehuda Bacon, an artist who spent his early teens in Auschwitz and whose connections with the *Sonderkommandos* afforded him an opportunity to study the interiors of the crematoria and gas chambers. He describes the pains he took to commit every last detail to memory in case he should survive and have the chance to put them down on paper. Although he subsequently went on to do so, Mitscherlich chooses not to include Bacon's drawings of the gas chamber in the film, despite showing some of his other images of camp life. Unlike *Shoah*, *Reisen ins Leben* refuses to grant us any form of visual access to this central trauma site.

Exceptional amongst these singular testimonies is the miraculous account we hear in *The Eighty-First Blow* (1974), a documentary by David Bergman, Jaquot Ehrlich and Haim Gouri. The film is composed predominantly of Nazi photographs and film footage which are accompanied on the soundtrack by a compilation of oral testimony from witnesses at the trial of Adolf Eichmann. The witness in question describes how he was selected for the gas chamber as a boy and waited for death in the darkness after the airtight doors had been closed. He informs the court, and the cinema audience, that he owes his survival to a last-minute change of plan on the part of the guards, who suddenly reopened the doors and chose fifty boys to be put to work, before proceeding to gas the rest. What makes this witness's deposition unique is that it addresses us from within the sealed chamber; he speaks from a position unavailable even to the *Sonderkommando* survivor. As such, his testimony supplies an (aural) counter-shot and corrective to the external perspective afforded by the spyhole in narrative films such as *Kornblumenblau* and *Schindler's List*. However, the relationship between his testimony and the images shown in *The Eighty-First Blow* is more ambiguous. He and the other witnesses heard in the film are never named or seen. By depriving them of a physical presence on the screen, the film downplays the specificity of their individual experiences.[8] Disturbingly, moreover, the relation between soundtrack and image-track is one not of counterpoint but of mutual corroboration: images recorded by the perpetrators are deployed in such a way as to illustrate and verify the words of the survivors (as if such verification were needed), just as the testimonies are edited to impose meaning and coherence on the images. No attempt is made to interrogate the disjunction between the points of view offered by the testimonies and the images, or to exploit discrepancies between them. For the film's viewers there is little escaping the geographic position of the Nazi camera-operator, the metaphorical violence of which is highlighted by a series of photographs of a mass execution of Jewish prisoners in a ditch, taken by one of the executioners. Yet in using these photographs to validate the witnesses' accounts, the film not only obscures the moral perspectives inscribed in the images, but also conflates them with the perspectives of the survivors.

Nevertheless, inviting us to listen to eyewitnesses speaking about their experiences is thus one way in which filmmakers can avoid the ethical risks that pertain, as discussed above, to visualising the gas chambers. By enlisting us as listeners as well as viewers, documentaries such as *Shoah*, *Reisen ins Leben* and *The Eighty-First Blow* place different ethical demands on us from fictional reconstructions of the trauma scene which tend to appeal first and foremost to our sense of sight. The spoken word can engage us in a form of ethical dialogue, particularly when accompanied by images of the remembering survivor, by appealing more insistently to our imagination and fantasy. In these films the eyewitness's words do not so much supplant the missing images of the gas chamber as evoke their absence. But in other documentaries testimonies on this subject are supplemented by images of the crematoria, or what remains of them, whose relationship to the absent image of death is more complicated. Typical is footage included in James Moll's *The Last Days* (1998), a film about the persecution of the Hungarian Jews produced by Spielberg for the Shoah Foundation. Here a handheld camera wanders around the restored Crematorium I at Auschwitz while Dario Gabbai, a Greek survivor of the camp's *Sonderkommando*, describes witnessing its lethal function for the first time. In their imitative relation to Gabbai's words, these images recall those that accompany Müller's account of his first impression of this crematorium in *Shoah* (a sequence discussed in chapter one). Shortly afterwards, however, Moll's images of the present find a correlate in an image from the past which seems to align us with a different point of view. As Gabbai remembers 'big shots from Berlin' visiting the camp to observe the gassings, we are shown a fragment of archive footage depicting an unidentified man looking through a grated spyhole into what we take to be a gas chamber. (The film does not specify the source of this footage, but the evidence available suggests that it was filmed just after the liberation of one of the death camps.) The camera continues to hover in front of the spyhole after the man has moved away, making this uncomfortably reminiscent of the equivalent shot in *Schindler's List*.

Discussing documentary spectatorship, Nichols argues that if in fiction film 'realism aligns itself with a scopophilia, a pleasure in looking …documentary realism aligns itself with an epistephilia, so to speak, a pleasure in knowing' (1991: 178). In this respect, documentary calls for 'the elaboration of an epistemology and axiology more than of an erotics' (ibid.). Yet the spyhole sequences in *Schindler's List* and *The Last Days* and the responses they solicit from the viewer suggest that the pleasures promised by the two films have more in common than Nichols' argument anticipates. *The Last Days* unquestionably arouses and purports to satisfy our curiosity, our desire to know. The oral testimonies, archive footage and present-day images of the crematorium and other atrocity sites follow a seamless logic of corroboration in line with documentary convention, which 'posits an organising agency that possesses information and knowledge, a text that conveys it, and a subject who will gain it' (1991: 31). However, the lingering shot of the spyhole is just one of a number of sequences in the film which simultaneously thematise the act of onlooking and exploit our desire to see. Its relationship to Gabbai's words is purely illustrative; it neither contradicts nor adds extra information to his account. It is presented simply as a visual dramatisation of the scene he describes, and thus becomes a source of visual gratification, despite the fact that it almost certainly features an Allied soldier discovering the chamber after the liberation rather than a visiting SS official during the war. *The Last Days* posits a subject who will gain pleasure from looking as well as from knowing, and whose desire to know is closely bound up with his or her desire to see.

Lea Rosh and Eberhard Jäckel's documentary *Der Tod ist ein Meister aus Deutschland* (*Death is a Master from Germany*, 1999) also adheres to its contractual obligation to impart knowledge while exploring the role that visual desire plays in this process. Newly-filmed images of the crematorium complex at Majdanek are accompanied by a traditional voice-over commentary which guides us around the shower room and gas chamber in time with the smoothly panning camera, explaining the significance of what we see (it points out, for example, the openings in the ceiling where Zyklon B was introduced). As in *The Last Days*, images of the present are supplemented by images of the past; here they are intercut with grainy footage filmed by the Soviet liberators at the same location. But the film also includes a sequence which visualises the atrocities more directly. Commenting on the industrial scale of the killing, the voice-over informs us that since imagination is insufficient in such a context we will be shown ex-tracts from a 'strictly authentic historical film'. There follow excerpts from Jack Gold's feature film *Escape from Sobibor* (1987), one of which recon-structs the final moments of a group of deportees and simulates the sounds of their dying in a gas chamber. At such moments, Rosh and Jäckel's docu-mentary brings our scopophilic and epistephilic impulses into alignment. Recontextualised here, Gold's reconstruction is supposed to make history more visible and tangible and to satisfy the curiosity aroused by the traces and remnants of violence we see in the archive footage and present-day images of the empty crematorium.[9]

According to Nichols, in documentary 'knowledge, as much or more than the imaginary identification between viewer and fictional character, promises the viewer a sense of plenitude or self-sufficiency' (1991: 31). But he warns too that 'like the ideal-ego figures or objects of desire suggested by the characters of narrative fiction', this knowledge may become 'a source of pleasure that is far from innocent' (ibid.). Nichols' remarks suggest that the documentary spectator may be no more of a neutral bystander than the spectator of narrative fiction, that his or her desires may be different but are no less complicit. Indeed, I want to argue that the pledge to provide knowledge and the illusory sense of mastery it affords could be seen as an alternative strategy for escaping ethical implication. In honouring this unwritten contract with their audiences, *The Last Days* and *Der Tod ist ein Meister aus Deutschland* reassure us of the security of our viewing posi-tions while discouraging us from taking responsibility for the knowledge we are given.

More hesitant about promising knowledge, less confident of its claim on the real, and more ethically exacting in relation to its viewer, I would suggest, is Resnais' exploration of Holocaust sites in *Nuit et brouillard*, a film which, like *Shoah*, has become a seminal point of reference in postwar debates about the ethics of representation. *Nuit et brouillard* has four prin-cipal components: black-and-white photographs and film footage from the archive are interpolated with freshly-shot colour images of the camps and accompanied by a voice-over commentary written by the survivor Jean Cayrol and a musical score by Hanns Eisler. Unlike some of the document-aries discussed above, however, Resnais' film incessantly interrogates the relationship between its visual and aural elements and the historical reality they purport to represent, registering doubts about its capacity to render the Holocaust visible, graspable or knowable. As Leo Bersani and Ulysse Dutoit have noted, our vision is constantly disturbed and disoriented by the dissonant relations between voice, music and image, which prevent us from becoming absorbed in what we see: 'to watch this film is to be turned away from it' (1993: 187).

Nuit et brouillard includes one and *The Last Days* two of the photographs taken by members of the *Sonderkommando* in and around Crematorium V at Auschwitz in August 1944. The photographs in question show bodies burning in a ditch, though in the versions recycled by Moll and Resnais the doorframe that featured prominently in the originals has been excised and, with it, the visible signs of the courage and resourcefulness of the photographer hiding in the gas chamber. In *Nuit et brouillard*, moreover, a film which famously elides the Jewish specificity of the genocide, the brief appearance of Alex's photograph in a sequence of images of corpses taken by the Allies further obscures the distinctions between the concentrationary system and the 'Final Solution'. However, whereas in Moll's film the photographs function straightforwardly as documentary evidence of the events described by the witnesses, Resnais' montage discourages us from viewing such images as transparent windows onto the past. As the camera tracks through empty barracks in Birkenau, Cayrol's commentary warns us that the reality of the camps is 'hard for us to uncover traces of now' and remains incommensurable with words and images as 'no description, no image can restore their true dimension'. These words call into question the testimonial status of the commentary and of the images of the present and the past, making explicit their precarious relation to history and drawing attention to the ambiguous role of film in the construction of historical knowledge.

In what is possibly the most devastating scene of the film, and one that might be viewed as emblematic of his project, Resnais' camera enters a gas chamber at Majdanek, eleven years after Alex hid with his camera inside the chamber at Auschwitz, and at least two decades before Lanzmann returns to the latter site in *Shoah*. Unlike Lanzmann, Resnais does not stop at the threshold. And unlike Alex, who had to steal his snapshots secretly while the guards were looking the other way, Resnais can film at his own pace. His mobile, exploratory camerawork implies a residual corporeal presence in the silent, desolate chamber, ghosting the passage and perspective of those who died there. As the voice-over explains that the guards used to shut the doors and observe, the camera comes to rest momentarily on a closed door with a spyhole. But as it pans across the rough, pitted ceiling, it becomes more difficult for us to reconcile what we hear with what we see. We strain to make out what the commentary identifies as the sole remaining physical indices of those murdered there: the marks made in the concrete by their fingernails. In a discussion of our haptic engagement with material details in the film, Wilson comments on the disarming effect of this panning shot: 'The relation between the human markings and the atrocity to which they bear witness, and of which they offer material proof, challenges rationality and sense-making ... The gouging of this seemingly

Nuit et brouillard: fingernail marks in the ceiling of a gas chamber at Majdanek

adamant substance, and the oxymoron it embodies, challenges and nauseates the viewer. We have no purchase on these images' (2005: 109). This lack of purchase is exacerbated, rather than redressed, as Resnais cuts from the clawed corner of the empty chamber to a series of harrowing archive images of disfigured and decomposing bodies, which pose new challenges to the viewer's understanding. In contrast to some of the other films, both fiction and documentary, examined in this chapter, *Nuit et brouillard* seeks neither to materialise the absent image of death in the gas chamber, nor to invent or import images that might stand in for it.[10] Here, as throughout the film, Resnais' images of the present are haunted by the missing images of the past. The same could be said of *Hiroshima mon amour*, where the mnemonic or imagined images of the female protagonist dragging her knuckles roughly along a wall and sucking her wounds distressingly recall the fingernail marks in the earlier film and the scene of death to which they bear indexical witness. Moreover, in *Nuit et brouillard* the archive images too, in their turn, become haunted, the emaciated, traumatised survivors and the mounds of corpses evoking, but not supplanting, the missing bodies of those who were murdered in the gas chamber, incinerated in the crematoria or recycled in the various appalling ways mentioned. By insisting on the incommensurability of image, word and the reality to which they allude, *Nuit et brouillard* confounds our desire to know and understand while implicating us bodily, affectively and ethically.

'In cinema', writes Sobchack, 'the visible representation of vision inscribes sight not only in an image but also as moral insight' (2004a: 243). This chapter has examined some of the moral perspectives inscribed in images of trauma and suggested ways in which *mise-en-scène*, montage and sound may translate into ethical insights that are open to scrutiny by the viewer. I have noted some of the strategies by which films sidestep ethical concerns about viewing violence or, conversely, foreground questions of agency and responsibility. In so doing, I have stressed the ethical implicatedness of both fiction and documentary spectatorship, an issue which gains urgency when we are faced with images of historical trauma. In Holocaust films the threshold of the gas chamber becomes a privileged locus of anxieties about the ethics of representation. Yet respecting the prohibition on depicting the atrocities directly can also be a means of escaping an ethical confrontation with the event, as in *Schindler's List* and other films.

Nevertheless, images of these sites can bring into focus the responsibilities viewing confers on spectators, whether violence unfolds on the screen or is alluded to but ultimately withheld from view. The geographical positions from which we watch these scenes cannot fully account for our affective and ethical responses to them. The most challenging representations discussed here disrupt scopophilic and epistephilic dynamics by interrogating the limits of vision and knowledge in the face of the Holocaust – and encouraging us to look beyond them. Rather than the 'integral image' of the genocide imagined by Chéroux, films such as *Kornblumenblau*, *Amen*, *The Grey Zone* and *Nuit et brouillard* offer us fleeting glimpses of its horror which engage us in difficult, painful and open-ended processes of ethical reflection.

4

Blindness and the Difficulty of Facing: The Gorgon, the Muselmann and the Fragile Face

In an article originally published in a 1988 issue of the *Nouvelle revue de psychanalyse*, which resembles a manifesto in its didactic tone and polemical force, Lanzmann writes:

> Not to understand was my iron law during all the years of developing and making *Shoah*: I braced myself on this refusal as the only possible attitude, at once ethical and operative. This vigilance, these blinkers, this blindness were for me the vital conditions of creation. Blindness should be understood here as the purest mode of looking, the only way not to avert our gaze from a reality which is literally blinding: clearsightedness itself. To direct a frontal look at horror requires that we renounce distractions and evasions. (1990a: 279)

This enigmatic yet suggestive passage serves as the lynchpin of Lanzmann's defence of his refusal, while making *Shoah*, to ask the question 'why?' Borrowing his title from an SS man encountered by Levi, 'Hier ist kein Warum' ('Here There is No Why'), Lanzmann argues, contentiously, that the attempt to understand the Nazi genocide as a rational phenomenon is not merely unethical, but more properly 'obscene'. He warns us that the search for coherent historical explanations can become an alibi for neglecting to face the ethical reality of the event.[1] From this argument he derives an apparently paradoxical imperative. The only way to confront the horror of the camps directly, without succumbing to the temptation of sense-making projects, he suggests, is to approach it 'blind', or, at least, wearing 'blinkers'. This claim appears particularly provocative in the light of Lanzmann's relationship with cinema, a medium which tends to privilege vision over the other senses, even if filmic images remain irreducible to the purely visible. However, Lanzmann proceeds to reconceptualise 'blindness' here as a form of 'vigilance', 'the purest mode of looking' and 'the vital condition of creation'. Rather than a strategy of self-defence, an amnesiac ploy or an excuse to look away or awry, 'blindness' becomes instead the condition of the possibility of seeing and witnessing – of facing the past clear-sightedly.

Lanzmann's concept of 'vigilant blindness' offers a fresh perspective on the questions about spectatorship addressed in the previous chapter. This final chapter pursues these questions in new directions by exploring the ways in which Lanzmann's insights into the relationship between blindness and facing intersect with philosophical writings on testimony and ethics, on the one hand, and with certain currents in filmmaking practice, on the other. Lanzmann's discussion of 'blindness' has so far received only limited attention even from his most illuminating commentators. Felman, LaCapra and Cathy Caruth, for example, all quote parts of the passage from 'Hier ist kein Warum' cited above, but none offers more than a cursory account of the possible meanings of the concept as it is mobilised by Lanzmann (Felman is cited in Lanzmann 1995: 204; Caruth 1996: 124). It seems to me, however, that his insistence on 'blindness' as a condition of witnessing cannot simply be dismissed as a figure of speech, or as a retreat from historical understanding. Certainly, 'blindness' implies a rejection of explanations that distract us from facing, through the witness, the reality of the death camps. Stephenie Young interprets Lanzmann's comments by saying that 'blindness is a way of conceptualising how we bear witness to testimony by facing our subject with the admission that we may never understand his or her experience' (2000: 108–9). But I would suggest that the term might also legitimately be interpreted in a more literal sense in relation to Lanzmann's work.

In commentary upon *Shoah*, Lanzmann borrows and reconfigures a verbal image from Gérard de Nerval and Julia Kristeva to articulate a perceptual disturbance: 'The Holocaust is very difficult to face. It is like a black sun' (cited in Felman 1992c: 252).[2] Weissman observes that allusions to the sun as a trope for the Holocaust 'typically express how [the event] cannot and must not be confronted straight-on' (2004: 149). To illustrate the use of this trope he quotes the survivor Aaron Appelfeld, who remarks: 'I would say that, artistically, it is impossible to deal with [the Holocaust] directly. It's like the sun. You cannot look at the sun' (cited in ibid.). Appelfeld's observation recalls one of François La Rochefoucauld's seventeenth-century maxims: 'Le soleil ni la mort ne se peuvent regarder fixement' ('Neither the sun nor death can be looked at with a steady eye') (2002: 138). But Lanzmann's viewing position is markedly different from Appelfeld's and La Rochefoucauld's. Rather than too bright to be seen, Lanzmann's sun is darkened or eclipsed; the source of the light which enables sight is extinguished. For Lanzmann, the black sun figures an impossibility of seeing which he, in contrast to Appelfeld, insists must nonetheless be faced directly.

The concept of 'blindness' is inevitably a charged one in the context of film, spectatorship and historical trauma. One way in which it might be understood in the particular context of *Shoah*, *Un vivant qui passe* and *Sobibor* is in relation to cinema's capacity to facilitate our vision precisely by impeding or disturbing it thereby compelling us to look differently. As LaCapra points out, Lanzmann's refusal to show us images of the past at first appears to contradict his injunction to 'direct a frontal look at horror' (1998: 101). But this refusal surely confirms that the 'frontal look' he seeks to offer us need not be predicated upon direct visual access to the event; indeed, does it not imply that such access may actually prevent us from facing the event head-on? At the same time, the form and content of *Shoah* reflect a preoccupation with the different ways in which the Holocaust interferes with or blocks the vision of bystanders, perpetrators and survivors as well as film spectators. Describing the Holocaust as a 'historical assault on seeing' (1992c: 209) Felman argues that the three kinds of witnesses interviewed by Lanzmann are differentiated 'not so much by what they actually see ... as by what and how they *do not see*, by what and how they *fail to witness*' (1992c: 208; emphasis in original). Lanzmann is careful to speak of 'blindness' to explanations and causal chains, rather than to facts, and a number of the interviews with perpetrators and bystanders in *Shoah* encourage us to be wary of the witness's liability to attempt to rationalise what he or she has seen in retrospect. Nevertheless, Lanzmann's concerns about the event's propensity to overwhelm or inhibit vision – as encapsulated in the image of the black sun – must be understood in the context of the privilege consistently accorded in *Shoah* to eyewitness testimony, to the deposition of those who were physically present at the atrocities, and who, with Jan Karski, the former courier of the Polish government in exile who secretly visited the Warsaw ghetto in order to report on the Jews' persecution to the Allies, can claim 'I saw it myself'.[3]

This chapter seeks to broaden the book's perspective on ethical issues in cinema by engaging with films and philosophical texts which look beyond the Holocaust to different testimonial and mnemonic scenarios, alongside others which respond more directly to this specific event. While Holocaust films pose forceful questions about the ethics of vision and blindness, I want to highlight the pertinence of these questions in other cinematic contexts too. In order to give a firmer theoretical grounding to the connections between witnessing and blindness alluded to above, the chapter turns first to two recent discussions of testimony which deal in different ways with the impaired or lost sight of the witness or his or her capacity to trouble others' vision. Derrida's reflections on the representation of the blind and the blindness of representation in *Mémoires d'aveugle: l'autoportrait et autres ruines* (1990) posit the blind as privileged witnesses. Agamben's *Remnants of Auschwitz* meanwhile traces an alternative history of testimony that, controversially, identifies the only true witness as the one who constitutes an 'impossibility of seeing' (1999: 54): the 'faceless presence' of the Muselmann (see Levi 1966: 103). The next section attempts to draw out some of the ethical implications of vision and blindness through analysis of Levinas's writings on the encounter with the 'visage', or face. The rest of the chapter examines how these theoretical perspectives illuminate film practice, focusing on films by Marker and Resnais. Both of these directors identify the face as the locus of an ethical meaning which, like that of the Levinasian 'visage', resides as much in the invisible as in the visible. My readings explore how their images attest to and contend with alterity and the other's trauma without visualising or appropriating it, and implicate our vision by limiting or blocking it.

Witnessing blind, witnessing by proxy

In *Mémoires d'aveugle*, the catalogue essay which accompanied the exhibition of images of the blind held at the Louvre in 1990–91, Derrida explores the act of bearing witness through the figure of the blind seer. Intrigued by the privileged vision so often accorded to the blind in Greek mythology and the Bible, he notes that blindness is often the price to pay for insight, for the gift of opening eyes, one's own or another's. From this he derives the concept of a 'revelatory' blindness, a 'blindness that reveals the very truth of the eyes' (1993: 127). Moreover, as visionaries and prophets, the blind are called to reveal the truth – in short, to bear witness. 'By a singular vocation', writes Derrida, 'the blind man becomes a witness; he must attest to the truth or the divine light'; he is, in this sense, 'an archivist of visibility' (1993: 20). Derrida is referring specifically here to the blind man who was healed by Christ. However, the restoration of physical sight is not a precondition of bearing witness. On the contrary, in Derrida's account, the most effective witnesses, the elected witnesses, are, paradoxically, the blind ones: 'the blind man becomes … the best witness, the chosen witness' (1993: 104). What is more, Derrida continues, 'a witness, as such, is always blind. Witnessing substitutes narrative for perception. The witness cannot see, show, and speak at the same time, and the interest of the attestation, like that of the testament, stems from this dissociation' (ibid.).

One of the stories Derrida draws upon to illustrate his discussion of the relationship between vision and blindness is the myth of Medusa. The classicist Jean-Pierre Vernant points out that the disparate episodes of this myth are linked by a shared preoccupation with eyes, gazes and the experience of seeing and being seen (1985: 77). More specifically, they explore how vision is disturbed by an encounter with radical alterity. They deal with *missing* eyes (Perseus steals the single eye shared by the Graiae, sisters of the Gorgons, in order to blind and escape from them), with invisibility (the *kunē*, the helmet of Hades, makes Perseus invisible and thus blinds the Gorgons to him) and thus with non-intersecting or blocked gazes. This, then, is a myth about threatened or lost vision, or, in Derrida's reading, about blindness as the condition of sight: since Medusa's gaze turns those who meet it to stone, Perseus, of course, has to go in 'blind' when he kills her, taking his bearings only from her reflection in his polished shield.

It is apt that the myth of Medusa should be one of the points where Derrida's text intersects with Agamben's, given that their otherwise divergent accounts of testimony are inflected, like Lanzmann's, by a common concern with disrupted vision. While the memory of the Holocaust is rarely an explicit presence in *Mémoires d'aveugle*, it haunts Derrida's writing in unsettling ways. The closest he comes to acknowledging this explicitly is an ironic caveat which contemplates the implications of his argument as grist to the mill of Holocaust denial: 'and as for the witnesses of Auschwitz, like those of all the extermination camps, there is here an abominable resource for all "revisionist" denials' (1993: 104). Derrida's insights into the 'too-much of sight', or excess of seeing, to be found 'at the heart of blindness itself' (1993: 16) echo Lanzmann's redefinition of 'blindness' as 'clearsightedness … the purest mode of looking' (1990a: 279), and, as we shall see, shed light on the particular predicament of *Shoah*'s spectators. But Derrida's central contention that the witness is always blind is more difficult to reconcile with the evidence presented in Lanzmann's film.

Taken literally this claim is simply false – none of the witnesses in *Shoah* is visually impaired. Interpreted metaphorically Derrida's assertion might remind us of the non-Jewish German and Polish witnesses in the film, who suffer from various forms of myopia; their vision, like their memories, remains selective. The paradigmatic 'blind' witness of this kind would be Maurice Rossel, the former Red Cross delegate interviewed by Lanzmann during the making of *Shoah* but featured instead in his later film *Un vivant qui passe*. Rossel inspected Auschwitz and Theresienstadt and, against every likelihood, published a favourable report. But insofar as they 'let the

Holocaust occur as an event essentially unwitnessed' (Felman 1992c: 211), these interviewees have nothing in common with Derrida's blind witness, who sees and speaks the truth. Instead, *Shoah* dramatises Derrida's point that the witness cannot see and narrate simultaneously both by 'substituting narrative for perception' (1990: 106) and by insisting on the distance between the past and the present, between the moments of perception and attestation. Lanzmann shows that the witness needs time before speaking and time to speak, while highlighting the capacity of memories to fade, change and disappear over time. The film's negotiation of this temporal gap as both a prerequisite for and a threat to testimony validates Derrida's assertion that testimony's interest stems from the dissociation between seeing, showing and speaking.

However, Derrida also refers to witnesses who are blind before and after the moment of testifying, and from this perspective his argument remains at odds with *Shoah*'s affirmation of the special status and value of eyewitness testimony, of the words of those who saw the crimes with their own eyes. Blindness remains a privileged term in Derridean thought; in negating the plenitude of vision, it troubles the 'metaphysics of presence' that is a central target of deconstruction. But by the same token, blindness seems to flout the conventions and conditions of possibility of witnessing. Erik Vogt points out that traditionally the structure of testimony 'has been predicated on a double presence, that is, on the witness's presence at the event witnessed and on the witness's presence at the moment of testifying' (2005: 81). 'What', however, he wonders, 'happens to testimony if those conditions of presence are marked by a double impossibility, if one is dealing with an attempt at bearing witness in which neither a third party present to some event to be witnessed nor a witness who would have experienced the event to be witnessed from beginning to end could be invoked?' (ibid.). What happens if the event in question destroyed the majority of its witnesses or deprived them of an overview? Is it possible for the dead to bear witness to their own deaths? Is it possible for survivors to bear witness on behalf of those who died?

These are some of the questions which preoccupy Agamben in *Remnants of Auschwitz*. If Derrida's argument prompts us to look for blind spots in the witness's vision, Agamben's account invites us to search for lacunae in his or her testimony. In *Remnants of Auschwitz*, which announces itself as a 'perpetual commentary on testimony' (1999: 13), the privileged witness is not the blind man but the Muselmann.[4] Variations on the word 'Muselmann' were used in the camps to refer to those prisoners who had lost the will to live, who had been reduced by extreme suffering to little more than the sum of their steadily weakening bodily functions.[5] For Agamben, 'in Auschwitz ethics begins precisely at the point where the

Muselmann, the "complete witness", makes it forever impossible to distinguish between man and non-man' (1999: 47). Agamben's discussion of the Muselmann is closely informed by the writings of Levi, who states, in *The Drowned and the Saved*:

> We, the survivors, are not the true witnesses … We survivors are not only an exiguous but also an anomalous minority: we are those who by their prevarications or abilities or good luck did not touch bottom. Those who did so, those who saw the Gorgon, have not returned to tell about it or have returned mute, but they are the 'Muslims', the submerged, the complete witnesses, the ones whose deposition would have a general significance. They are the rule, we are the exception … We who were favoured by fate tried, with more or less wisdom, to recount not only our fate, but also that of the others, the submerged; but this was a discourse on 'behalf of third parties', the story of things seen from close by, not experienced personally. When the destruction was terminated, the work accomplished was not told by anyone, just as no one ever returned to recount his own death. Even if they had paper and pen, the submerged would not have testified because their death had begun before that of their body. Weeks and months before being snuffed out, they had already lost the ability to observe, to remember, to compare and express themselves. We speak in their stead, by proxy. (1988: 63–4)

Paradoxically, then, for Levi, the 'true' witness, the 'complete' witness is the one who is 'drowned', 'submerged', dead or 'mute', and thus unable to bear witness. If the survivor is to 'speak in their stead' she or he faces the possibly impossible task of 'bearing witness to a missing testimony' (Vogt 2005: 83).

Agamben's text is haunted by the 'missing' deposition of the Muselmann and the daunting implications of this absence. Asserting that 'testimony contain[s] at its core an essential lacuna', he describes his project as 'interrogating this lacuna or, more specifically, attempting to listen to it' (1999: 13). In view of this emphasis, it is all the more surprising that Agamben 'leaves the last word' (1999: 165) to the Muselmann; the final six pages of his text are devoted exclusively to quotations from witnesses who claim to have once been *Muselmannër* (1999: 166–71). However, rather than subjecting these testimonies to close analysis, Agamben advises us in advance that they 'fully verify' Levi's paradox, and bases his argument instead on readings of a selection of other testimonies, observing that they 'bore witness to something it is impossible to bear witness to' (1999: 13). The texts with which Agamben engages figure the Muselmann in divergent ways and position themselves differently in relation to the Muselmann's 'missing' testimony. While some, such as the writings of Levi and Bruno Bettelheim (1960), offer lengthy and detailed reflections on the Muselmann's identity and fate, others devote only the most cursory attention to this figure. Jean Améry makes this omission explicit when he admits that this 'bundle of physical functions in its last convulsions [who] no longer had room in his consciousness for the contrasts good or bad, noble or base' (1980: 9), has no place in his account of the camps: 'As hard as it may be for us to do so, we must exclude [the Muselmann] from our considerations' (ibid.). Likewise, the Muselmann is only a marginal presence in Antelme's *L'Espèce humaine*, which focuses instead on the possibility of *resisting* being reduced to something less than human. (As Agamben points out, it is revealing in this context that the title of Antelme's testimony seems to place it in ironic dialogue with the book Levi published in the same year, the more interrogatively entitled *If This is a Man* (see 1999: 58).) Agamben's readings of these and other texts lead him to the conclusion that while 'all witnesses speak of [the Muselmann] as a central experience' (1999: 52), the Muselmann remains 'the untestifiable, that to which no one has borne witness' (1999: 41). The 'complete witness' turns out to be 'the absolutely unwitnessable' (1999: 156): 'let us ... posit the *Muselmann* as the absolute impossibility of bearing witness' (1999: 164).

According to Agamben, then, the survivor's testimony can never be complete because it cannot adequately bear witness to the central experience of which it speaks. Before examining this assertion in the light of evidence presented in *Shoah*, it is worth examining a further line of enquiry pursued in *Remnants of Auschwitz*, where Agamben's account coincides not only with Levi's again but also, unexpectedly, with Derrida's and Lanzmann's, and which holds particular implications for visual forms of testimony such as film. Agamben notes that survivors tend to speak of the Muselmann as a figure who was universally avoided, whom 'no one want[ed] to see' (Aldo Carpi, cited in 1999: 50), indeed, the sight of whom was 'unbearable to human eyes' (1999: 51). Other prisoners feared recognising themselves in the Muselmann's empty eyes and emaciated face, a face which was generic, bereft of the distinguishing features of humanity. Remembering that 'not a trace of a thought [was] to be seen' on the face and in the eyes of the *Muselmänner*, Levi refers to them as 'faceless presences' (1966: 103). So what is it that has destroyed or negated the Muselmann's face? Agamben advances a further explanation for the disturbance these figures created in the perceptual field of those around them: something was wrong with the Muselmann's vision too. Another way in which Levi describes the *Muselmänner* is 'those who saw the Gorgon' (1988: 64). In order to gloss this elliptical formulation, Agamben turns to Françoise Frontisi-Ducroux's *Du masque au visage* (1995), which informs us that ancient Greek representations of the Gorgon's face broke with the iconographical tradition in vase-painting of showing the human figure only in profile (see also Vernant 1985: 31–2). Depicted head-on, this 'prohibited face, which cannot be seen because it produces death' (Agamben 1999: 53), and which in this sense 'represents the impossibility of vision' is also that which 'cannot *not* be seen' (ibid.; emphasis in original). Unlike Perseus, the *Muselmänner* have no polished shield, either real or metaphorical; they encounter the Gorgon face to face. Agamben continues:

> If to see the Gorgon means to see the impossibility of seeing, then the Gorgon does not name something that exists or happens in the camp, something that the *Muselmann*, and not the survivor, would have seen. Rather, the Gorgon designates the impossibility of seeing that belongs to the camp inhabitant, the one who has 'touched bottom' in the camp and has become a non-human … This is why to bear witness to the *Muselmann*, to attempt to contemplate the impossibility of seeing, is not an easy task … The Gorgon and he who has seen her and the *Muselmann* and he who bears witness to him are one gaze; they are a single impossibility of seeing. (1999: 54)

Žižek, drawing on Agamben, surmises that the Muselmann's 'desubjectivised, transfixed gaze [is] frozen into immobility by seeing too much, seeing what one should not see' (2001: 79–80). In Žižek's account, this excessive, blinding vision refocuses attention on the gaze itself:

> Since the subject cannot directly see *that*, the lethally fascinating Thing, he accomplishes a kind of reflection-into-self by means of which the object that fascinates him becomes *the gaze itself* […] This zero-level at which it is no longer possible to distinguish clearly between the gaze and the object it perceives, the level at which the horrified gaze itself becomes the ultimate object of horror, is what characterises the Muslim. (2001: 80–1; emphasis in original)

For Agamben and Žižek, then, Levi's description of the Muselmann tells us something about the nature of visual relations in the camps and the capacity of atrocity to threaten the vision both of those who experience it directly and of those who study it afterwards. In both accounts the look becomes conflated with its object; the Gorgon signifies an 'impossibility of seeing' (Agamben) which reflects the gaze back onto itself (Žižek). Looking results in terror or blindness and yet somehow remains a source of knowledge: 'we will not understand what Auschwitz is if we do not first understand who or what the Muselmann is – if we do not learn to gaze with him upon the Gorgon' (1999: 52).

Remnants of Auschwitz has provoked lively debate and a range of stimulating critiques. While most commentators acknowledge the originality and importance of Agamben's insights and agree that the book maps fertile new ethical territory, many also have reservations about his methodology and the broader implications of his discussion of the Muselmann. Philippe Mesnard and Claudine Kahan (2001), Fethi Benslama (2001: 69–78), Robert Eaglestone (2002) and Colin Davis (2004: 85–8) amongst others have charged Agamben variously with rejecting historiography, reading his sources selectively or *mis*reading or pre-empting them, and arbitrarily idealising a specific, but ultimately partial, experience of the Holocaust. Mesnard and Kahan, who devote an entire book to dismantling Agamben's argument, sum up the concerns of many of his critics when they query the extent to which his elevation of the Muselmann into the exemplary or paradigmatic witness marginalises or devalues the testimonies of others (see, for example, 2001: 11). This risk is highlighted if we consider Agamben's conclusions in the light of the testimonies presented in *Shoah*.

Lanzmann's film proposes a different answer to the question that resonates throughout Agamben's text: 'Who is the subject of testimony?' (1999: 120). In chapter one I discussed the privileged position *Shoah* accords to the recollections of those who have seen the extermination process, the crematoria and gas chambers first-hand: the survivors of the death camps, such as Chelmno, Treblinka and Auschwitz-Birkenau, and especially those who worked in the *Sonderkommandos* and haircutting detail, who are presented by the film as the eyewitnesses *par excellence*. Contrary to claims Lanzmann makes outside the film, Müller's, Bomba's, Podchlebnik's and Srebnik's testimonies confirm that the reality of the camps and the machinery of mass murder was neither 'invisible' (1991: 99) nor 'literally blinding' (1990a: 279). In sharp contrast to some of the non-Jewish German and Polish witnesses, who are reluctant to admit to what they saw, Müller, Bomba and Srebnik insist upon their physical presence at and direct visual access to the events they recall and repeatedly invoke the acts of looking, seeing and witnessing. Müller emphasises, for example, that while the Czech Jews from the Theresienstadt 'family camp' were 'blinded' by floodlights on their arrival at Crematorium II, he himself witnessed everything.[6]

The *Sonderkommando* survivor's singular status as an eyewitness to the epicentre of the genocide not only calls into question Derrida's identification of the blind as the privileged witnesses and Felman's contention that the witnesses in *Shoah* enact a series of failures to witness; it is also one of the bases on which Mesnard and Kahan take issue with Agamben: 'If one figure is to be made into the exemplary witness, we would have to look for him in the *Sonderkommandos*' (2001: 15).[7] Simply by virtue of their survival and retained capacity for speech, neither Müller, Podchlebnik nor

Srebnik, nor any of the survivors in *Shoah*, meet the criteria which, for Levi, define the 'complete witness'. To what extent, then, do their accounts bear out Agamben's contentions that the survivor can only bear witness 'by proxy', and that testimony 'has truth and a reason for being only if it is completed by [the Muselmann]' (1999: 150)? Querying the validity of Agamben's claim that 'all witnesses speak of [the Muselmann] as a central experience', Davis points out that there isn't a single reference in *Shoah* to this figure. But he concedes, too, that Agamben's argument is 'in its way irrefutable', since the Muselmann's 'absence from testimony could always be explained as a significant omission' (2004: 86). The most likely reason why none of the witnesses in *Shoah* mentions the Muselmann is that they rarely or never encountered such figures. The film accords a central place to survivors of the Operation Reinhard camps at Belzec, Sobibor and Treblinka, where the figure of the Muselmann was unknown. So in these cases his absence from testimony is unremarkable and cannot be seen as an omission at all. Agamben's argument that 'the survivor and the Muselmann, like the tutor and the incapable person and the creator and his material, are inseparable' (1999: 150) implies that the Muselmann somehow featured in the experience of all survivors, whether or not they came face to face with him. But to hear echoes of the Muselmann in the words, falterings and silences of witnesses such as Bomba or Glazar, slave workers at Treblinka, would signal a pre-emptive failure of listening, one which distracts from the other realities, no more nor less terrible, that they charge us to face.

The discrepancies between Agamben's and Lanzmann's understandings of testimony arise from their divergent conceptions of the defining experience of those persecuted by the Nazis. *Shoah* and *Remnants of Auschwitz* map out different topographies of the Holocaust. While these topographies coincide in Auschwitz, the former centres on the wider programme of systematic killing and locates the gas chambers as the core of the violence, and the latter focuses on suffering in Auschwitz specifically as the emblematic consequence of the Nazi enterprise. For Lanzmann the paradigmatic experience is annihilation; for Agamben it appears to be prolonged privation. The privileged witnesses to these experiences are the *Sonderkommando* member and the Muselmann respectively. However, the irreconcilable contradictions which emerge when Agamben's text and Lanzmann's film are read against each other highlight the dangers involved in attributing an exemplary or iconic status to any single kind of witness. Just as the importance accorded to the Muselmann in Agamben's model of testimony does not reflect the experiences of all survivors, so Lanzmann's attribution of the role of 'spokespeople for the dead' to the *Sonderkommando* survivors (cited in Rabinowitz 1994: 30) has been challenged by other witnesses; after all, none speaks of or for the Muselmann. For survivors like Levi, the *Sonderkommando* are highly equivocal figures, whose testimony is neither exemplary nor emblematic: 'One cannot expect from men who have known such extreme destitution a deposition in the juridical sense, but something that is at once a lament, a curse, an expiation, an attempt to justify and rehabilitate oneself' (1988: 36). In suggesting that one figure can bear witness on behalf of others, both Agamben and Lanzmann implicitly de-emphasise the irreplaceability attributed to the witness by Derrida in *Demeure* (1998: 46–7, 126) and the 'radically unique, noninterchangeable and solitary burden' which Felman ascribes to him or her in *Testimony* (1992a: 3). Both Derrida and Felman quote Paul Celan's well-known lines in this context: 'No-one/bears witness for the/witness'.[8]

Despite their conflicting testimonial paradigms, however, both Lanzmann and Agamben are concerned with aspects of the Holocaust which troubled the vision of witnesses and those who contemplate the event afterwards, concerns which are resonant in the context of a discussion of film. In inviting us 'to attempt to contemplate the impossibility of seeing' (1999: 54), Agamben's discussion of the Muselmann's encounter with the Gorgon returns us, via the Derridean figure of the blind seer, to Lanzmann's coupling of a vigilant blindness and the facing position. Moreover, another recent critical intervention serves to establish a closer relationship between, though not to reconcile, Agamben's and Lanzmann's distinctive topographies. In the essay cited in the introduction, Nancy offers an alternative commentary upon Levi's designation of the *Muselmänner* as 'those who saw the Gorgon'. Like Agamben, Nancy stresses the loss of vision occasioned by this confrontation, which he describes as a 'blind face-to-face', a 'face-to-face with the one without a gaze' ('le sans-regard' refers to both the Gorgon and death itself) (2003: 92). However, Nancy proceeds to introduce a 'third partner' into this face-to-face encounter: the *Sonderkommando* Jew, 'who gathers upon himself the intersection of the two empty gazes' (ibid.). Nancy observes that the *Muselmänner* were not the only 'faceless presences' in the camps; he quotes from the testimony of Hermann Langbein, according to whom the *Sonderkommando* members no longer had a human face.[9] For Nancy, this loss or violation has direct implications for representation: 'The question of the representation of the camps is none other than that of the representation of a face which has itself been deprived of a representation and a gaze ... At Auschwitz, the space of representation was crushed and reduced to the presence of a gaze appropriating death, which became impregnated with the dead gaze of the other' (2003: 92–3).

Nancy's account identifies the face of the persecuted (the Muselmann, the *Sonderkommando* member) as the primary locus of the challenges to representation posed by the camps. In the light of his remarks, I would like to turn now to the work of a philosopher whose writings offer a different ethical perspective on the limits of visuality and the perils of representation, before exploring the relevance of these different theoretical perspectives to filmic images of trauma and alterity. If Levinas had little to say explicitly about the Holocaust, his writings are nonetheless haunted by the event's traumatic legacy. They supply further insights into the significance of the violence which, according to Levi and Nancy, was inflicted not only on the body, but also, precisely, on the face in the camps.

Levinas: an ethics of facing

Levinas locates the origin of ethics in an encounter with the 'visage', or face, of the Other. Describing the 'visage' as 'the way in which the Other presents himself, exceeding *the idea of the Other in me*' (1969: 50; emphasis in original), Levinas argues in *Totalité et infini: essai sur l'extériorité* that 'the epiphany of the face is ethical' because it confronts the self with the irreducible and unassimilable reality of the Other, which calls the self into question (1969: 199). For Levinas, whose account differs in this respect from those of many other ethical thinkers, the relation or non-relation between self and Other is asymmetrical; I have an obligation to the Other which is non-reciprocal. This singular obligation is revealed to me in the encounter with the face – the *face-à-face*. Levinas's term 'visage' allows him to articulate the way in which the Other makes its presence known to me without linguistically or philosophically violating its alterity by incorporating it into a pre-existing totality or restoring symmetry to the relation. In his account, the 'facing position' (1969: 196) makes manifest the proximity of the Other whilst preserving its separation from the self. This position issues a 'moral summons' (ibid.), compelling me to question my own position in the world while awakening me to my absolute responsibility towards the Other.

What interests me in the current context about Levinas's writings is the light they shed on three of the intersecting lines of enquiry pursued in this chapter: the violation of the face (distinct from the 'visage', which Levinas describes as ultimately inviolable) in the Holocaust touched upon above; the relationships between facing and blindness posited by Lanzmann, Agamben and Nancy; and the possible implications of these relationships for visual representation in general and film practice and spectatorship in particular. While Levinas himself remained all but silent about cinema, film critics are beginning to recognise the potential of his philosophy to enrich our understanding of the ethical dimensions of moving images (see, for example, Botting & Wilson 2001; Downing 2004: 106–30; Renov 2004:

148–67; Cooper 2006). Indeed, the 'optical' qualities of Levinasian ethics (1969: 23) and his identification of the face as a site of 'revelation' (1969: 81) initially appear conducive to reflection on a medium that habitually privileges our sense of sight. However, any endeavour to view film through a Levinasian lens must engage with his abiding misgivings about the aesthetic and the visual. Like many of the filmmakers and thinkers discussed in this book, though for reasons that do not derive primarily from concerns about the particular horror of the Holocaust, Levinas is preoccupied with the ethical risks of representation and, in particular, of the image.

Totalité et infini is imbued with scepticism about the privilege granted in the West to visuality and the gaze, which Levinas sees as conducive to forms of oppression: 'inasmuch as the access to beings concerns vision, it dominates those beings, exercises a power over them', where 'the identity of the I envelops the alterity of the object' (1969: 194). Commentators have linked these concerns about vision back to Levinas's training in Judaism (see, for example, Jay 1993: 550–1, 555), and Levinas makes explicit the extent to which the Second Commandment, the prohibition on creating graven images, inflects the horizon of his ethical thought (see 1984a). In reflections informed by this interdiction, he explains that his concept 'visage' alludes first and foremost neither to a visible object which appears in the phenomenal world (such as the human face), nor to something that can be captured in representation: 'The face with which the Other turns to me is not reabsorbed in a representation of the face' (1969: 215; see also, for example, Levinas 1982: 91; 1984b: 344).[10] In the unique expression of the face the Other is revealed 'without the intermediary of any image' (1969: 200):

> The way in which the Other presents himself ... does not consist in figuring as a theme under my gaze, in spreading itself forth as a set of qualities forming an image. The face of the Other at each moment destroys and overflows the plastic image it leaves me, the idea existing to my own measure. (1969: 51–1)

Any image I form of the face will be unable to encompass its infinite alterity. Any attempt to visualise the face in representation works instead to reappropriate its otherness by reducing it to immobility and silencing its appeal. Levinas reiterates: 'To hear [the Other's] destitution which cries out for justice is not to represent an image to oneself, but is to posit oneself as responsible' (1969: 215).

So the face of the Other cannot be encountered in images, and its ethical summons cannot be issued in representation; in Levinas's thought, it marks the limits of the figurable. Philippe Crignon spells out some of the implications of Levinas's argument for the visual arts:

If the face is not seen, it is at least that which sees: the orientation of the gaze is exactly reversed in the case of artistic representation, where the work – a drawing, painting, sculpture, film, or image of any kind – abandons itself entirely and immoderately to the eye of the spectator. [...] The work of art gives itself to be seen but remains, itself, blind or enucleated. The work does not see us, does not *look at* us – and thus does not reveal anything. (2004: 104, 113; emphasis in original)

As Crignon's comments intimate, the suspicion of the eye which permeates Levinas's writings on the face poses a series of questions to film viewers, some of which I have endeavoured to outline elsewhere (Saxton 2007). I have argued, however, that Lanzmann's images in *Shoah*, especially in their hesitancy about visualising the past, might be viewed as hospitable to Levinasian thought at once in spite and because of Levinas's hostility towards vision and representation. The readings which follow aim to forge further connections between Levinas's ideas and cinema by exploring how the asymmetrical ethical relation with the 'visage' might enable us to rethink the exchanges between viewers and films often less reluctant to reconstruct the past. My focus here will be on images of the face and figures of facing in films by Marker and Resnais, two directors whose acclaimed explorations of memory and trauma investigate the capacity of images to reveal alterity. It is my contention that resonant parallels can be drawn between Levinas's warning against visual appropriation and the films' attempts to bear witness to alterity without reducing the other to an object of perception. Levinas's description of a 'visage' that must be faced but cannot quite be seen, Lanzmann's redefinition of 'blindness' as a prerequisite of facing and Agamben's and Nancy's discussions of the 'blind *face-à-face*' between the Muselmann, the Gorgon and (in Nancy's case) the *Sonderkommando* member intersect in the idea that alterity can only be encountered somewhere beyond the perceptual field. Like the Levinasian 'visage', the 'faceless presences' of the Muselmann and the *Sonderkommando* member at once threaten and implicate my look; in Levinasian terms, they 'call into question my presence and my responsibility' (1991: 140). This is also the function, I would like to suggest, of some of the fragile faces which Marker and Resnais invite us to contemplate or, in other cases, withhold from our sight.

Screening the face, facing the screen

'To film a face', writes Jacques Aumont in *Du visage au cinéma*, 'is to confront all the problems of film, all its aesthetic problems and thus all its ethical problems' (1992: 84). Aumont's book contains only a handful of references to Levinas for, unlike the Levinasian 'visage', the faces which concern Aumont are exclusively human and rendered in representation. Nevertheless, Aumont too locates the on-screen face as a privileged ethical figure and is interested in how it can elude and transform our gaze, becoming something more than an object to be looked at. Identifying the face as the very origin of representation, *Du visage au cinéma* opens by tracing the history of the face in art. According to Aumont, cinema is born into this history just as a fissure is emerging in the humanist conception of the face as a site of plenitude and transcendence. The 'cracking', 'splitting', 'defeat' or 'effacement' of the face that begins in modernist painting (he mentions the work of Pablo Picasso and Francis Bacon, amongst others) persists in cinema, where we begin to see a 'dévisagéification' ('defacialisation') of the face (1992: 34, 163, 183). Moreover, Aumont proposes a connection between these developments and the legacy of twentieth-century atrocities: 'As the last visible refuge, after Hiroshima, after Auschwitz, of a belief in man, it is the very excess of this belief which has led [cinema] to manhandle, to destroy the face' (1992: 184).

If the progressive 'defacialisation' or 'destruction' of the face on film is related to the aftermath of the Holocaust and other historical traumas, to what extent might it also be seen as a reflection of the violation, both physical and symbolic, of the face in the camps, to which the 'faceless presences' of the Muselmann and the *Sonderkommando* member bear witness? Furthermore, what does cinema's evolving relationship to the face reveal about ethics and alterity? This second question emerges as a preoccupation in Daney's writings on the circulation of images in contemporary visual media. Like Aumont, Daney observes a progressive endangerment, even erasure, of the face in visual representation: 'Anyone who has followed the adventures of the image will have witnessed, over the last ten, twenty or thirty years, the strange "effacement" of the human face' (1991b: 15). At the same time, however, he finds in cinema a potential site of resistance to the deleterious effects of this 'effacement'. In essays discussing media coverage of the first Gulf War Daney posits an opposition between his *bête noire*, the inexhaustible flood of television images which he dubs 'le visuel' (literally, 'the visual'), and 'l'image', which is unique to cinema. The former is defined by the unitary perspective inscribed in its images: '[*the*] *point of view of power*, in other words, of a shot without a counter-shot (of a shot which annihilates its counter-shot)' (1991a: 185; emphasis in original); he goes on to assert that 'le visuel ... lacks nothing, it is a closed system, a feedback loop ... in the image of a pornographic spectacle' (1991a: 192). Daney argues, however, that the homogenising closure and symbolic violence of 'le visuel' can be redressed by 'l'image', which is defined, in contrast, by heterogeneity and lack, and thus 'dedicated to bearing witness to a certain *alterity*':

What the cinematic image affirms is that ... there is also *the other* ... If the image informed us ... it never did so solely from the point of view of the stronger party, but from a position in-between [*à partir d'un entre-deux*] where, sometimes *in extremis*, the face of the weaker party would take shape. (1991a: 193; emphasis in original)

There are unmistakable echoes of Levinas here, the phenomenality and distinctive political meanings of Daney's 'visage' notwithstanding. Daney's argument also anticipates Comolli's claim that cinema has the power to 'return people to each other. Return them face-to-face' (1997: 22). Crucial to this process, in Daney's account, is the medium's ability to reverse the televisual erasure of the other's face (which may be at the root of Godard's claim that television does not produce 'images' at all).[11] Filmic images can 'bear witness to alterity' by teaching me 'tirelessly to probe with my gaze the distance from myself at which the other begins' (Daney 1992: 19). For Daney, this capacity to sensitise us to the proximity and distance between self and other is what defines cinema as a site of ethical reflection.

Marker: the *regard caméra*

One of the filmic gazes that proves conducive to such reflection is known in French as the 'regard caméra': the glance of an imaged subject catching and returning the gaze of the camera. This reciprocated look is one of the most ambiguous and disruptive in cinema. Whether it is a look at the person behind the camera, at the camera itself or at an imaginary future spectator, the *regard caméra* destabilises the boundaries between on-screen and off-screen space, representation and reality, image and viewer. Though it has been largely avoided by classical and mainstream cinema, elsewhere it has been actively solicited and privileged as an event which captures the essence of the medium. Relating this look to 'the Feuillade effect' (a reference to its occurrence in early works shot on location such as Louis Feuillade's *Fantômas* (1913–14)), Jean-Pierre Jeancolas argues that the later 'cinéastes du réel' such as Jean Rouch and Marker came to view it 'no longer ... as an effect, but as the very nature of filmmaking' (1990: 118). What was originally an unguarded, accidental glance, and then, in later films, a vestige of cinematic innocence (witness, for example, the to-camera glances of curious passers-by in the Champs Elysées sequence of Godard's *À bout de souffle* (*Breathless*, 1959)), has been exploited in more recent filmmaking practice to a range of subversive effects.[12]

It is significant in the current context that the *regard caméra* is the first in de Baecque's list of 'specifically cinematographic figures that testify to the obsessive presence of the concentrationary palimpsest' (2000: 66). This look has entered collective memory as part of the iconography of the camps, specifically in the form of images of recently liberated deportees staring silently back at Allied camera-operators through barbed wire (a series of which are seen towards the end of *Nuit et brouillard*, for instance). This encounter is restaged by Radu Milhaileanu in his Holocaust comedy *Train de vie* (*Train of Life*, 1998), where Shlomo's final look to the camera from behind the fence of the camp in which he is imprisoned is privileged as the only authentic gaze in a work of fiction. In *Train de vie* and other narrative films, the *regard caméra* often functions as an allusion to documentary. But in documentary too it can rupture the diegetic reality, creating a rift through which history unexpectedly intrudes. Elizabeth Cowie accounts for this rupture as follows:

The look back at the camera disturbs the actuality shot by reversing the object of fascination from inside the scene to outside – a disjunction not merely because the spectator becomes aware of her or his look as well as becoming the – imagined – object of another's look, but also because such a look rivals the spectacle which is the 'topic' of the actuality, for the camera's gaze is narratively undercut when all the bystanders appear quite uninterested in the scene behind them, which we are being shown, and are instead avidly watching the camera. (1997b: n.p.)

Nuit et brouillard: the concentrationary palimpsest

The *regard caméra* reconfigures the relationship between viewer and image posited by some of the most influential theories of the cinematic apparatus. It does so by deflecting our attention from the on-screen spectacle back into the off-screen space of the shot and into the cinema auditorium, reminding us of our presence as spectators and implicating us inescapably in the production of meaning (this is why it remains the forbidden gaze of classical narrative film). In this respect, we might describe it in Levinasian terms as an encounter with the other which calls the self into question. However, the uncomfortable impression that the imaged other is actually looking at us is of course an illusion, since the encounter is mediated by the apparatus (as Cowie points out, we are only ever the 'imagined' object of the other's look). This recognition reminds us of Crignon's Levinasian characterisation of the work of art as 'blind' or 'enucleated'. Moreover, as we have seen, Levinas reiterates that the *face-à-face* does not take place in the field of the visible, where the other's face remains prey to the risk of violence.

One of the filmmakers who has most inventively interrogated the disruptive potential of the *regard caméra* is Chris Marker. Marker's interest in this look is already apparent in a pivotal sequence from *La Jetée* (*The Pier*, 1962), a film haunted by the ghosts of the Nazi camps as well as by the more recent memory of the Franco-Algerian war and the future possibility of nuclear destruction. The film's central protagonist, often described as a time-traveller, is introduced by the voice-over as a man 'marked by an image from his childhood'. This memory-image is the genesis of the film's narrative, yet it only resurfaces when the man's captors cover his eyes with surgical pads, physically blocking his vision and symbolically blinding him. As it ponders the relationship between remembering and seeing, *La Jetée* also disturbs the vision of its spectators. Announcing itself as a 'photo-roman' ('photo-novel'), it consists of a succession of still images, with one significant exception. In the sequence in question, a cluster of close-up photographs of the sleeping face of the woman loved by the time-traveller melt into each other through a series of cross-fades and superimpositions which begin to create the impression of movement. Suddenly, as the accompanying crescendo of birdsong reaches a climax, the woman opens her eyes, stares straight at the camera and blinks several times. Catherine Lupton describes this fragment of movement as a 'brief flight into life, out of the fixed frames and inexorable logic of the fated narrative' (2005: 93), while Philippe Dubois views the woman's blinking as encapsulating the very essence of cinema (2002: 36). The sequence reminds us that it is precisely as time breathes motion and life into the still image that cinema comes into being. Furthermore, this infinitesimal motion locates the origin of the medium in the instant when the imaged eye opens to meet the viewer's eye, an encounter mediated by the camera-eye. *La Jetée* identifies the *regard caméra* as the originary gaze of cinema.

Twenty years later, Marker revisits this gaze in his essay-film *Sans soleil* (*Sunless*, 1982), where it is the subject of explicit commentary. In *Sans soleil* the meditation on time, memory and the image initiated in *La Jetée* is reframed within an exploration of cross-cultural visual relations between self and other. A fictional cameraman, identified in the credits as Sandor Krasna, travels around the world collecting images and investigating what he calls 'the magical func-

La Jetée: moving images

tion of the eye'.[13] In an early sequence shot on the island of Fogo, we see locals glancing curiously but often sidelong and warily at Krasna's camera, prompting him to complain, 'frankly, have you ever heard of anything stupider than to say to people, as they teach in film schools, not to look at the camera?' At which moment, right on cue, a girl and an elderly woman turn to look directly at us. Reversing *La Jetée*'s passage from stasis to motion, Marker now freezes the image, giving his viewers time to contemplate a look which fascinates Krasna more than any other. As confirmation of this, in a later sequence we find him endeavouring to capture the gazes of women in the Praia marketplace in Guinea-Bissau, initially with little success. Eventually, though, his camera comes to rest on a young woman's face and records motionlessly as she lowers her gaze, smiles almost imperceptibly, and finally, after a delay of many seconds, glances straight into the lens. This time there is no freeze-frame; the woman meets our gaze for what Krasna tells us is precisely the duration of a single frame of film, only for time immediately to reassert itself and transform this meeting into yet another memory.

Like the moving images of *La Jetée*, this beguiling sequence is also one of the film's most enigmatic. The woman's prolonged refusal to acknowledge the camera's presence followed by her fleeting acquiescence in its look raise questions about the ethical dynamics of the encounter between camera-operator, viewer and viewed. One of the letters from Krasna read out in voice-over by the female narrator (Florence Delay in the French version of the film, Alexandra Stewart in the English version) provides a commentary on this sequence and an insight into the kind of relationship he is trying to establish with his filmic subjects here:

Sans soleil: the 'real look'

> It was in the marketplaces of Bissau and Cape Verde that I rediscovered *the equality of the gaze*, and that series of figures so close to the ritual of seduction: I see her – she saw me – she knows that I see her – she offers me her gaze, but just at an angle where it is still possible to act as though it was not addressed to me – and at the end *the real look*, straight forward, that lasted 1/24 of a second, the length of a film frame. [emphasis added]

Earlier in the film, as he captures and freezes the *regard caméra* of a man in a bar in Namidabashi, Japan, Krasna explains, via Delay/Stewart, that the 'equality of the gaze' can be understood in relation to a 'threshold below which any man is as good as any other, and knows it'. Implicit in his remarks about these 'real looks' is a seductive invitation to read the *regard caméra* as a reciprocal exchange which affirms the face of the other as equal subject. Critical commentary on the modes of relatedness described and enacted in *Sans soleil* has dwelt on the ethical implications of such encounters. Catherine Gillet's essay on Marker's faces suggests they privilege 'proximity' and 'intimacy' (2002: 79). Barbara Lemaître's analysis emphasises the relation of equality that makes such closeness possible. Reading the film as an attempt to trace 'the contours of the experience of alterity' (2002: 73), Lemaître argues that Marker is seeking to establish a 'precarious equilibrium between the one who is looking and the one who is being looked at' (2002: 70):

> The film *Sans soleil* allows us to recognise the movement through which an individual finally comes to apprehend the other through his or her images. The whole film works to construct the relation between an individual positioned as an observer, and that knot of singular realities which define the other ... To surrender one's gaze to another is to consent to being looked at in one's turn – or at least to the risk of this ... The equality of the gaze is a primary contract between the traveller and what he films. (2002: 70–1)

Yet the terms of this contract, this purportedly 'equal' or reciprocal exchange, remain ambiguous. The complex, shifting relations between voice and image in *Sans soleil* invite us to read the *regard caméra* against as well as with Krasna's commentary, which is crucial if we are to avoid reducing what is an anxiety-laden exploration of otherness and difference to a series of encounters mired in the comfort and security of sameness. As an aspiration, a posited *telos*, the 'equality of the gaze' remains a compelling foundation for a mutually respectful encounter with alterity, but *Sans soleil* at the same time prompts us to question the extent to and conditions under which such equality is ultimately attainable, as has been emphasised in feminist and postcolonial critiques of the film (see, for example, Russell 1999; Bruzzi 2000). The relationship of equality conceptualised by Krasna downplays the inescapable ambivalence of the viewing positions he adopts; as a Western male collecting images of women from different cultures, he has been charged with 'superimposing a scopophilic frame onto the ethnographic gaze' (Russell 1999: 306). While the *regard caméra* upsets the acquisitive relationship to the other's face as spectacle often fostered in cinema, these exchanges place neither Krasna nor his audience on a more equal footing with the subjects he films, and highlight the voyeuristic inclinations of his project. In so doing, however, they become one of the mechanisms of distancing and displacement that I would argue are crucial to the establishment of more ethical relations between camera-operator, film viewer and imaged subject.

The sense of intimacy, immediacy and intensity frequently created by the facial close-up prompts Aumont to identify this shot as the locus of a privileged relationship to the real (1992: 98). This privilege might be traced back to traditional conceptions of the eyes as a 'window on the soul' or of the face as the veracious expression of interiority. 'When you photograph a face, you photograph the soul that lies behind it', remarks Bruno Forestier in Godard's *Le Petit soldat* (*The Little Soldier*, 1960). Forestier's interlocutor and photographic subject here is Véronique Dreyer, whose name brings to mind Carl Theodor Dreyer's celebrated images of Marie Falconetti's face in *La Passion de Jeanne d'Arc* (*The Passion of Joan of Arc*, 1928), which seem to bear out Forestier's claim. While Jeanne's anguished gaze returns the look of the camera, it refuses to return the gaze of her judges, to participate in the relay of gazes which condemn it. Dreyer's avoidance of counter-shots and matching eyelines ensures that her face remains, quite literally, a picture of innocence, the place where truth is made manifest. In conspicuous contrast, Krasna's images of the woman in the Praia marketplace in *Sans soleil* work to dismantle the myth of the face as an expressive totality promising unmediated insights into otherwise inaccessible truths. A gap opens up between the visuals and the accompanying commentary as the woman's eyes make contact with Krasna's and our own. Rather than satisfying the desire for intimacy, authenticity, contact and knowledge implicit in his allusions to the 'real look' and 'seduction', her face retains an essential impenetrability as it silently warns us to keep our distance. Unlike Jeanne's, her look draws attention to the cinematic apparatus, the presence of the camera and the work of the film, and later, when she reappears at its very end, to the materiality of the images as they are fed into Hayao Yamaneko's synthesiser, de-naturalised and, finally, frozen. In so doing, the woman's gaze shows up the twin fallacies of the 'real look' and the all-seeing, omniscient viewer, reminding us that the other can never be reduced to the sum of his or her images. In *Sans soleil* the 'equality of the gaze' is posited only to be permanently threatened and infinitely deferred; instead, it is the viewing self who is called into question by the blind spots preserved in the face of the other.

In this respect, the structure of these exchanges returns us to the asymmetry and separation of the Levinasian *face-à-face*, and to the 'visage' which, in its absolute alterity, will not participate in an encounter between two equals. Cooper argues that *Sans soleil* 'creates a space … in which the other is positioned beyond the viewing self's perspective rather than being contained within it from the outset' (2006: 58).[14] I would suggest that the *regard caméra* plays an important role in this process, piercing the surface of the image to point beyond it to an alterity which eludes our gaze. The subjects of these looks ultimately resist reduction to objects of our vision and knowledge. Viewed through a Levinasian lens, the faces of *Sans soleil* thus shed retrospective light on the traumatic memory-images of *La Jetée*, as well as on the potentially ethical dimensions of the *regard caméra*, as cinema's originary gaze. If, as the enigma of the opening eyes in *La Jetée* and of the glance of the woman in *Sans soleil* suggest, something crucial remains withheld by this look, a Levinasian reading helps to account for the ethical insights these limited and distancing visions may nonetheless provide.

Resnais: figures of facing

Given their preoccupation with the challenges posed to representation by personal and collective trauma, Resnais' early films might seem more immediately hospitable to Levinasian thought than Marker's work. I alluded in chapters two and three to parallels between Resnais' and Lanzmann's projects deriving from shared concerns about the referentiality of images, the quality of the access they offer to the past, concerns that, as mentioned above, are also resonant in a Levinasian context. If *Nuit et brouillard*, unlike *Shoah*, allows us to look directly upon the faces of the dead, like *Hiroshima mon amour* and *Muriel, ou le temps d'un retour*, this film betrays an awareness that such images can at best merely allude to rather than fully capture the horror of the realities they depict. Moreover, these films offer distinctive takes on the difficulties of facing alterity and the perceptual disruption that such facing entails. Prey to the vicissitudes of time and memory, Renais' faces are also subject to processes of effacement which threaten to impede the face-to-face encounter (with Hiroshima, with Algeria, with the Holocaust). From a Levinasian perspective, however, this effacement may be seen to foster openness to an otherness which exceeds the confines of the frame.

Daney's readings of Resnais' images offer insights that are pertinent in this context. Given Daney's belief in cinema's privileged capacity and ethical responsibility as a witness to traumatic history, it is no surprise that Resnais' films occupy a pivotal place in his writings (indeed, Nezick identifies *Nuit et brouillard* as Daney's 'opus absolutum' (1998: 163)). Daney is intrigued by the ways in which Resnais' early work seems to disrupt the relay of gazes structuring classical narrative cinema. Attempting to account for this disturbance, he describes his impression that the entwined emaciated corpses in *Nuit et brouillard* and the living, caressing bodies in the celebrated opening sequence of *Hiroshima mon amour* are looking back at him as he watches them (1992: 8). This disconcerting sensation leads him to suggest that cinematic 'forms' might be read as 'faces looking at us' (1992: 18). To read Resnais' images of trauma, with Daney, as 'faces', I would suggest, is to contemplate the ways in which they interpellate, implicate and impose an obligation on us as viewers.

Curiously, Daney's intuition is echoed by Krasna in *Sans soleil*: 'The more you watch Japanese television', he muses, 'the more you feel it's watching you.' If the feedback loop into which Krasna is drawn by the hypnotic televisual flux of Manga, horror and pornography has little to do with the ethical address which Daney discerns in Resnais' images, Resnais' early collaborations with Marker suggest that these divergent encounters derive from complementary concerns about the structure of exchanges between viewer and viewed. *Les Statues meurent aussi* (*Statues Also Die*, 1953) explores the political and ethical dynamics of the Western viewer's encounter with African art. In counterpoint to the visual focus on the faces of African statues, the voice-over repeatedly evokes and mourns the loss of vision. 'An object is dead', it informs us, 'when the living eyes that came to rest on it have disappeared.' The dead eyes of the statues stare blindly back at us, reflecting our own blinkered vision: 'As colonisers of the world, we want everything to speak to us: animals, the dead, statues. And yet these statues are mute. They have mouths and do not speak. They have eyes and do not see us.' Like the eyes of the corpses in *Nuit et brouillard* (another project with which Marker assisted), the statues' sculpted eyes cannot physically see, yet in spite of this we have the uncomfortable feeling that they are watching us. In line with Daney's discussion of form as face, at such moments, it is as if vision is symbolically restored to the enucleated Levinasian artwork.

In *Muriel, ou le temps d'un retour* the face of the other, like the Levinasian 'visage', addresses and commands protagonists and viewers from a position beyond the field of the visible. This film departs from the same basic premise as *La Jetée*: Bernard, like the time-traveller of Marker's film, is haunted by a memory-image from his past, which centres, once again, on a woman's face. But Resnais, unlike Marker, withholds this memory-image from the viewer. In the pivotal sequence of *Muriel, ou le temps d'un retour*, Bernard confesses to his role in the torture and murder of a young Algerian resistance fighter and describes the moment when her eyes met his: 'She stared at me. Why me? She closed her eyes and then began to vomit.' In this fleeting face-to-face encounter between the torturer and his victim, the woman's staring then closing eyes recall the unseeing but vigilant and accusing eyes in *Les Statues meurent aussi* and *Nuit et brouillard*. Moreover, Resnais' image-track is complicit in her refusal to solidify into an image or an object under our gaze. Crucially, the exchange of looks between Bernard and his victim is unwitnessed by the spectator, for Bernard's testimony is accompanied not by flashback images of her battered face and body but by amateur footage depicting routine scenes of army life in Algeria.

Naomi Greene describes the missing scenes of torture as 'a black hole at the centre of *Muriel*' (1999: 48). As the blind spot of the diegesis, they are readable not only as an oblique critique of the French authorities' censorship during the Algerian war (as witnessed, for example, in the banning of *Le Petit soldat*), but also as an acknowledgement of the propensity of direct images to betray the other's trauma. (In this respect, as well as in their fantasy status, the missing images of the tortured body in *Muriel, ou le temps d'un retour* bring to mind the hypothetical footage of the gas chamber at the heart of the debate between Lanzmann and Godard.) Drawing parallels between the non-coincidence of sound and image at certain points in *Nuit et brouillard* and during Bernard's confession in *Muriel, ou le temps d'un retour*, Bersani and Dutoit suggest that the distractions created by these discrepancies 'make it impossible for us to keep our distance from the scene of torture; it is not *out there*, sequestered within the cinematic frame, offering itself up to be judged' (1993: 195; emphasis in original). We encounter the torture scene without the mediation of any image which might allow us to contemplate it from a distant position of safety and non-complicity. So while, on the one hand, the absence of these images attests to the difficulty of facing up to the troubled memory of the Algerian war, on the other, their exclusion paradoxically enables us to confront the past, and thus also the present, more clearsightedly.

Muriel, ou le temps d'un retour, then, raises questions about blindness and facing as an ethical relation, questions with which Resnais had already begun to engage in *Hiroshima mon amour*. Both films revolve around the same aporia as *Nuit et brouillard*, self-consciously acknowledging the impossibility of their projects. Indeed, Duras' often-quoted remark that 'all that we can do is speak of the impossibility of speaking of Hiroshima' (1960: 10) anticipates Robert's warning to Bernard, in which the ethical issue is inadvertently highlighted by a political injunction: 'You want to talk about Muriel? But Muriel can't be talked about.' In *Hiroshima mon amour*, as in *Muriel, ou le temps d'un retour*, the difficulty of speech, narration and testimony is compounded by the visual inaccessibility of the traumatic event and explored through figures of blindness. The film opens with an extended montage sequence composed of eclectic fragments of visible evidence, including museum exhibits, photographs, archive footage and fictional reconstructions, each of which offers an imperfect form of visual access to the past. Newsreel images of survivors with blind or mutilated eyes hint disturbingly at the film's preoccupation with lost or damaged vision.

At the same time, the Japanese architect's repeated denial of the French actress's claim to have seen – 'You saw nothing at Hiroshima. Nothing' – compels us to reconsider what it means to be a witness to such an atrocity.[15] For Caruth, the Japanese man's insistent assertion suggests that 'the act of seeing, in the very establishing of a bodily referent, erases, like an empty grammar, the reality of an event. Within the insistent grammar of sight, the man suggests, the body erases the event of its own death' (1996: 29). Caruth's equation of seeing with erasing and discussion of the 'ceaseless betrayal of bodily sight' (1996: 33) recall both Levinas's critique of vision and Lanzmann's advocation of blindness as a method of facing. *Hiroshima mon amour* redefines the relation between seeing and witnessing, for while neither protagonist saw the explosions at Hiroshima and Nagasaki, both in their own ways become effective witnesses. In this respect, their 'blindness' might be contrasted with the myopia of Rossel in *Un vivant qui passe*, who was present at Auschwitz but failed to grasp its reality and went on to deliver a false report. (With self-conscious irony, Lanzmann's words to Rossel echo those of Resnais' protagonist: 'You saw nothing at Theresienstadt.') In contrast to Rossel, the Japanese man and the French woman missed the event itself, and yet through them the film succeeds in testifying to its indelible impact and ongoing physical and emotional fallout. Like *Muriel, ou le temps d'un retour*, then, *Hiroshima mon amour* ultimately stages witnessing as a *missing*.[16] These films bear witness to history through a series of missed encounters which implicate the vision of their spectators precisely by denying us visual access to the traumatic events they compel us to face.

This chapter has argued that, contrary to traditional understandings of the act, witnessing is intimately connected to non-seeing, blocked vision and blindness, and that such perceptual disruptions form a locus of ethical inquiry in filmic practice as much as in philosophical theory. My readings have drawn parallels between theoretical writings on testimony, alterity and ethics which look beyond the field of the visible and privilege figures which exceed our vision or disturb visual relations. I have suggested, moreover, that film can dramatise these 'blind' encounters, and that this is another means by which it can implicate viewers as ethical subjects, as opposed to disavowing their responsibility. While concepts of blindness and prohibited vision have immediate resonance in the context of the debates about the representability of the Holocaust which are the primary focus of this book, I have tried to show how they are also relevant to films dealing with other kinds of violence and alterity, and thereby to broaden the scope of my discussion of the ethical dimensions of film. In distinct yet complementary ways, Marker's and Resnais' images of memory and trauma work to preserve an opening onto forms of alterity that escape reduction to the vision of filmmaker, protagonist or spectator. Ethical insight emerges here in the disjunctive relationship between the on-screen or off-screen filmic face and the unrepresentable 'visage' to which Levinas alludes. In the films discussed above the face of the other sets in motion an interrogation of the self rather than exposing interiority. These films offer us no firm purchase on the history, memory or trauma of others who elude our gaze or slip from our grasp. In line with Derrida's discussion of the witness's blindness, Agamben's invitation to us to 'gaze with the Muselmann upon the Gorgon' might be understood in this context as a call to attend to the sites of non-seeing – the blind spots – that structure spectatorship when the screen becomes a trauma site. Face to face with atrocities such as the Holocaust, this vigilant 'blindness' may be the condition of our witnessing and the price we pay for the privilege of insight.

Conclusion

In an essay written shortly before his death, Serge Daney recalls watching shots of Western celebrities intercut with images of starving African children in a *Live Aid* broadcast and finding himself reminded of another unpalatable juxtaposition. In this televisual montage he sees 'the current face of abjection' and 'the improved form of my travelling de *Kapo*' (1992: 18). Daney's reflections on the competing regimes of 'le visuel' and 'l'image' bring him incessantly back to 'the indisputable axiom, the limit of all debate' (1992: 6) inadvertently furnished by Pontecorvo's domestication of death at Auschwitz. Daney is not proposing any kind of equivalence between the Nazi genocide and an African famine or any other atrocity or disaster. Rather, the parallel he draws suggests that Rivette's critique of the aestheticisation of suffering is still relevant and resonant today, that its implications reach far beyond the field of Holocaust films, and that the 'abjection' emblematised by Pontecorvo's tracking shot is evolving into new visual forms.

This book has explored some of the ways in which the Holocaust continues to haunt the moving image. Rather than interrupting or exceeding representation, the event has led, on the contrary, to a proliferation of visual witness. While the dearth of images of the experience of mass death in the extermination camps poses particular challenges to filmmakers, it has prompted them to invent and innovate in an attempt to capture and communicate a glimpse of its violence. At the same time, Holocaust films remain preoccupied with moral and religious prohibitions on representing the industrial forms of murder peculiar to this genocide. We have seen how a recurrent motif in both fiction and documentary films in the genre, shots which approach and then halt at the threshold of the gas chamber, attests to persistent concerns about the so-called 'limits' of representation. Within critical discourse too, the programme of extermination is often seen as a 'limit experience' which confronts testimony and reconstruction with insurmountable cognitive challenges. The dispute between Lanzmann and Godard about the 'pellicule maudite' and the discussions about the photographs taken by the Auschwitz *Sonderkommando* echo some of these doubts about representation, but cumulatively they are helping to advance the debate beyond the ultimately sterile obsession with 'limits'. Throughout this book I have sought to question the legitimacy and validity of interdictions, taboos and discourses of 'ineffability'. My point is not that representation should be free from moral constraints, but that the unreflective reiteration of perceived limits and prohibitions can lead to the prioritisation of a prescriptive/proscriptive moral framework over an ethical one concerned with the relationships of responsibility between filmmaker, viewer and imaged subject. In contrast, films such as *Shoah* and *Histoire(s) du cinéma* look beyond prohibitions on representation and complicate the binary opposition between showing and not showing in their self-conscious explorations of these ethical relations.

The films discussed in this book progressively undermine any clear or stable distinction between ethics and aesthetics. My readings have repeatedly troubled this distinction, arguing that even an apparent prioritisation of aesthetic concerns over ethical ones is *de facto* an ethical choice. My underlying contention has been that all films occupy ethical positions, just as all films occupy political ones, whether or not they seek to make these explicit. Ethics is one of the inescapable yet critically under-acknowledged contexts in which our encounters with films take place. I have sought to identify ways in which Holocaust films and critical debates around them distract us from or disavow this context, sidestepping ethical issues or subordinating them to moral concerns, as well as the means by which the ethical is foregrounded. These means are diverse and sometimes contradictory, as demonstrated in my comparative analysis of *Histoire(s) du cinéma* and *Shoah*. Pontecorvo's infamous 'travelling' may be recapitulated in disconcertingly literal ways in films such as *Schindler's List* and *The Grey Zone*. But Rivette's polemic is just one of many possible starting points for inquiry into the ethical dimensions of Holocaust films; camera movements are one of a potentially infinite number of means by which a filmmaker articulates his or her ethical vision. In chapters three and four I suggested that ethical meaning emerges most insistently in the heterogeneous encounters between viewers and images. Yet it is important to point out that distinctions between films which protect us as innocent bystanders and those which implicate us as ethical subjects, often by obstructing or disturbing our vision, are rarely clear-cut. Films such as *Shoah* and *Nuit et brouillard* are often perceived as models of virtuous filmmaking instructing in virtuous viewing, yet their much-discussed elisions and blindspots at times prioritise political agency over ethical reflection. In this way, they pose prescient questions about the relationship between a politics and an ethics of spectatorship: to what extent does politically engaged viewing lead to an evasion of ethical responsibility? Conversely, to what extent does a properly ethical response entail a retreat from politics in the face of an atrocity which was perpetrated as a political tactic?

Such questions gain importance as our culture becomes progressively mired in unprocessed images of abjection. Another of the contentions underpinning this book is that analysis of Holocaust films can *open* rather than foreclose the wider debate about film and ethics, as intimated by my readings of films by Marker and Resnais in chapter four. But do the critical hermeneutics elaborated here stand up and remain relevant in other contexts? Daney warns that 'le travelling de *Kapo*' will continue to mutate and that the critical approach it symbolises will need to evolve as advances in technology open up new aesthetic possibilities. His discussions of the visual media as a key front in the first Gulf War anticipate the progressive implication of media and military technologies. Indeed, in the years since Daney's death, we have seen a proliferation both of image technologies and mediatised atrocities. What currency and power do the haunted images of Holocaust films retain in a society where we are increasingly bombarded with images of the pain and suffering of others?

While this book has been in preparation, the circulation of new forms of images of torture and death has prompted fresh debates about what kinds of experience should and should not be filmed and seen. Of numerous possible examples, three will serve to illustrate the range of issues at stake here. In July 2007, Paul Watson's television documentary about pianist and composer Malcolm Pointon's struggle with Alzheimer's sparked a furore when it was revealed that the publicity material falsely implied that the film captured the moment of Pointon's death.[1] Commentary on this controversy attested to the resilience of the social taboo on filming death and attacked the media's willingness to exploit it. In April 2004, digital photographs of American soldiers abusing Iraqi detainees in the prison at Abu Ghraib were broadcast and published around the world. These images came to emblematise both the war in Iraq and the convergence of torture, pornography and new technologies of visual representation.[2] As witnessed by ongoing discussions about the moral, political, legal and economic ramifications of these images, the questions formulated in the course of this book about the ethics of images gain a fresh urgency at a time when new technologies are transforming our relationship to history by bringing it to unprecedented visibility as pure media spectacle. The attack on the World Trade Center on 11 September 2001 – my third example – is often cited as the archetypal postmodern 'spectacle of the real': an event staged for the media, witnessed in real time by spectators around the world and immediately subjected to the endless repetition that structures televisual representation. Events of this kind challenge conventional conceptions of the relation between images and history in ways that have already been the subject of extensive commentary (see, for example, Baudrillard 2002; Virilio 2002; Žižek 2002). Critical debate has dwelt on the progressive retreat of reality and the Real behind an omnivorous media flux, which casts doubt upon the referentiality of the image, its celebrated indexical bond with profilmic reality. Such doubts are exacerbated by the advent of digital images, which, for Thomas Elsaesser, confirm 'the now definitively "traumatic" status of the moving image in our culture as the symptom without a cause, as the event without a trace' (2001: 197). At the same time, contemporary forms of mediation are reconfiguring time and space in ways which call into question traditional understandings of history and the 'historical event'. Live reportage collapses the temporal gap between reality and its representation, according the present an unprecedented historicity. As Sobchack puts it in the prophetic introduction to her edited volume *The Persistence of History: Cinema, Television, and the Modern Event*, 'event and its representation, immediacy and its mediation, have moved increasingly towards simultaneity ... Today, history seems to happen right now' (1996: 5). This movement 'towards simultaneity' dissociates the image from the processes of memory and mourning in which visual representation has long played a crucial role. Moreover, it has particular implications for representations of trauma, for it elides the complex processes of delay and deferral – commonly conceptualised by trauma theorists in terms of latency and *Nachträglichkeit* – which define traumatic experience, and which time-based media and moving images in particular have helped to figure and interrogate.[3]

What future for cinema as witness in this increasingly mediatised and (in Elsaesser's terms) 'traumatised' landscape? This book has argued that Holocaust films can be read as commemorative, imaginative and enabling responses to a visual lacuna, an absence of images. But filmmakers approaching recent atrocities more often have to grapple with a surfeit of visual witness. At a time when technology is draining images of their testimonial power, can cinema reinvest them with mnemonic value and a claim on the real? Sontag has affirmed the capacity of photography to preserve memory in an era of information overload: 'Nonstop imagery (television, streaming video, movies) is our surround, but when it comes to remembering, the photograph has the deeper bite' (2003: 22). Hartman has described how the videographic testimonies of Holocaust survivors can counteract the media's deleterious 'unreality-effect' (2000: 4). Yet the achievements of the filmmakers discussed in this book suggest that cinema may provide an even more resilient and versatile site of resistance to the potentially pernicious influence of competing technologies. Indeed, contemporary filmmakers are testing this resistance by incorporating the alien image-systems of 'le visuel' into their work in a bid to confront and challenge them. In Mexican filmmaker Alejandro González Iñárritu's contribution to the portmanteau film *11'09"01 – September 11* (2002), images of bodies falling past blue sky and glinting glass and concrete erupt onto a black screen in a series of searing flashes, confounding our senses and resisting comprehension.[4] In Marker's video-essay *Chats perchés* (*The Case of the Grinning Cat*, 2004), an intertitle 'flashback' introduces an image of the cityscape of Paris, over which is superimposed, phantom-like, a shot of the exploding Twin Towers, creating a composite image which brings to mind the devastated post-apocalyptic Paris featured in *La Jetée*. Such provocative reappropriations of traumatic media images act as a corrective to the deleterious effects of televisual looping, reinvesting them with the power to shock, and a purchase on history.

González Iñárritu's and Marker's attempts to reclaim the image as testimonial trace serve to highlight the wider relevance of the questions raised principally in relation to film and the Holocaust in this book. In particular, they underline the currency of the questions at stake in the dispute between Lanzmann and Godard. Do direct images of atrocities screen the past *for* us or *from* us? In what circumstances and contexts, cinematic or otherwise, can they solicit an ethical response? It is not my contention that the various filmic approaches to the Holocaust considered here translate into universal ethical principles or systems. Rather than normative formulations and moral prescriptions, my aim has been to offer some points of orientation for continued ethical reflection on cinema. Films such as *Shoah*, *Histoire(s) du cinéma* and others discussed in the book constitute seminal interventions in ongoing processes of remembering and mourning which individually they fail to complete or circumscribe. Rather, they advocate 'the persistence of always fallible and contestable representation' (Rose 1996: 41). Together they attest to the continued importance of seeking truthful and creative ways of bearing witness to events which demand new modes of representation, and demonstrate the vital roles which the moving image can play in this process. They highlight the multiple functions of the image as witness, as trace, as evidence, as screen, as shield and as ethical lens, as interface between self and other. At a time when new technologies are redefining the role of the image as vector of memory, these films constitute prescient prolegomena to future cinema and future testimony, to the haunted images which have yet to be invented. They suggest that we should look back to the Holocaust for insights into the future of the image as witness.

Notes

Introduction

1 The name 'cyanide' comes from the Greek word 'kyanos', meaning 'blue'.

2 For remarks on the difficulty of naming the event and detailed accounts of the meanings and limitations of the different names and epithets which have been used to refer to it, see the chapter on 'Names of the Holocaust' in James E. Young's *Writing and Rewriting the Holocaust: Narrative and the Consequences of Interpretation* (1988: 83–98) and Bergoffen (2000: 27–9). Like many scholars, I use the word 'Holocaust' in this study since, in spite of its unfortunate implications, it remains the term most commonly employed in this context. 'Holocaust' refers here to the Nazis' persecution not only of the Jews but also of groups whose suffering has received less attention, such as the Roma, Communists, gays and lesbians and the disabled.

3 All translations from French and German are my own, except where published translations are cited in the bibliography.

4 See, for example, Semprun (1994: 23–4), Rose (1996: 41–3), Agamben (1999: 31–3), Rancière (2001), Didi-Huberman (2001: 230–1), Nancy (2003). Arguments along intersecting lines are advanced by Levi (1988: 68–9), Bersani & Dutoit (1993: 224), Lang (2000: 18) and Žižek (2001: 66–8).

5 On evolving perceptions of the Holocaust in France, see Wieviorka (1992), Kritzman (1995), Wolf (2004) and Suleiman (2006).

6 See Insdorf (1983), Doneson (1987), Avisar (1988) and Colombat (1993).

7 For an extended discussion of the evolving meanings of Adorno's concept of 'poetry after Auschwitz' and different interpretations of it by other scholars, see chapters one and two of Michael Rothberg's *Traumatic Realism: The Demands of Holocaust Representation* (2000: 17–96).

8   Alongside representations of the Holocaust, Rancière's discussion of the concept of the 'unrepresentable' mentions the Kantian 'sublime', Marcel Duchamp's *Le Grand Verre* (1915–23) and Kazimir Malevich's *White Square on White* (1918) (2001: 81).

9   Significantly, Nancy qualifies this conclusion by interrogating the relationship between representation and presence and rethinking the Nazi project in these terms. Reflecting on the privileged political role ascribed to representation by the Nazi regime, with its penchant for spectacular parades and monumental art and architecture, Nancy describes the death camps as 'an enterprise of over-representation [*sur-représentation*]', where a desire for 'total, saturated presence' stages 'the spectacle of the destruction of that which, in its eyes, is non-representation' (2003: 61, 80, 81). In this account, the Aryan is cast as the absolute 'representative of representation', while his or her victim is 'drained of the possibility of representation' (2003: 79, 90). This leads Nancy to venture that the camps precipitated 'an ultimate crisis of representation' insofar as they aimed at 'a crushing [*écrasement*] of representation itself' (2003: 70, 71). Only in this precise context, Nancy argues, is it legitimate to speak of 'la représentation interdite'. The French adjective 'interdit' can be translated not only as 'banned', 'forbidden' or 'prohibited' but also as 'dumbfounded', 'taken aback' or 'disconcerted'. According to Nancy, representation of the camps is 'interdite' in this latter sense: not 'prohibited' but 'taken by surprise', 'suspended' or 'put to the test' by a reality which is 'not of the order of presence', an ultimately irrecuperable prior moment of absence (ibid.).

10 On the concept of representational limits see especially Saul Friedländer's landmark edited collection *Probing the Limits of Representation: Nazism and the 'Final Solution'*. Friedländer writes: 'The extermination of the Jews of Europe is as accessible to both representation and interpretation as any other historical event. But we are dealing with an event which tests our traditional conceptual and representational categories, an "event at the limits"' (1992: 2–3). Discussing the intractable 'limits to representation *which should not be but can easily be transgressed*', he points out that such limits are difficult to define, marking 'intangible but nonetheless perceived boundaries', which have less to do with 'gross transgression' than with 'a kind of uneasiness' (1992: 3; emphasis in original).

11 Horowitz (1992) is troubled, for example, by Felman and Laub's uncritical use of a psychoanalytic model as an interpretative framework for Holocaust testimony and by their failure to distinguish with sufficient rigour between different kinds of witnesses and witnessing. LaCapra too argues that Felman's essay on *Shoah* collapses crucial distinctions in traumatic experience and threatens 'to confuse life with both self-reflexive art and self-dramatizing criticism' (1998: 13). Again in a related vein, Joshua Hirsch accuses Felman and Laub of 'promoting a boundariless contagion of trauma that erases the distinctions

between specific historical experiences' (2004: 26). Further objections to Felman's reading of Lanzmann's film are addressed in chapter one.

12 From the testimonies of survivors and perpetrators and also historians' research, we learn, for example, that the victims' bodies were incinerated in crematoria or ditches and their ashes dispersed by the wind, while archives documenting the mass murder were destroyed towards the end of the war. Further details can be found in the sections entitled 'Concealment' and 'Erasure' in Raul Hilberg's *The Destruction of the European Jews* (1985: 240–3, 249–51). The *Nacht und Nebel* ('Night and Fog') decree of 1941, which authorised the clandestine deportation of resisters and the suppression of information about their whereabouts, might also be seen as emblematic of the Nazis' exploitation of secrecy as a political strategy.

13 Janina Struk emphasises that photography was 'integral to the operation of some of the concentration camps' (2004: 102). For discussion of the different kinds of photographs which were taken there, from prisoner identification, anthropometric portraiture and documentation of medical experiments to personal mementos, see About (2001) and Struk (2004: 99–123). See also Ireneusz Dobrowolski's *Portrecista* (*The Portraitist*, 2005), a documentary about the experiences of Wilhelm Brasse, a Polish political prisoner who worked at Auschwitz as a photographer in the reconnaissance commando and managed to save many of the photographs he took.

14 See the illuminating analysis of the first images of the camps to enter the public domain in newsreels, their impact upon public consciousness and their subsequent circulation in cinema, including discussion of Alain Resnais' *Nuit et brouillard* (*Night and Fog*, 1955), Arnaud des Pallières' *Drancy Avenir* (1996) and *Shoah*, in chapter four of Sylvie Lindeperg's *Clio de 5 à 7: Les Actualités filmées de la Libération: archives du futur* (2000: 155–209).

15 There is, however, a substantial body of work devoted to the legal and moral rights of imaged subjects (see, for example, Pryluck 1976; Gross, Katz & Ruby 1988; Ruby 1988), ethical issues which lie outside the scope of my own study. For a summary of the questions at stake in these debates and a case for moving beyond them, see Cooper (2006: 3).

16 The recently-released DVD of *Kapo* (Carlotta, 2006) includes a 9-minute extra entitled 'Le polémique *Kapo*' ('The *Kapo* Polemic') which retraces the chequered history of the film and addresses the debates provoked by Rivette's and Daney's reactions to it.

17 While this dictum was originally formulated by Godard, during a round-table discussion of what remains one of the most celebrated cinematic representations of historical trauma, Resnais' *Hiroshima mon amour* (1959) (in Domarchi *et al.* 1959: 5), Godard was in fact simply inverting a phrase coined by Luc Moullet earlier the same year: 'la morale est affaire de travellings' ('morality is a question of tracking shots') (1959: 14). Two years later, Rivette

(who also participated in the round-table discussion) revisits both versions in 'De l'abjection'. For a more detailed history of this dictum, see de Baecque (1991 II: 48–9; 2003: 206–9).

18 Further important recent analyses of cinema along ethical lines, which are less directly relevant to the concerns of this book, can be found in Kaja Silverman's *The Threshold of the Visible World* (1996) and Robert Samuels' *Hitchcock's Bi-textuality: Lacan, Feminisms and Queer Theory* (1998). Silverman's interweaving explorations of looking and loving aim to offer 'an ethics of the field of vision, and a psychoanalytic politics of visual representation' (1996: 2), while Samuels draws on Lacanian ethics and recent theories of feminine and queer subjectivity to reread a series of canonical Hitchcock films against the heterosexual grain.

Chapter 1

1 Lanzmann describes, for example, how after a screening of the first part of *Shoah* in New York, a rabbi returned to the empty cinema to recite the *Kaddish*, the Jewish prayer of mourning and praise (reported in Forges 1997: 115).

2 On the relation between male and (largely absent) female testimony in *Shoah*, see also Alfredo Montferré (in Lanzmann 1991: 98).

3 For charges of such kinds, besides those mentioned later in the paragraph, see, for example, Bonnaud & Viviant (1998: 28) and Rothberg (2000: 234).

4 See Koch (1993b) for a detailed analysis of concepts of the *Bilderverbot* in the context of cinema and Critical Theory.

5 For a discussion of the Wiener film, see Hirsch (2004: 1–3).

6 Lanzmann reiterates these remarks in an article in *Le Monde*: 'If I had found an existing film – a secret film because it was strictly prohibited – made by an SS man showing how 3,000 Jews, men, women and children, died together, asphyxiated in the gas chamber of Crematorium II at Auschwitz; if I had found that, not only would I not have shown it, I would have destroyed it. I am not capable of saying why. It goes without saying' (1994: vii). For further discussion of this hypothetical film, see Lanzmann (2001a).

7 For a variety of further reactions to Lanzmann's incendiary comments about the Nazi footage of the gas chamber, see Bensoussan (2003: 161–2), Delfour (2000a) and Didi-Huberman (2003: 122). Delfour's defence of Lanzmann's position is discussed in chapter three.

8 Lanzmann famously insists that *Shoah* is not a documentary (see, for example, 1991: 96).

9 For a summary and discussion of critics' responses to Spielberg's experimentation with documentary style in *Schindler's List*, see Zelizer (1997: 27–8).

10 The role of the *Sonderkommandos* is discussed in detail in Müller (1980), Levi

(1988: 34–43), Mesnard and Kahan (2001: 13–22), Didi-Huberman (2003: 11–15) and Greif (2005). Their activities are also depicted at length in Tim Blake Nelson's film *The Grey Zone* (2001), which is discussed in chapter three.

11 I am grateful to Barry Langford for drawing my attention to this common misapprehension about Bomba and the discrepancies between his testimony and others which position the Treblinka barbers' work in the undressing huts or at the beginning of the *Schlauch*.

12 Felman's remarks are particularly resonant in the case of Srebnik, who, as we are informed by the titles at the beginning of *Shoah*, survived a bullet to the head in January 1945, when the Nazis executed the remaining Jews in Chelmno in advance of the arrival of Soviet troops. Objections to Lanzmann's presentation of the *Sonderkommando* survivors as 'spokespeople for the dead' (cited in Rabinowitz 1994: 30) are discussed in chapter four.

Chapter 2

1 For a more detailed account of much of the history of the proposed joint project and some of its implications, see Frodon (1999).

2 For further discussion and evaluation of this strand of Godard's argument, see Williams (1999: 308, 310–11), Witt (1999: 334), Rancière (2001a: 227–32) and Didi-Huberman (2003: 176–8).

3 An alternative reading of the Stevens/Giotto sequence, which explicitly takes issue with Rancière's conclusions, is offered by Didi-Huberman (2003: 180–7). Two other important analyses of this sequence are to be found in Williams (2000: 134–7) and Wright (2000). For both Williams and Wright, as for Rancière, this sequence is central to an understanding of the whole work: Williams finds in it 'a new and unheralded form of touching across form, encompassing art, cinema and video', which constitutes 'a metapoetic comment on Godard's own process' (2000: 135), while Wright interprets it as a precise representation of the director's 'unattainable idea of montage' (2000: 51).

4 While both the Greek terms used in this sentence signify a 'likeness' or an 'image', *eikôn* implies a truthful representation in contrast to the false image implied by *eidôlon*.

5 Godard contentiously suggests, for example, that cinema might be able to assist scientists in the search for a cure for AIDS: 'AIDS has to do with culpability and morality. Cinema exists to make these connections, to teach us to think' (1998a II: 427).

6 Bellour used this adjective during a panel discussion at *For Ever Godard*, a conference held at the Tate Modern in London on 21–24 June 2000.

7 The montage of *Histoire(s)* also exhibits some of the symptoms Derrida associates with the 'mal d'archive' ('archive fever'), a desire to consign to memory which is at once created and threatened by the apparently conflicting impulse

to forget and destroy. Drawing on the work of Sigmund Freud, Derrida argues that the archive cannot be conceptualised purely in terms of mnemonic or anamnesiac functions because it is infected and inflected by the death drive. Paradoxically, then, the archive 'takes place at the place of originary and structural breakdown of the said memory ... the archive always and *a priori* works against itself' (1995: 26–7). On the one hand, Godard's video-essay compulsively revisits existing archives, recovering lost fragments of film and reassembling them in an archive of its own. On the other, in so doing, it simultaneously attests to the necessity of forgetting. In *Amnésies: fictions du cinéma d'après Jean-Luc Godard* Jacques Aumont reasons that amnesia constitutes the condition not only of history and memory but also of montage, which must inevitably 'forget' certain fragments and possible constellations in order to 'remember' others (1999: 26). Even as it works to remember and preserve, Godard's montage explores and enacts processes of loss and mourning, whose pathos is intensified, as Williams observes, by the fact that the very material of which film is made is steadily decomposing (1999: 311).

8   The name 'la pellicule maudite' has also been applied to photographs taken by *Sonderkommando* members in Auschwitz-Birkenau in August 1944 (which are discussed later in this chapter). Following Delfour, I use the phrase here to refer instead to hypothetical film footage of the gas chambers.

9   For similar claims, see also, for example, Godard (1998a II: 247) and Dulaure & Parnet (1985: 21).

10 See also Lanzmann's objections to Eyal Sivan's documentary *Un spécialiste, portrait d'un criminel moderne* (*The Specialist*, 1999), which is composed entirely of Leo Hurwitz's footage of the Adolf Eichmann trial and is informed by Arendt's thesis (in Perraud 1999).

11 Guerrin's article includes a detailed description of the exhibition. For further discussion of the photographs on display, see Chapuis (2001).

12 For further information about the history of the photographs taken by the *Sonderkommando* members, see Struk (2004: 112–15).

13 Besides making this claim, Chéroux also lists a number of historical sources which refer to photographic or filmic images of the interior of the gas chamber, and concludes, confirming Godard's suspicions, that it is quite possible that such images exist or existed (Chéroux 2001: 215–16). A different take on the status of the *Sonderkommando* members' photographs is offered by a sequence in the television series *Holocaust*, which includes one of the two photographs of burning pits while simultaneously drawing attention to the absence of images depicting the killing itself. Two SS officers watch a slideshow of real black-and-white photographs of the camps as one explains to the other the procedures involved in the 'special treatment' of the deportees. But as the speaker identifies photographs of the killing itself – 'the interior of a gas chamber before the Zyklon B is released ... during ... and, finally,

afterwards' – the camera cuts from the slides to close-ups of the faces of the viewers, acknowledging the lack of images of the death scene, before Alex's photograph of its aftermath concludes the slideshow.

14 For a critical account and further evaluation of the debate between Lanzmann, Godard, Didi-Huberman, Wajcman and Pagnoux, see Frodon (2004).

15 While images of the extermination are Wajcman's primary subject here, I find that his argument does not always sufficiently acknowledge the value of other Holocaust-related photographs. The testimonial function of photographs of the Nazi crimes as well as photographic art remembering and responding to them is perceptively explored by Andrea Liss in *Trespassing through Shadows: Memory, Photography, and the Holocaust* (1998), Ulrich Baer in *Spectral Evidence: The Photography of Trauma* (2002) and Struk in *Photographing the Holocaust: Interpretations of the Evidence* (2004). See also Philippe Mesnard's *Consciences de la Shoah: critique des discours et des représentations*, (2000), which contains a critical overview of the ways in which a wide variety of archive photographs and footage have been used to evoke the Holocaust in films, including Resnais' *Nuit et brouillard*, Sivan's *Un spécialiste, portrait d'un criminel moderne* and Alain Jaubert's *Auschwitz, l'album, la mémoire* (*Auschwitz, the Album, the Memory*, 1985) (see Mesnard 2000: 286–306).

16 Lanzmann explains his objections to Resnais' film in a statement dating from May 1987 cited in Lowy (2001: 85–6) and in interviews in a radio programme produced for France Culture and included on the DVD of *Nuit et brouillard* (Arte, 2003), '*Nuit et brouillard, 1954–1994*'.

17 Wilson has suggested that Resnais' film has more in common with Lanzmann's in this respect than is often acknowledged by its commentators. Analysing the 'hesitant, even tremulous relation … between Resnais' images and the inaccessible real he seeks yet to represent' in *Nuit et brouillard*, she argues that 'Resnais' manipulation of images … as much as Cayrol's commentary, betrays an awareness of the extent to which these images are screening us from the reality of the camps, rather than screening it for us' (2005: 95). (Resnais' work is discussed in more detail in chapters three and four.)

18 As MacCabe reminds us, when Godard refused to be honoured by the New York Film Critics' Circle in 1995, he listed nine aspects of American cinema upon which he had not been able to exert an influence, starting with this failure.

19 For Lanzmann's views on the difficulty of recuperating the genocide within a straightforward chronological historical narrative, see, for example, 1990b: 315–16 and Kaganski & Bonnaud 1998: 21.

20 See Cheyette for further discussion of Spielberg's allusions to Lanzmann's film (1997: 231).

21 *Vrai faux passeport* was commissioned by the Centre Pompidou for the exhibition 'Voyages en utopie, Jean-Luc Godard, 1946–2006'.

Chapter 3

1   Another, more sensational reconstruction of mass killing in a gas chamber appears in the ABC television series *War and Remembrance* (1988).

2   The gas chamber sequence in *Kornblumenblau* is accompanied, in ironic counterpoint, by the final chorale of Beethoven's Ninth Symphony, the Schillerian 'Ode an die Freude' ('Ode to Joy'), which also happens to be the soundtrack to the scene in Stanley Kubrick's *A Clockwork Orange* (1971) where the delinquent Alex has his eyelids clamped open and is forced to view images showing or suggesting violence, including documentary footage of Nazi rallies and wartime activities. In different ways, both scenes explore the morality of viewing violent images, fictional and documentary, and foreground our potential complicity in the violence we see.

3   Further accounts of spectatorship which pursue these insights in a variety of directions include Clover (1992), Cowie (1997a) and Staiger (2000).

4   Of the different types of representation of death discussed in Sobchack's essay, the 'pellicule maudite' bears perhaps the closest relation to another hypothetical kind of film: the 'snuff' movie. An extreme sub-genre of pornography in which the actors are supposedly killed on-screen, 'snuff' remains a popular urban myth despite inconclusive evidence of its existence. Like the Nazi filming the gas chamber, the camera-operator in a snuff film would be complicit in the death shown, however, unlike the Nazi footage, snuff 'teases the viewer as to its undecidable ontological status' (Sobchack 2004a: 247) and is produced solely for commercial rather than documentary or scientific purposes – for pleasure rather than knowledge.

5   Horowitz, for example, writes 'the appeal to the audience's voyeurism is repeated in the shower room scene at Auschwitz, a scene pornographic both for its depiction of terrified, naked Jewish women and for its use of the gas chamber to provoke the viewer's sense of suspense' (1997b: 128).

6   Critiques of Spielberg's eroticisation of some of the Jewish women in *Schindler's List* echo responses to Liliana Cavani's controversial *Il Portiere di notte* (*The Night Porter*, 1974), a film about the sadomasochistic relationship between a former SS officer and a Jewish survivor of the camps, which has also been criticised for its ambiguous conflation of traumatic, erotic and cinematic spectacle. *Il Portiere di notte* contains flashbacks in which a fully-clothed Max films a naked Lucia in close-up as she waits in line to be registered in a camp, the viewfinder of his camera acting as a peep-hole.

7   Horowitz goes further, arguing that the spray of water from the showerheads effectively 'refutes the reality of the gas chamber' (1997b: 128). Comparing references to gas earlier in the film with Jean-François Lyotard's paraphrase of the logic behind revisionist Robert Faurisson's argument that gas chambers did not exist, Horowitz reasons that 'the film's treatment of the phe-

nomenon of the gas chamber seemingly confirms not the testimony of Holocaust survivors but the claims of Holocaust deniers that the Nazi genocide never occurred' (1997b: 129). A parallel emerges between Spielberg's film and Schogt's in this context. *Zyklon Portrait* also substitutes water for gas, but inverts the logic underpinning Spielberg's substitution; via the metonymic chain established by Schogt the images of water come to testify to the reality of the gas chambers, as suggested in my reading in the introduction.

8   See Omar Bartov for a critique of *The Eighty-First Blow* which demonstrates how the film inadvertently perpetuates an image of the 'Jew' as victim (2005: 56–63).

9   This is also the function of the CGI reconstruction of Crematorium II at Auschwitz in Leslie Woodhead's documentary *The Holocaust on Trial* (2000). Woodhead uses digital technology to enable the viewer to explore the undressing room and gas chamber as they would have appeared when in use.

10   As Hirsch points out, 'no attempt is made to substitute the gas chamber shot for the missing image of the gassing itself. *Night and Fog* thus suggests that the spectator understand the image of gassing precisely as missing, something that can only be confronted through the image of its ruins' (2004: 52).

Chapter 4

1   Todorov (1991: 254–5), Georges Bensoussan (2003: 160–2) and Alain Douchevsky (n. d.: 12–18, 23–4) amongst others have highlighted the problematic implications of Lanzmann's argument. Žižek meanwhile has defended Lanzmann's prohibition of the question 'why?' against some of their objections (2001: 65–6). My own focus here is more specifically on the concept of 'blindness' which Lanzmann formulates in the course of his argument.

2   Lanzmann is borrowing imagery from Nerval's poem 'El Desdichado', originally published in 1854 (1958 I: 693), as well as from Kristeva's *Soleil noir: dépression et mélancolie* (1987). For both de Nerval and Kristeva, the black sun is an image of melancholia.

3   Karski describes in *Shoah* how a Jewish leader persuaded him to visit the ghetto: 'I know the Western world. You are going to deal with the English. Now you will give them your oral reports. I am sure it will strengthen your report if you will be able to say "I saw it myself"'.

4   See especially the chapter entitled 'The *Muselmann*' (Agamben 1999: 41–86).

5   For a discussion of the disputed origins and etymology of the term 'Muselmann' and its synonyms, see Agamben (1999: 44–5).

6   On this occasion, moreover, rather than observing passively from a viewing position located safely outside the action, Müller witnessed it from the perspective of an active participant. The traumatic past anticipates the testi-

monial present as he explains to Lanzmann that the plight and courage of his fellow Czechs prompted him to resolve to die with them, before he was persuaded to leave the gas chamber at the last minute by a woman who reminded him of his future responsibility as a witness. Müller's testimony exemplifies one of the principal tropes informing Holocaust narrative, as described by Horowitz: 'the victim of the Nazi atrocity resolves to survive the genocidal onslaught … in order to testify against the perpetrators and on behalf of the victims' (1992: 45). It is thus at once paradigmatic – insofar as every testimonial narrative is essentially the story of how the witness survived to tell his or her story – and unique – we presume that none of the others who witnessed this scene survived to tell this story.

7 Agamben's text does refer to the *Sonderkommandos*, but views them primarily as 'the extreme figure of [Levi's] "grey zone"' (Agamben 1999: 24–6).

8 These lines can be found in the poem 'Aschenglorie', from a collection originally published in 1967 (Celan 1983 II: 72).

9 Antelme also refers to a loss or 'permanent negation' of the face in the camps which is not specific to the Muselmann. In *L'Espèce humaine* he describes the faces of the deportees as 'twice denied'; firstly by the gaze of the SS, to whom all the deportees looked alike, and secondly by the deportees themselves, as they endeavoured to make themselves invisible to avoid attracting undue attention from their guards (see 1957: 57–8). As Georges Perec puts it in his moving essay on Antelme's testimony, 'the deportee could no longer afford to have a face' (1996: 180).

10 Davis discusses the confusion created by Levinas's account in this regard, noting that certain commentators (Derrida amongst them) have succumbed to the 'inevitable temptation' to account for the face in phenomenal terms (1996: 133–5).

11 See Witt (1999) for discussion of Godard's misgivings about 'the televisual mutation' and its impact on cinema.

12 Documentary filmmaker, Errol Morris, for instance, has developed the Interrotron, a network of cameras and monitors which allows the person interviewed to look directly at the camera lens, rather than slightly to the side at the interviewer. Disrupting the representational conventions of reality television, this device experiments with the possibility of first-person address in moving images by 'closing the dynamic circuit between camera and viewer' (Rosenheim 1996: 222).

13 Quotations from *Sans soleil* are translated from the French version of the film, rather than taken from the English version, which differs in places.

14 Cooper's 'Chris Marker: Love, Death and Documentary' (2006: 48–61) offers an illuminating and much more extended Levinasian reading of *Sans soleil*, which shows how the ethics of vision at work in the film are 'based not on an openness to the other but the displacement of the self' (2006: 57). My own

focus here is more narrowly on the potentially Levinasian resonances of the *regard caméra*.

15 'If the [actress] is witness to all these signs of Hiroshima's past yet "sees" – understands – nothing, then how can we, at an additional move from them, trust our eyes?', asks John W. Moses, who draws parallels between Resnais' use of archive images paradoxically to undermine the act of vision in *Hiroshima mon amour* and *Nuit et brouillard* (1987: 159).

16 I am drawing here on Felman's reading of Albert Camus's *La Chute*, in which, she argues, 'the event is witnessed insofar as it is *not experienced*, insofar as it is literally *missed* ... *The Fall* bears witness, paradoxically enough, to the *missing* of the fall' (1992b: 168–9; emphasis in original). Caruth's discussion of 'Traumatic Awakenings: Freud, Lacan, and the Ethics of Memory' (1996: 91–112) also offers compelling insights into the relationship between witnessing and missing.

Conclusion

1 *Malcolm and Barbara: Love's Farewell* was screened on ITV1 on 8 August 2007.

2 See Sontag (2004) for an analysis of the moral and political meanings of these photographs.

3 On the intersections between trauma theory and screen studies see Elsaesser (2001) and Radstone (2001).

4 The images of people jumping from the World Trade Centre recorded by professional and amateur camera-operators on 11 September 2001 were beamed all over the world in the immediate aftermath of the attacks, but swiftly disappeared from the US media in the wake of angry public reactions. For further discussion of these images see Jousse (2001).

Filmography

11'09"01 – September 11 11 (Youssef Chahine, Amos Gitai, Alejandro González Iñárritu, Shohei Imamura, Claude Lelouch, Ken Loach, Samira Makhmalbaf, Mira Nair, Idrissa Ouedraogo, Sean Penn, Danis Tanović, 2002, Bosnia Herzegovina/Burkina Faso/France/Egypt/India/Iran/Israel/Japan/Mexico/UK/USA)

À bout de souffle (*Breathless*, Jean-Luc Godard, 1959, France)

Allemagne année 90 neuf zéro (*Germany Year 90 Nine Zero*, Jean-Luc Godard, 1991, France)

Amen (Constantin Costa-Gavras, 2002, France/Germany/Romania/USA)

Les Anges du péché (*Angels of the Streets*, Robert Bresson, 1943, France)

Au nom de tous les miens (*For Those I Loved*, Robert Enrico, 1983, France/Canada/Hungary)

Auschwitz, l'album, la mémoire (*Auschwitz, the Album, the Memory*, Alain Jaubert, 1985, France)

Chats perchés (*The Case of the Grinning Cat*, Chris Marker, 2004, France)

Child of the Death Camps: Truth and Lies (Christopher Olgiati, 1999, UK)

A Clockwork Orange (Stanley Kubrick, 1971, UK)

David (Peter Lilienthal, 1979, West Germany)

Drancy Avenir (Arnaud des Pallières, 1996, France)

The Eighty-First Blow (David Bergman, Jaquot Ehrlich and Haim Gouri, 1974, Israel)

Éloge de l'amour (*In Praise of Love*, Jean-Luc Godard, 2001, France/Switzerland)

Escape from Sobibor (Jack Gold, 1987, Yugoslavia/UK)

Europa, Europa (Agnieszka Holland, 1991, Germany/France/Poland)

Der ewige Jude (*The Eternal Jew*, Fritz Hippler, 1940, Germany)

Fantômas (Louis Feuillade, 1913–14, France)

Une femme mariée (*A Married Woman*, Jean-Luc Godard, 1964, France)

The Great Dictator (Charlie Chaplin, 1940, USA)

The Grey Zone (Tim Blake Nelson, 2001, USA)

Hiroshima mon amour (Alain Resnais, 1959, France/Japan)

Histoire(s) du cinéma (Jean-Luc Godard, 1988–98, France)

Holocaust (Marvin J. Chomsky, 1978, USA)

The Holocaust on Trial (Leslie Woodhead, 2000, UK)

La Jetée (*The Pier*, Chris Marker, 1962, France)

Kapo (Gillo Pontecorvo, 1960, Yugoslavia/France/Italy)

Korczak (Andrzej Wajda, 1990, Poland/Germany/UK)

Kornblumenblau (Leszek Wosiewicz, 1988, Poland)

The Last Days (James Moll, 1998, USA)

Malcolm and Barbara: Love's Farewell (Paul Watson, 2007, UK)

Muriel, ou le temps d'un retour (*Muriel, or the Time of Return*, Alain Resnais, 1963, France/Italy)

Notre musique (*Our Music*, Jean-Luc Godard, 2004, France/Switzerland)

Nuit et brouillard (*Night and Fog*, Alain Resnais, 1955, France)

The Old Place (Jean-Luc Godard and Anne-Marie Miéville, 1999, France/USA)

Pasazerka (*The Passenger*, Andrzej Munk, 1962, Poland)

La Passion de Jeanne d'Arc (*The Passion of Joan of Arc*, Carl Theodor Dreyer, 1928, France)

Le Petit soldat (*The Little Soldier*, Jean-Luc Godard, 1960, France)

The Pianist (Roman Polanski, 2002, France/Germany/UK/Poland)

A Place in the Sun (George Stevens, 1951, USA)

Il Portiere di notte (*The Night Porter*, Liliana Cavani, 1974, Italy)

Portrecista (*The Portraitist*, Ireneusz Dobrowolski, 2005, Poland)

La Règle du jeu (*The Rules of the Game*, Jean Renoir, 1939, France)

Reisen ins Leben: Weiterleben nach einer Kindheit in Auschwitz (*Journey into Life: Aftermath of a Childhood in Auschwitz*, Thomas Mitscherlich, 1995, Germany)

Sans soleil (*Sunless*, Chris Marker, 1982, France)

Saving Private Ryan (Steven Spielberg, 1998, USA)

Schindler's List (Steven Spielberg, 1993, USA)

Shoah (Claude Lanzmann, 1985, France)

Sobibor, 14 octobre 1943, 16 heures (*Sobibor, October 14, 1943, 4pm*, Claude Lanzmann, 2001, France)

Un spécialiste, portrait d'un criminel moderne (*The Specialist*, Eyal Sivan, 1999, Israel/France/Germany/Austria/Belgium)

Les Statues meurent aussi (*Statues Also Die*, Alain Resnais and Chris Marker, 1953, France)

Der Tod ist ein Meister aus Deutschland (*Death is a Master from Germany*, Lea Rosh and Eberhard Jäckel, 1999, Germany)

Train de vie (*Train of Life*, Radu Mihaileanu, 1998, France/Belgium/Netherlands/ Israel/Romania)

Triumph of the Spirit (Robert M. Young, 1989, USA)

Les Uns et les autres (*Bolero*, Claude Lelouch, 1981, France)

La Vita è bella (*Life is Beautiful*, Roberto Benigni, 1997, Italy)

Un vivant qui passe (*A Visitor from the Living*, Claude Lanzmann, 1997, France/ Germany)

Vrai faux passeport (*True False Passport*, Jean-Luc Godard, 2006, France)

War and Remembrance (Dan Curtis and Tommy Groszman, 1988, USA)

The Warsaw Ghetto (Hugh Burnett, 1968, UK)

Zyklon Portrait (Elida Schogt, 1999, Canada)

Bibliography

Aaron, M. (2007) 'Ethics and Spectatorship: Response, Responsibility and the Moving Image', in *Spectatorship: The Power of Looking On*. London: Wallflower Press, 87–123.

About, I. (2001) 'La Photographie au service du système concentrationnaire national-socialiste (1933–1945)', in C. Chéroux (ed.) *Mémoire des camps: photographies des camps de concentration et d'extermination nazies (1933–1999)*. Paris: Marval, 29–53.

Adorno, T. (1973) 'Meditationen zur Metaphysik', in *Gesammelte Schriften*, 21 vols, XI. Frankfurt am Main: Suhrkamp, 354–400.

_____ (1974) 'Engagement', in *Gesammelte Schriften*, 21 vols, XI. Frankfurt am Main: Suhrkamp, 409–30.

_____ (1977) 'Kulturkritik und Gesellschaft', in *Gesammelte Schriften*, 21 vols, X.I. Frankfurt am Main: Suhrkamp, 11–30.

Agamben, G. (1999) *Remnants of Auschwitz: The Witness and the Archive*, trans. D. Heller-Roazen. New York: Zone.

Alphen, E. van (1997) *Caught by History: Holocaust Effects in Contemporary Art, Literature, and Theory*. Stanford, CA: Stanford University Press.

Améry, J. (1980) *At the Mind's Limits: Contemplations by a Survivor on Auschwitz and its Realities*, trans. S. and S. P. Rosenfeld. Bloomington: Indiana University Press.

Antelme, R. (1957 [1947]) *L'Espèce humaine*. Paris: Gallimard.

Arendt, H. (1964) *Eichmann in Jerusalem: A Report on the Banality of Evil*. New York: Viking.

Arthur, P. (1998) 'On the Virtues and Limitations of Collage', *Documentary Box*, 11. Online. Available at: http://www.yidff.jp/docbox/11/box11-1-e.html (accessed 3 March 2006).

Aumont, J. (1992) *Du visage au cinéma*. Paris: Cahiers du cinéma.

_____ (1999) *Amnésies: fictions du cinéma d'après Jean-Luc Godard*. Paris: POL.

Avisar, I. (1988) *Screening the Holocaust: Cinema's Images of the Unimaginable*. Bloomington: Indiana University Press.

Baecque, A. de (1991) *Les Cahiers du cinéma: histoire d'une revue*, 2 vols. Paris: Cahiers du cinéma.

_____ (2000) 'Premières images des camps: quel cinéma après Auschwitz?', *Cahiers du cinéma*, November, hors série, 62–66.

_____ (2003) *La Cinéphilie: invention d'un regard, histoire d'une culture 1944–1968*. Paris: Fayard.

Baecque, A. de and C. Delage (eds) (1998) *De l'histoire au cinéma*. Brussels: Complexe.

Baecque, A. de and C. Vassé (2000) 'Les Photos jaunies ne m'émeuvent pas' [interview with Alain Resnais], *Cahiers du cinéma*, November, hors série, 70–5.

Baer, U. (2002) *Spectral Evidence: The Photography of Trauma*. Cambridge, MA and London: MIT Press.

Barthes, R. (1980) *La Chambre claire: note sur la photographie*. Paris: Gallimard.

Bartov, O. (1996) *Murder in our Midst: The Holocaust, Industrial Killing, and Representation*. New York and Oxford: Oxford University Press.

_____ (2005) *The 'Jew' in Cinema: From 'The Golem' to 'Don't Touch My Holocaust'*. Bloomington: Indiana University Press.

Baudrillard, J. (2002) *L'Esprit du terrorisme*. Paris: Galilée.

Bauman, Z. (1993) *Postmodern Ethics*. Oxford: Blackwell.

Beauvoir, S. de (1985) 'La Mémoire de l'horreur', in C. Lanzmann *Shoah*. Paris: Fayard, 7–10.

Beddock, F. (1988) *L'Héritage de l'oubli: de Freud à Claude Lanzmann*. Nice: Z'Éditions.

Bellour, R. and M. L. Bandy (eds) (1992) *Jean-Luc Godard: Son + Image, 1974–1991*. New York: Museum of Modern Art.

Benayoun, R. (1980) 'Les Rendez-vous manqués', in *Alain Resnais: arpenteur de l'imaginaire de Hiroshima à Mélo*. Paris: Stock, 106–16.

Benslama, F. (2001) 'La Représentation et l'impossible', in J.-L. Nancy (ed.) *L'Art et la mémoire des camps: représenter exterminer*. Paris: Seuil, 59–80.

Bensoussan, G. (2000) 'La Shoah, fait d'histoire', *Le Monde*, 7 July, 15.

_____ (2003) *Auschwitz en héritage? D'un bon usage de la mémoire*. Paris: Mille et une nuits.

Bergala, A. (1999) *Nul mieux que Godard*. Paris: Cahiers du cinéma.

Bergoffen, D. B. (2000) 'Improper Sites', in A. Rosenberg, J. R. Watson and D. Linke (eds) *Contemporary Portrayals of Auschwitz: Philosophical Challenges*. Amherst, NY: Humanity Books, 27–42.

Bernstein, M. A. (1994) *Foregone Conclusions: Against Apocalyptic History*. Berkeley and London: University of California Press.

Bersani, L. and U. Dutoit (1993) *Arts of Impoverishment: Beckett, Rothko, Resnais.* Cambridge, MA: Harvard University Press.

Besançon, A. (1994) *L'Image interdite: une histoire intellectuelle de l'iconoclasme.* Paris: Gallimard.

Bettelheim, B. (1960) *The Informed Heart.* Glencoe, IL: Free Press.

Blouin, P., F. Nouchi and C. Tesson (2001) 'Sur le courage' [interview with Claude Lanzmann], *Cahiers du cinéma*, 561, 46–57.

Blümlinger, C. and K. Sierek (2001) *Das Gesicht im Zeitalter des bewegten Bilders.* Vienna: Sonderzahl.

Boltanski, L. (1993) *La Souffrance à distance: morale humanitaire, médias et politique.* Paris: Métailié.

Bonnaud, F. and A. Viviant (1998) 'La légende du siècle' [interview with Jean-Luc Godard], *Les Inrockuptibles*, 21 October, 20–8.

Botting, F. and S. Wilson (2001) *The Tarantinian Ethics.* London: Sage.

Bruzzi, S. (2000) 'The Woman's Voice: *Sunless*', in *New Documentary: A Critical Introduction.* New York and London: Routledge, 57–64.

Burdeau E. and C. Tesson (2000) 'Avenir(s) du cinéma' [interview with Jean-Luc Godard] *Cahiers du cinéma*, April, hors série, 8–19.

Burke, P. (2001) *Eyewitnessing: The Uses of Images as Historical Evidence.* London: Reaktion.

Burleigh, M. (1997) *Ethics and Extermination.* Cambridge: Cambridge University Press.

Butler, J. (1990) *Gender Trouble: Feminism and the Subversion of Identity.* New York and London: Routledge.

Camus, A. (1956) *La Chute.* Paris: Gallimard.

Cantor, J. (1996) 'Death and the Image', in C. Warren (ed.) *Beyond Document: Essays on Nonfiction Film.* Hanover, NH and London: University Press of New England, 23–49.

Carr, J. (1985) 'A Muted Godard Awaits US Bow of Hail Mary', *Boston Globe*, 7 October, 28.

Caruth, C. (ed.) (1995) *Trauma: Explorations in Memory.* Baltimore, MD and London: Johns Hopkins University Press.

____ (1996) *Unclaimed Experience: Trauma, Narrative, and History.* Baltimore, MD and London: Johns Hopkins University Press.

Cayrol, J. (1946) *Poèmes de la nuit et du brouillard; suivis de Larmes publiques.* Paris: P. Seghers.

Celan, P. (1983 [1975]) *Gedichte, 2 vols. Frankfurt am Main: Suhrkamp.*

Chapuis, F. (2001) 'L'Horreur vue de l'intérieur', *Télérama*, 13 January, 2661, 6–10.

Chéroux, C. (2001) 'Les Chambres noires ou l'image absente?', in C. Chéroux (ed.) *Mémoire des camps: photographies des camps de concentration et d'extermination nazies (1933–1999).* Paris: Marval, 213–17.

Chevrie, M. and H. Le Roux (1990 [1985]) 'Le Lieu et la parole' [interview with Claude Lanzmann] in B. Cuau, M. Deguy, R. Ertel, S. Felman, E. de Fontenay, E. Huppert, G. Koch, S. Naïr, M. Ophuls, A. Dayan-Rosenman, P. Vidal-Naquet, A. Brumberg, N. Ascherson, T. Garton Ash, J. Kuron, J.-C. Szurek and C. Lanzmann (eds). *Au sujet de 'Shoah', le film de Claude Lanzmann*. Paris: Belin, 293–305.

Cheyette, B. (1994) 'The Holocaust in the Picture-House', *Times Literary Supplement*, 18 February, 18–19.

_____ (1997) 'The Uncertain Certainty of Schindler's List', in Y. Loshitzky (ed.) *Spielberg's Holocaust: Critical Perspectives on 'Schindler's List'*. Bloomington: Indiana University Press, 226–38.

Ciment, M. and S. Goudet (1999) 'Jean-Luc Godard: des traces du cinéma', *Positif*, 456, 50–7.

Clendinnen, I. (1999) *Reading the Holocaust*. Cambridge: Cambridge University Press.

Clover, C. (1992) *Men, Women, and Chain Saws: Gender in the Modern Horror Film*. Princeton, NJ: Princeton University Press.

Cole, T. (1999) *Images of the Holocaust: The Myth of the 'Shoah Business'*. London: Duckworth.

Colombat, A. P. (1993) *The Holocaust in French Film*. New Jersey: Scarecrow Press.

Comolli, J.-L. (1997) 'Le Miroir à deux faces', in J.-L. Comolli and J. Rancière *Arrêt sur histoire*. Paris: Éditions du Centre Pompidou, 11–45.

Cooper, S. (2006) *Selfless Cinema?: Ethics and French Documentary*. Oxford: Legenda.

Coquio, C. (ed.) (1999) *Parler des camps, penser les génocides*. Paris: Albin Michel.

Cowie, E. (1997a) *Representing the Woman: Cinema and Psychoanalysis*. Basingstoke: Macmillan.

_____ (1997b) 'The Spectacle of Reality and Documentary Film', *Documentary Box*, 10. Online. Available at: http://www.yidff.jp/docbox/10/box10-1-e.html (accessed 3 March 2006).

_____ (2000) 'Traumatic Memories of Remembering and Forgetting', in M. Rossington and A. Whitehead (eds) *Between the Psyche and the Polis: Refiguring History in Literature and Theory*. Aldershot: Ashgate, 191–204.

Crignon, P. (2004) 'Figuration: Emmanuel Levinas and the Image', *Yale French Studies*, 104, 100–25.

Critchley, S. (1992) *The Ethics of Deconstruction: Derrida and Levinas*. Oxford: Blackwell.

Crowley, M. (2003) *Robert Antelme: Humanity, Community, Testimony*. Oxford: Legenda.

_____ (2005) 'Frightful, Yes Frightful!', *French Studies*, 59, 1, 17–24.

Cuau, B., M. Deguy, R. Ertel, S. Felman, E. de Fontenay, E. Huppert, G. Koch, S. Naïr, M. Ophuls, A. Dayan-Rosenman, P. Vidal-Naquet, A. Brumberg, N. Ascherson, T. Garton Ash, J. Kuron, J.-C. Szurek and C. Lanzmann (1990) (eds) *Au sujet de 'Shoah', le film de Claude Lanzmann*. Paris: Belin.

Damisch, H. (2005) 'Montage du désastre', *Cahiers du cinéma*, 599, 72–4, 76–8.

Daney, S. (1991a) *Devant la recrudescence des vols de sacs à main: cinéma, télévision, information*. Lyon: Aléas.

_____ (1991b) 'Du visuel au visage', *Libération*, 4 February, 15.

_____ (1992) 'Le Travelling de *Kapo*', *Trafic*, 4, 5–19.

Davis, C. (1996) *Levinas: An Introduction*. Oxford: Polity.

_____ (2000) *Ethical Issues in Twentieth-Century French Fiction: Killing the Other*. Basingstoke: Macmillan.

_____ (2004) 'Can the Dead Speak to Us? De Man, Levinas and Agamben', *Culture, Theory & Critique*, 45, 1, 77–89.

Davis, J. (ed.) (1986) *Film, History and the Jewish Experience: A Reader*. London: The National Film Theatre.

Dawidowicz, L. (1978) 'Visualizing the Warsaw Ghetto: Nazi Images of Jews Refiltered by the BBC', *Shoah: A Review of Holocaust Studies and Commemorations*, 1, 1, 5–6, 17–18.

Debray, R. (1992) *Vie et mort de l'image: une histoire du regard en Occident*. Paris: Gallimard.

Deleuze, G. (1983) *Cinéma 1: l'image-mouvement*. Paris: Minuit.

_____ (1985) *Cinéma 2: l'image-temps*. Paris: Minuit.

Delfour, J.-J. (2000a) 'La Pellicule maudite: sur la figuration du réel de la *Shoah*', *L'Arche*, 508, 14–17.

_____ (2000b) 'Bénie soit la belle vie à Auschwitz?', *Trafic*, 35, 61–80.

_____ (2000–01) 'La Shoah, fait métaphysique', *Temps modernes*, 611–12, 327–32.

Delorme, M.-L. and G. Herzlich (2000) 'L'Écriture ravive la mémoire' [interview with Jorge Semprun], *Le Monde des débats*, 14, 11–13.

Derrida, J. (1993) *Memoirs of the Blind: The Self-Portrait and Other Ruins*, trans. P.-A. Brault and M. Naas. Chicago: University of Chicago Press.

_____ (1995) *Mal d'archive: une impression freudienne*. Paris: Galilée.

_____ (1998) *Demeure: Maurice Blanchot*. Paris: Galilée.

Didier, E., B. Hazan, C. Chalier, J. J. Moscovitz, F. Beddock, G. Szwec, A. M. Houdebine, L. Kaplan, G. Rabinovitch, D. Oppenheim, S. Reznik, E. Macedo, P. Mathis, A.-L. Stern and C. Lanzmann (1990) *Shoah, le film: des psychanalystes écrivent*. Paris: J. Grancher.

Didi-Huberman, G. (2001) 'Images malgré tout', in C. Chéroux (ed.) *Mémoire des camps: photographies des camps de concentration et d'extermination nazies (1933–1999)*. Paris: Marval, 219–41.

_____ (2003) *Images malgré tout*. Paris: Minuit.

Dieckmann, K. (1993) 'Godard's Counter Memory', *Art in America*, 81, 10, 65–7.

Domarchi, J., J. Doniol-Valcroze, J.-L. Godard, P. Kast, J. Rivette, E. Rohmer (1959) 'Hiroshima, notre amour', *Cahiers du cinéma*, 97, 1–18.

Doneson, J. (1987) *The Holocaust in American Film*. Philadelphia: The Jewish Publication Society.

Douchevsky, A. (n. d.) 'L'Épreuve de la représentation: mémoire et historiographie de la Shoah'. Online. Available at: http://controv.free.fr/pdf/ricoeur.pdf (accessed 12 August 2006).

Downing, L. (2004) 'The Ethics of the Couple', in *Patrice Leconte*. Manchester: Manchester University Press, 106–30.

Dubois, P. (2002) '*La Jetée* ou le cinématogramme de la conscience', in P. Dubois (ed.) *Recherches sur Chris Marker*. Paris: Presses Sorbonne Nouvelle, 8–45.

Dulaure, A. and C. Parnet (1985) 'Entretien avec Jean-Luc Godard', *L'Autre journal*, 2, 12–27.

Duras, M. (1960) *Hiroshima mon amour: scénario et dialogues*. Paris: Gallimard.

Eaglestone, R. (2002) 'On Giorgio Agamben's Holocaust', *Paragraph*, 25, 2, 52–67.

Elsaesser, T. (1996) 'Subject Positions, Speaking Positions: From *Holocaust, Our Hitler*, and *Heimat* to *Shoah* and *Schindler's List*', in V. Sobchack (ed.) *The Persistence of History: Cinema, Television, and the Modern Event*. New York and London: Routledge, 145–83.

_____ (2001) 'Postmodernism as Mourning Work', *Screen*, 42, 2, 193–201.

Epstein, J. and L. H. Lefkovitz (eds) (2001) *Shaping Losses: Cultural Memory and the Holocaust*. Urbana, IL: University of Illinois Press.

Evans, C. and L. Gamman (1995) 'The Gaze Revisited or Revisiting Queer Viewing', in P. Burston and C. Richardson (eds) *A Queer Romance: Lesbians, Gay Men and Popular Culture*. New York and London: Routledge, 13–56.

Felman, S. (1992a) 'Education and Crisis, or the Vicissitudes of Teaching', in S. Felman and D. Laub *Testimony: Crises of Witnessing in Literature, Psychoanalysis, and History*. New York and London: Routledge, 1–56.

_____ (1992b) 'The Fall, or the Betrayal of the Witness', in S. Felman and D. Laub *Testimony: Crises of Witnessing in Literature, Psychoanalysis, and History*. New York and London: Routledge, 165–203.

_____ (1992c) 'The Return of the Voice: Claude Lanzmann's *Shoah*', in S. Felman and D. Laub *Testimony: Crises of Witnessing in Literature, Psychoanalysis, and History*. New York and London: Routledge, 204–83.

Felman, S. and D. Laub (1992) 'Foreward', in *Testimony: Crises of Witnessing in Literature, Psychoanalysis, and History*. New York and London: Routledge, xiii–xx.

Ferro, M. (1973) 'De l'interview chez Ophuls, Harris et Sédouy', in *Cinéma et histoire*. Paris: Denoël, 53–7.

Finkelstein, N. G. (2000) *The Holocaust Industry: Reflections on the Exploitation of Jewish Suffering*. London: Verso.

Flitterman-Lewis, S. (1998) 'Documenting the Ineffable: Terror and Memory in Alain Resnais's *Night and Fog*', in B. K. Grant and J. Sloniowski (eds) *Documenting the Documentary: Close Readings of Documentary Film and Video*. Detroit, MI: Wayne State University Press, 204–22.

Forges, J.-F. (1997) *Éduquer contre Auschwitz: histoire et mémoire*. Paris: ESF.

_____ (2000) '*Shoah*: histoire et mémoire', *Temps modernes*, 608, 30–41.

Frappat, H. (2001) 'Les Chemins de la liberté', *Cahiers du cinéma*, 561, 77–8.

Friedländer, S. (1982) *Reflets du nazisme*. Paris: Seuil.

_____ (1992) 'Introduction', in S. Friedländer (ed.) *Probing the Limits of Representation: Nazism and the 'Final Solution'*. Cambridge, MA and London: Harvard University Press, 1–21.

Frodon, J.-M. (1997a) 'Le long voyage de *Shoah* à travers l'actualité et la mémoire', *Le Monde*, 12 June, 27.

_____ (1997b) 'Ne pas comprendre a été ma loi d'airain' [interview with Claude Lanzmann], *Le Monde*, 12 June, 27.

_____ (1999) '"Le fameux débat": Lanzmann–Godard: le parti des mots contre le parti des images', *Le Monde* (*Supplément Télévision*), 28 June, 5.

_____ (2001a) 'On ne peut pas raconter une histoire sans faire de l'Histoire' [interview with Jean-Luc Godard], *Le Monde*, 17 May, 29.

_____ (2001b) 'L'Éphémère Silence des images', *Le Monde*, 13 November, 18.

_____ (2004) 'Juste des images', *Cahiers du cinéma*, 587, 19–22.

_____ (ed.) (2007a) *Le Cinéma et la Shoah: un art à l'épreuve de la tragédie du 20e siècle*. Paris: Cahiers du cinéma.

_____ (2007b) 'Le Travail du cinéaste' [interview with Claude Lanzmann], in *Le Cinéma et la Shoah: un art à l'épreuve de la tragédie du 20e siècle*. Paris: Cahiers du cinema, 111–25.

Frodon, J.-M., F. Delay, M.-J. Mondzain, J. Narboni, J. Rancière, G. Agamben (1995) 'Face au cinéma et à l'Histoire, à propos de Jean-Luc Godard', *Le Monde* (*Supplément Livres*), 6 October, i, x–xi.

Frontisi-Ducroux, F. (1995) *Du masque au visage*. Paris: Flammarion.

Furman, N. (1995) 'The Languages of Pain in *Shoah*', in L. D. Kritzman (ed.) *Auschwitz and After: Race, Culture, and 'the Jewish Question' in France*. New York and London: Routledge, 299–312.

Fuss, D. (1995) *Identification Papers*. New York and London: Routledge.

Gaillac, J.-Y., T. Morgue and J.-P. Guerand (2001) 'Godard: le grandeur d'un petit commerce de cinema', *Epok*, 16, 8–15.

Gantheret, F. (1990 [1986]) 'Les Non-lieux de la mémoire' [interview with Claude Lanzmann] in B. Cuau, M. Deguy, R. Ertel, S. Felman, E. de Fontenay, E. Huppert, G. Koch, S. Naïr, M. Ophuls, A. Dayan-Rosenman, P. Vidal-Naquet, A. Brumberg, N. Ascherson, T. Garton Ash, J. Kuron, J.-C. Szurek and

C. Lanzmann (eds). *Au sujet de 'Shoah', le film de Claude Lanzmann*. Paris: Belin, 280–92.

Gillet, C. (2002) 'Visages de Marker', in P. Dubois (ed.) *Recherches sur Chris Marker*. Paris: Presses Sorbonne Nouvelle, 74–82.

Ginsberg, T. (2004) 'Towards a Critical Pedagogy of Holocaust and Film', *Review of Education, Pedagogy, and Cultural Studies*, 26, 1, 47–59.

Godard, J.-L. (1963) 'Feu sur Les Carabiniers', *Cahiers du cinéma*, 146, 1–4.

_____ (1980) *Introduction à une véritable histoire du cinéma*. Paris: Albatros.

_____ (1996) 'À Propos de cinéma et d'histoire', *Trafic*, 18, 28–32.

_____ (1998a) *Jean-Luc Godard par Jean-Luc Godard*, ed. A. Bergala, 2 vols. Paris: Cahiers du cinéma.

_____ (1998b) *Histoire(s) du cinéma: introduction à une véritable histoire du cinéma la seule la vraie*, 4 vols. Paris: Gallimard.

Godard, J.-L. and Y. Ishaghpour (2000) *Archéologie du cinéma et mémoire du siècle: dialogue*. Tours: Farrago.

Godmilow, J. (1997) 'How Real is the Reality in Documentary Film?', *History and Theory*, 36, 4, 80–101.

Goetschel, W. (1997) 'Zur Sprachlosigkeit von Bildern', in M. Köppen and K. R. Scherpe (eds) *Bilder des Holocaust: Literatur, Film, bildende Kunst*. Köln: Böhlau, 131–44.

Goudet, S. (1999) 'Splendeurs et apories de la dernière écume', *Positif*, 456, 58–9.

Greene, N. (1999) *Landscapes of Loss: The National Past in Postwar French Cinema*. Princeton, NJ: Princeton University Press.

Greif, G. (2005) *We Wept Without Tears: Testimonies of the Jewish Sonderkommando from Auschwitz*. New Haven, CT and London: Yale University Press.

Gross, L., J. S. Katz and J. Ruby (eds) (1988) *Image Ethics: The Moral Rights of Subjects in Photographs, Film and Television*. Oxford: Oxford University Press.

Guerrin, M. (2001a) 'Entre mémoire et histoire des camps, le rôle de la photographie', *Le Monde*, 19 January, 28.

_____ (2001b) 'La question n'est pas celle du document, mais celle de la vérité' [interview with Claude Lanzmann], *Le Monde*, 19 January, 29.

Haggith, T. (2005) 'Filming the Liberation of Bergen-Belsen', in T. Haggith and J. Newman (eds) *Holocaust and the Moving Image: Representations in Film and Television since 1933*. London: Wallflower Press, 33–49.

Hand, S. (ed.) (1996) *Facing the Other: The Ethics of Emmanuel Levinas*. Richmond: Curzon.

Hansen, M. B. (1996) '*Schindler's List* is Not *Shoah*: Second Commandment, Popular Modernism and Public Memory', *Critical Inquiry*, 22, 2, 292–312.

Hartman, G. H. (1996) *The Longest Shadow: In the Aftermath of the Holocaust*. Bloomington: Indiana University Press.

_____ (2000) 'Memory.com: Tele-Suffering and Testimony in the Dot Com Era', *Raritan*, 19, 3, 1–18.

Henochsberg, M. (2000) 'Loin d'Auschwitz, Roberto Benigni, bouffon malin', *Temps modernes*, 608, 42–59.

Herzlich, G. (2000) 'Parler pour les morts' [interview with Claude Lanzmann], *Le Monde des débats*, 14, 14–16.

Hilberg, R. (1985) *The Destruction of the European Jews*. New York: Holmes and Meier.

Hirsch, J. (2004) *Afterimage: Film, Trauma, and the Holocaust*. Philadelphia: Temple University Press.

Hirsch, M. and L. Spitzer (1993) 'Gendered Translations: Claude Lanzmann's *Shoah*', in M. Cooke and A. Woollacott (eds) *Gendering War Talk*. Princeton: Princeton University Press, 3–19.

Hochhuth, R. (1963) *Der Stellvertreter: ein christliches Trauerspiel*. Reinbek bei Hamburg: Rowohlt.

Horowitz, S. R. (1992) 'Rethinking Holocaust Testimony: The Making and Unmaking of the Witness', *Cardozo Studies in Law and Literature*, 4, 1, 45–68.

_____ (1997a) *Voicing the Void: Muteness and Memory in Holocaust Fiction*. Albany: State University of New York Press.

_____ (1997b) 'But Is It Good for the Jews? Spielberg's Schindler and the Aesthetics of Atrocity', in Y. Loshitzky (ed.) *Spielberg's Holocaust: Critical Perspectives on 'Schindler's List'*. Bloomington: Indiana University Press, 119–39.

Howland, J. (1995) 'Reflections on Lanzmann's *Shoah*', *Proteus*, 12, 2, 42–6.

Insdorf, A. (1983) *Indelible Shadows: Film and the Holocaust*. New York: Random House.

Jay, M. (1993) *Downcast Eyes: The Denigration of Vision in Twentieth-Century Thought*. Berkeley and London: University of California Press.

Jeancolas, J.-P. (1990) 'Beneath the Despair, the Show Goes On: Marcel Carné's *Les Enfants du paradis*', in S. Hayward and G. Vincendeau (eds) *French Film: Texts and Contexts*. New York and London: Routledge, 117–26.

Jousse, T. (2001) 'New York, 11 septembre, l'envers du spectacle', *Cahiers du cinéma*, 561, 10–11.

Joyard, O. (2001) '11 septembre, image zéro', *Cahiers du cinéma*, 561, 45.

Kaes, A. (1989) *From Hitler to Heimat: The Return of History as Film*. Cambridge, MA and London: Harvard University Press.

Kaganski, S. and F. Bonnaud (1998) 'Témoin de l'immémorial' [interview with Claude Lanzmann] *Les Inrockuptibles*, 28 January, 14–21.

Kandel, L., R. Redeker and G. Wajcman (2000) 'La Shoah face à l'Histoire', *Le Monde*, 27 July, 12.

Keilbach, J. (2003) 'Des images nouvelles', *Trafic*, 47, 71–82.

Khalfa, J. (2002) 'Seeing the Present', in S. Kemp and L. Saxton (eds) *Seeing Things: Vision, Perception and Interpretation in French Studies*. London and Bern: Peter Lang, 235–49.

Knaap, E. van der (2006) *Uncovering the Holocaust: The International Reception of Night and Fog*. London: Wallflower Press.

Koch, G. (1990) 'Transformations esthétiques dans la représentation de l'inimaginable', trans. C. Weinzorn, in B. Cuau, M. Deguy, R. Ertel, S. Felman, E. de Fontenay, E. Huppert, G. Koch, S. Naïr, M. Ophuls, A. Dayan-Rosenman, P. Vidal-Naquet, A. Brumberg, N. Ascherson, T. Garton Ash, J. Kuron, J.-C. Szurek and C. Lanzmann (eds). *Au sujet de 'Shoah', le film de Claude Lanzmann.* Paris: Belin, 157–66.

_____ (1993a) 'Der Engel des Vergessens und die Black Box der Faktizität: Zur Gedächtniskonstruktion in Claude Lanzmanns Film *Shoah*', in A. Haverkamp, R. Lachmann and R. Herzog (eds) *Memoria: Vergessen und Erinnern.* Munich: Fink, 67–77.

_____ (1993b) 'Mimesis and Bilderverbot', *Screen*, 34, 3, 211–22.

Köppen, M. (1997) 'Von Effekten des Authentischen – *Schindler's List*: Film und Holocaust', in M. Köppen and K. R. Scherpe (eds) *Bilder des Holocaust: Literatur, Film, bildende Kunst.* Köln: Böhlau, 145–70.

Kristeva, J. (1987) *Soleil noir: dépression et mélancolie.* Paris: Gallimard.

Kritzman, L. D. (ed.) (1995) *Auschwitz and After: Race, Culture, and 'the Jewish Question' in France.* New York and London: Routledge.

Kulakowska, E. (2000) 'Des Personnages dans la tourmente' [interview with Andrzej Wajda], *Le Monde des débats*, 14, 16–17.

Lacan, J. (1973) *Les Quatre Concepts fondamentaux de la psychanalyse.* Paris: Seuil.

LaCapra, D. (1994) *Representing the Holocaust: History, Theory, Trauma.* Ithaca and London: Cornell University Press.

_____ (1998) *History and Memory after Auschwitz.* Ithaca: Cornell University Press.

_____ (2001) *Writing History, Writing Trauma.* Baltimore, MD and London: Johns Hopkins University Press.

Landes, D. (1983) 'Modesty and Self-Dignity in Holocaust Films', in A. Grobman and D. Landes (eds) *Genocide: Critical Issues of the Holocaust.* Los Angeles: Simon Wiesenthal Center; New York: Rossel Books, 11–13.

Lang, B. (1992) 'The Representation of Limits', in S. Friedländer (ed.) *Probing the Limits of Representation: Nazism and the 'Final Solution'.* Cambridge, MA: Harvard University Press, 300–17.

_____ (1999) *The Future of the Holocaust: Between History and Memory.* Ithaca and London: Cornell University Press.

_____ (2000) *Holocaust Representation: Art Within the Limits of History and Ethics.* Baltimore: Johns Hopkins University Press.

Langer, L. L. (1995) *Admitting the Holocaust.* New York and Oxford: Oxford University Press.

Langford, B. (1999) '"You Cannot Look At This": Thresholds Of Unrepresentability In Holocaust Film', *Journal of Holocaust Education*, 8, 3, 23–40.

Lanzmann, C. (1980) 'Preface', in F. Müller *Trois ans dans une chambre à gaz d'Auschwitz*, trans. P. Desolneux. Paris: Pygmalion, 9–17.

_____ (1985) *Shoah.* Paris: Fayard.

_____ (1990a [1988]) 'Hier ist kein Warum', in B. Cuau, M. Deguy, R. Ertel, S. Felman, E. de Fontenay, E. Huppert, G. Koch, S. Naïr, M. Ophuls, A. Dayan-Rosenman, P. Vidal-Naquet, A. Brumberg, N. Ascherson, T. Garton Ash, J. Kuron, J.-C. Szurek and C. Lanzmann (eds). *Au sujet de 'Shoah', le film de Claude Lanzmann*. Paris: Belin, 279.

_____ (1990b [1979]) 'De l'holocauste à Holocauste ou comment s'en débarrasser', in B. Cuau, M. Deguy, R. Ertel, S. Felman, E. de Fontenay, E. Huppert, G. Koch, S. Naïr, M. Ophuls, A. Dayan-Rosenman, P. Vidal-Naquet, A. Brumberg, N. Ascherson, T. Garton Ash, J. Kuron, J.-C. Szurek and C. Lanzmann (eds). *Au sujet de 'Shoah', le film de Claude Lanzmann*. Paris: Belin, 306–16.

_____ (1991) 'Seminar with Claude Lanzmann, 11 April 1990', ed. D. Rodowick, *Yale French Studies*, 79, 82–99.

_____ (1994) 'Holocauste, la représentation impossible', *Le Monde* (*Supplément Arts–Spectacles*), 3 March, i, vii.

_____ (1995) 'The Obscenity of Understanding', ed. C. Caruth and D. Rodowick, in C. Caruth (ed.) *Trauma: Explorations in Memory*. Baltimore, MD and London: Johns Hopkins University Press, 200–20.

_____ (2001a) 'Le Monument contre l'archive?', *Cahiers de médiologie*, 11, 271–9.

_____ (2001b) 'The Disaster', *Temps modernes*, 615–16, 1–3.

_____ (2002) 'Réponse à Marcel Ophuls', *Cahiers du cinéma*, 567, 54–55.

Laub, D. (1992) 'An Event Without a Witness: Truth, Testimony and Survival', in S. Felman and D. Laub *Testimony: Crises of Witnessing in Literature, Psychoanalysis, and History*. New York and London: Routledge, 75–92.

Lemaître, B. (2002) '*Sans soleil*, le travail de l'imaginaire', in P. Dubois (ed.) *Recherches sur Chris Marker*. Paris: Presses Sorbonne Nouvelle, 60–73.

Leutrat, J.-L. (1994) '*Histoire(s) du cinéma*: comment devenir le maître d'un souvenir', *Cinémathèque*, 5, 28–39.

Levi, P. (1966) *If This is a Man*, trans. S. Woolf. London: Bodley Head.

_____ (1988) *The Drowned and the Saved*, trans. R. Rosenthal. London: Michael Joseph.

Levinas, E. (1969) *Totality and Infinity: An Essay on Exteriority*, trans. A. Lingis. Pittsburgh: Duquesne University Press.

_____ (1982) *Éthique et infini: dialogues avec Philippe Nemo*. Paris: A. Fayard et Radio-France.

_____ (1984a) 'Interdit de la représentation et "Droits de l'homme"', in A. and J.-J. Rassial (eds) *L'Interdit de la représentation. Colloque de Montpellier, 1981*. Paris: Seuil, 107–13.

_____ (1984b) 'Paix et proximité', in J. Rolland (ed.) *Cahiers de la nuit surveillée*, 'Emmanuel Levinas', 3, 339–46.

_____ (1991) *Entre nous: essais sur le penser-à-l'autre*. Paris: Grasset et Fasquelle.

Liebman, S. (ed.) (2007) *Claude Lanzmann's 'Shoah': Key Essays*. New York and Oxford: Oxford University Press.

Lindeperg, S. (1997) *Les Écrans de l'ombre: la Seconde Guerre mondiale dans le cinéma français (1944–1969)*. Paris: CNRS.

_____ (2000) *Clio de 5 à 7. Les Actualités filmées de la Libération: archives du futur.* Paris: CNRS.

_____ (2007) *'Nuit et brouillard': un film dans l'histoire*. Paris: Odile Jacob.

Liss, A. (1998) *Trespassing through Shadows: Memory, Photography, and the Holocaust*. Minneapolis: University of Minnesota Press.

Listoe, D. (2006) 'Seeing Nothing: Allegory and the Holocaust's Absent Dead', *SubStance*, 110, 35, 2, 51–70.

Lopate, P. (2001) '*Sobibor, October 14, 1943, 4pm*', *Film Comment*, 37, 6, 67–70.

Loshitzky, Y. (1997) 'Holocaust Others: Spielberg's *Schindler's List* versus Lanzmann's *Shoah*', in Y. Loshitzky (ed.) *Spielberg's Holocaust: Critical Perspectives on 'Schindler's List'*. Bloomington: Indiana University Press, 104–18.

_____ (1999) 'Fantastic Realism: *Schindler's List* as Docudrama', in A. Rosenthal (ed.) *Why Docudrama? Fact–Fiction on Film and TV*. Carbondale, IL: Southern Illinois University Press, 357–69.

Lowy, V. (2001) *L'Histoire infilmable: les camps d'extermination nazis à l'écran*. Paris: L'Harmattan.

Lupton, C. (2005) *Chris Marker: Memories of the Future*. London: Reaktion.

Lyotard, J.-F. (1983) *Le Différend*. Paris: Minuit.

MacCabe, C. (2003) *Godard: A Portrait of the Artist at 70*. London: Bloomsbury.

Mandelbaum, J. (1997a) 'Trente films sur les génocides', *Le Monde*, 12 June, 27.

_____ (1997b) 'Des yeux pour ne pas voir', *Le Monde* (*Supplément Radio–Télévision*), 10 November, 5.

_____ (2001) 'La Shoah et ces images qui nous manquent', *Le Monde*, 25 January, 17.

Mayne, J. (1990) *The Woman at the Keyhole: Feminism and Women's Cinema*. Bloomington: Indiana University Press.

_____ (1993) *Cinema and Spectatorship*. New York and London: Routledge.

Mesnard, P. (2000) *Consciences de la Shoah: critique des discours et des représentations*. Paris: Kimé.

_____ (2001) 'Représenter l'irreprésentable', *Télérama*, 13 January, 2661, 11–13.

Mesnard, P. and C. Kahan (2001) *Giorgio Agamben à l'épreuve d'Auschwitz: témoignages/interprétations*. Paris: Kimé.

Metz, C. (1982 [1977]) *The Imaginary Signifier: Psychoanalysis and the Cinema*, trans. C. Britton, A. Williams, B. Brewster and A. Guzetti. Bloomington: Indiana University Press.

Mikles, L. (2001) '*Sobibor, 14 octobre 1943, 16 heures*', *Positif*, 489, 61–2.

Moses, J. W. (1987) 'Vision Denied in *Night and Fog* and *Hiroshima mon amour*', *Literature/Film Quarterly*, 15, 3, 159–63.

Moullet, L. (1959) 'Sam Fuller sur les brisées de Marlowe', *Cahiers du cinéma*, 93, 11–19.

Müller, F. (1980) *Trois ans dans une chambre à gaz d'Auschwitz*, trans. P. Desol- neux. Paris: Pygmalion.

Mulvey, L. (1975) 'Visual Pleasure and Narrative Cinema', *Screen*, 16, 3, 6–18.

Nancy, J.-L. (2003 [2001]) 'La Représentation interdite', in *Au fond des images*. Paris: Galilée, 57–99.

Nerval, G. de (1958) *Œuvres*, ed. H. Lemaître, 2 vols. Paris: Garnier Frères.

Nezick, N. (1998) 'Le Travelling de *Kapo* ou le paradoxe de la morale', *Vertigo*, 17, 160–4.

Nichols, B. (1991) *Representing Reality: Issues and Concepts in Documentary*. Bloomington: Indiana University Press.

Niney, F. (2000) *L'Épreuve du réel à l'écran: essai sur le principe de réalité documen- taire*. Brussels: De Boeck.

Nouchi, F. (2001) 'Le jour où fut sauvée l'humanité', *Cahiers du cinéma*, 558, 20.

Novick, P. (2000) *The Holocaust and Collective Memory: The American Experi- ence*. London: Bloomsbury.

Olin, M. (1997) 'Lanzmann's *Shoah* and the Topography of the Holocaust Film', *Representations*, 57, 1–23.

Pagnoux, E. (2001) 'Reporter photographe à Auschwitz', *Temps modernes*, 613, 84–108.

Pauly, R. M. (1992) 'From Shoah to Holocaust: Image and Ideology in Alain Resnais's *Nuit et brouillard* and *Hiroshima mon amour*', *French Cultural Stud- ies*, 3, 9, 253–61.

Perec, G. (1996 [1963]) 'Robert Antelme ou la vérité de la littérature', in Rob- ert Antelme, *textes inédits sur 'L'Espèce humaine': essais et témoignages*. Paris: Gallimard, 173–90.

Perraud, A. (1999) 'Simplisme obscur et tendancieux' [interview with Claude Lanzmann], *Télérama*, 31 March, 2568, 32.

Pressac, J.-C. (1993) *Les Crématoires d'Auschwitz: la machinerie du meurtre de masse*. Paris: CNRS.

Pryluck, C. (1976) 'Ultimately We are All Outsiders: The Ethics of Documentary Filming', *Journal of the University Film Association*, 28, 1, 21–9.

Rabinowitz, P. (1994) *They Must Be Represented: The Politics of Documentary*. London: Verso.

Radstone, S. (2001) 'Trauma and Screen Studies: Opening the Debate', *Screen*, 42, 2, 188–93.

Rancière, J. (1997) 'L'Inoubliable', in J.-L. Comolli and J. Rancière *Arrêt sur his- toire*. Paris: Éditions du Centre Pompidou, 47–70.

_____ (1999) 'La Sainte et l'héritière: à propos des *Histoire(s) du cinéma*', *Cahiers du cinéma*, 537, 58–61.

_____ (2001) 'S'il y a de l'irreprésentable', in J.-L. Nancy (ed.) *L'Art et la mémoire des camps: représenter exterminer*. Paris: Seuil, 81–102.

_____ (2003) *Le Destin des images*. Paris: La Fabrique.

_____ (2006) *Film Fables*, trans. E. Battista. Oxford: Berg.

Renaud, Y. (2001) 'Donner des coups: la construction du lien social (3)', *Le Philosophoire*, 13, 107.

Renov, M. (1993) 'The Truth about Non-Fiction', in M. Renov (ed.) *Theorizing Documentary*. New York and London: Routledge, 1–11.

_____ (2004) *The Subject of Documentary*. Minneapolis: University of Minnesota Press.

Rivette, J. (1961) 'De l'abjection', *Cahiers du cinéma*, 120, 54–5.

Robson, K. (2006) '*Shoah*', in P. Powrie (ed.) *The Cinema of France*. London: Wallflower Press, 165–73.

Rochefoucauld, F. La (2002 [1678]) *Réflexions ou Sentences et Maximes morales et Réflexions diverses*. Paris: Honoré Champion.

Rodowick, D. N. (1997) *Gilles Deleuze's Time Machine*. Durham, NC: Duke University Press.

Ropars-Wuilleumier, M.-C. (1990) 'How History Begets Meaning: Alain Resnais' *Hiroshima mon amour*', in S. Hayward and G. Vincendeau (eds) *French Film: Texts and Contexts*. New York and London: Routledge, 173–85.

Rose, G. (1996) *Mourning Becomes the Law: Philosophy and Representation*. Cambridge: Cambridge University Press.

Rosenbaum, J. (1997) 'Bande-annonce pour les *Histoire(s) du cinéma* de Godard', *Trafic*, 21, 5–18.

Rosenberg, A., J. R. Watson and D. Linke (eds) (2000) *Contemporary Portrayals of Auschwitz: Philosophical Challenges*. Amherst, NY: Humanity Books.

Rosenheim, S. (1996) 'Interrotroning History: Errol Morris and the Documentary of the Future', in V. Sobchack (ed.) *The Persistence of History: Cinema, Television, and the Modern Event*. New York and London: Routledge, 219–34.

Rosenstone, R. A. (1995) *Visions of the Past: The Challenges of Film to Our Ideas of History*. Cambridge, MA and London: Harvard University Press.

Roth, J. K. (ed.) (1999) *Ethics after the Holocaust: Perspectives, Critiques, and Responses*. St. Paul, MN: Paragon.

Roth, M. S. (1995) '*Hiroshima mon amour*: You Must Remember This', in R. A. Rosenstone (ed.) *Revisioning History: Film and the Construction of a New Past*. Princeton: Princeton University Press, 91–101.

Rothberg, M. (2000) *Traumatic Realism: The Demands of Holocaust Representation*. Minneapolis: Minnesota University Press.

Rousseau, J.-J. (1985 [1755]) *Discours sur l'origine et les fondements de l'inégalité parmi les hommes*. Paris: Gallimard.

Rousso, H. (1987) *Le Syndrome de Vichy*. Paris: Seuil.

Ruby, J. (1988) 'The Ethics of Imagemaking; or, "They're Going to Put Me in the Movies. They're Going to Make a Big Star Out of Me…"', in A. Rosenthal (ed.) *New Challenges for Documentary*. Berkeley: University of California Press, 308–18.

Russell, C. (1999) '*Sans soleil*: The Infirmities of Time', in *Experimental Ethnography: The Work of Film in the Age of Video*. Durham, NC: Duke University Press, 301–11.

Samuels, R. (1998) *Hitchcock's Bi-textuality: Lacan, Feminisms and Queer Theory*. Albany: State University of New York Press.

Santner, E. L. (1990) *Stranded Objects: Mourning, Memory, and Film in Postwar Germany*. Ithaca and London: Cornell University Press.

Sartre, J.-P. (1943) *L'Être et le néant: essai d'ontologie phénoménologique*. Paris: Gallimard.

Saxton, L. (2007) 'Fragile Faces: Levinas and Lanzmann', *Film-Philosophy*, 11, 2, 1–14.

Schneider, S. (ed.) (1998) *Formen von Erinnerung: eine Diskussion mit Claude Lanzmann. Ein anderer Blick auf Gedenken, Erinnern und Erleben. Eine Tagung*. Marburg: Jonas.

Semprun, J. (1997) *Literature or Life*, trans. L. Coverdale. London: Viking.

Shandler, J. (1999) *While America Watches: Televising the Holocaust*. New York and Oxford: Oxford University Press.

Silverman, K. (1996) *The Threshold of the Visible World*. New York and London: Routledge.

Smith, G. (1996) 'Jean-Luc Godard', *Film Comment*, 32, 2, 31–41.

Sobchack, V. (1996) 'Introduction: History Happens' in V. Sobchack (ed.) *The Persistence of History: Cinema, Television, and the Modern Event*. New York and London: Routledge, 1–14.

_____ (2004a [1984]) 'Inscribing Ethical Space: Ten Propositions on Death, Representation, and Documentary', in *Carnal Thoughts: Embodiment and Moving Image Culture*. Berkeley: University of California Press, 226–57.

_____ (2004b) 'The Charge of the Real: Embodied Knowledge and Cinematic Consciousness', in *Carnal Thoughts: Embodiment and Moving Image Culture*. Berkeley and London: University of California Press, 258–85.

Sontag, S. (2003) *Regarding the Pain of Others*. New York: Farrar, Straus and Giroux.

_____ (2004) 'Regarding the Torture of Others', *New York Times Magazine*, 23 May, 24–9.

Sorlin, P. (2001) 'La Shoah: une représentation impossible', in J.-P. Bertin-Maghit and B. Fleury-Vilatte (eds) *Les Institutions de l'image*. Paris: EHESS, 179–86.

Staiger, J. (2000) *Perverse Spectators: The Practices of Film Reception*. New York and London: New York University Press.

Steiner, G. (1985) *Language and Silence: Essays 1958–1966*. London and Boston: Faber and Faber.

Struk, J. (2004) *Photographing the Holocaust: Interpretations of the Evidence*. London: I. B. Tauris.

Suleiman, S. R. (2006) *Crises of Memory and the Second World War*. Cambridge, MA and London: Harvard University Press.

Temple, M., J. S. Williams and M. Witt (eds) (2004) *For Ever Godard: The Work of Jean-Luc Godard 1950–2000*. London: Black Dog.

Tesson, C. (1998) 'Une machine à montrer l'invisible: conversation avec Bernard Eisenschitz à propos des *Histoire(s) du cinéma*', *Cahiers du cinéma*, 529, 52–6.

_____ (2001) 'Retour à l'envoyeur', *Cahiers du cinéma*, 561, 77–8.

Todorov, T. (1991) *Face à l'extrême*. Paris: Seuil.

Torner, C. (2001) *Shoah, une pédagogie de la mémoire*. Paris: Atelier.

Turim, M. (1989) *Flashbacks in Film: Memory and History*. New York and London: Routledge.

Vernant, J.-P. (1985) *La Mort dans les yeux: figures de l'Autre en Grèce ancienne*. Paris: Hachette.

Vernet, M. (1988) *Figures de l'absence: de l'invisible au cinéma*. Paris: Cahiers du cinéma.

Virilio, P. (1984) *Guerre et cinéma*. Paris: L'Étoile.

_____ (2002) *Ce qui arrive*. Paris: Galilée.

Vogt, E. (2005) 'S/Citing the Camp', in A. Norris (ed.) *Politics, Metaphysics, and Death: Essays on Giorgio Agamben's Homo sacer*. Durham, NC: Duke University Press, 74–106.

Wajcman, G. (1998) *L'Objet du siècle*. Lagrasse: Verdier.

_____ (1999) '"Saint Paul" Godard versus "Moïse" Lanzmann, le match', *Infini*, 65, 121–7.

_____ (2000) 'Oh Les Derniers Jours', *Temps modernes*, 608, 2–29.

_____ (2001) 'De la croyance photographique', *Temps modernes*, 613, 47–83.

Walker, J. (2005) *Trauma Cinema: Documenting Incest and the Holocaust*. Berkeley and London: University of California Press.

Weissman, G. (2004) *Fantasies of Witnessing: Postwar Efforts to Experience the Holocaust*. Ithaca and London: Cornell University Press.

Wiesel, E. (1978) 'Trivializing the Holocaust: Semi-Fact and Semi-Fiction', *New York Times* (*Arts and Leisure*), 16 April, 1, 29.

Wiesel, E. and J. Semprun (1995) *Se taire est impossible*. Paris: Mille et une nuits.

Wieviorka, A. (1998) *L'Ère du témoin*. Paris: Plon.

_____ (1992) *Déportation et genocide: entre la mémoire et l'oubli*. Paris: Plon.

Wilkomirski, B. (1995) *Bruchstücke*. Frankfurt am Main: Suhrkamp.

Williams, J. S. (1999) 'The Signs Amongst Us: Jean-Luc Godard's *Histoire(s) du cinéma*', *Screen*, 40, 3, 306–15.

_____ (2000) 'European Culture and Artistic Resistance in *Histoire(s) du cinéma*: Chapter 3A, "La Monnaie de l'absolu"', in J. S. Williams and M. Temple (eds) *The Cinema Alone: Essays on the Work of Jean-Luc Godard 1985–2000*. Amsterdam: Amsterdam University Press, 113–39.

Williams, J. S. and M. Temple (1998) 'Jean-Luc Godard: Images, Words, Histories', *Dalhousie French Studies*, 45, 99–110.

Williams, L. (1993) 'Mirrors without Memories: Truth, History and the New Documentary', *Film Quarterly*, 46, 3, 9–21.

Williams, L. (1995) 'Introduction', in L. Williams (ed.) *Viewing Positions: Ways of Seeing Film*. New Brunswick, NJ: Rutgers University Press, 1–20.

Wilson, E. (1999) *French Cinema Since 1950: Personal Histories*. London: Duckworth.

____ (2005) 'Material Remains: *Night and Fog*', *October*, 112, 1, 89–110.

____ (2006) *Alain Resnais*. Manchester: Manchester University Press.

Witt, M. (1999) 'The Death(s) of Cinema According to Godard', *Screen*, 40, 3, 331–46.

____ (2000) 'Qu'était-ce que le cinéma, Jean-Luc Godard? An Analysis of the Cinema(s) at Work in and around Godard's *Histoire(s) du cinéma*', in E. Ezra and S. Harris (eds) *France in Focus: Film and National Identity*. Oxford: Berg, 23–41.

Wolf, J. B. (2004) *Harnessing the Holocaust: The Politics of Memory in France*. Stanford, CA: Stanford University Press.

Wood, N. (1999) *Vectors of Memory: Legacies of Trauma in Postwar Europe*. Oxford: Berg.

Wright, A. (2000) 'Elizabeth Taylor at Auschwitz: JLG and the Real Object of Montage', in J. S. Williams and M. Temple (eds) *The Cinema Alone: Essays on the Work of Jean-Luc Godard 1985–2000*. Amsterdam: Amsterdam University Press, 51–60.

Young, J. E. (1988) 'Names of the Holocaust', in *Writing and Rewriting the Holocaust: Narrative and the Consequences of Interpretation*. Bloomington: Indiana University Press, 83–98.

____ (2000) *At Memory's Edge: After-Images of the Holocaust in Contemporary Art and Architecture*. New Haven, CT and London: Yale University Press.

Young, S. (2000) 'Trauma, Testimony and the Survivor: Calling Forth the Ghosts of Bosnia-Herzegovina', in M. Rossington and A. Whitehead (eds) *Between the Psyche and the Polis: Refiguring History in Literature and Theory*. Aldershot: Ashgate, 108–20.

Zelizer, B. (1997) 'Every Once in a While: *Schindler's List* and the Shaping of History', in Y. Loshitzky (ed.) *Spielberg's Holocaust: Critical Perspectives on 'Schindler's List'*. Bloomington: Indiana University Press, 18–35.

____ (1998) *Remembering to Forget: Holocaust Memory through the Camera's Eye*. Chicago: University of Chicago Press.

Zelizer, B. (ed.) (2001) *Visual Culture and the Holocaust*. New Brunswick, NJ: Rutgers University Press.

Žižek, S. (2000a) *The Art of the Ridiculous Sublime: On David Lynch's 'Lost Highway'*. Seattle: University of Washington/Walter Chapin Simpson Center for the Humanities.

____ (2000b) 'Camp Comedy', *Sight and Sound*, 10, 4, 26–9.

____ (2001) *Did Somebody Say Totalitarianism?: Five Essays in the (Mis)Use of a Notion*. London: Verso.

____ (2002) *Welcome to the Desert of the Real! Five Essays on September 11 and Related Dates*. London: Verso.

Index